CONTENTS

Why a book on React? ... 1
Reading guide ... 2
1 – ES6 JavaScript ... 3
2 – Hello React ... 50
3 – React & JSX ... 72
4 – State object ... 99
5 – Interactions in React Components ... 118
6 – Manage the elements of a list ... 130
7 – Manage forms with React ... 171
8 – Use create-react-app to create a React application ... 242
9 – Redux ... 265
10 – React & Redux ... 285
11 – Use the react-redux module ... 304
12 – React Router ... 328

WHY A BOOK ON REACT?

As a developer, who has not heard of ReactJS (or shortened React) yet? This JavaScript library, originally written for Facebook (in 2013), is now widely used in the corporate world. It can effectively structure a web application, but can also be used in a so-called native version, to write mobile applications for iPhone or Android.

READING GUIDE

The book is written in a progressive way for the reader. Each chapter provides knowledge that will be used in subsequent chapters. It is therefore not recommended to skip a chapter.

The ultimate goal is to understand, step by step, how React works in order to use it professionally. The book is organized in 12 chapters:

1 - "ES6 JavaScript": discover the new JavaScript syntax used by React.

2 - "Hello React": introduction to React to write the first program.

3 - "React & JSX": write React code more easily using JSX syntax.

4 - "State object": understand how states work in React components.

5 - "Interactions in React Components": manage external events, such as clicks on buttons.

6 - "Manage the elements of a list": complete example to interact on the elements of a list (add, modify and delete).

7 - "Manage forms with React": use each form element for the most common uses with React.

8 - "Use create-react-app to create a React application": use specific software that creates the architecture of the React application.

9 - "Redux": use the Redux library to manage the states of the application.

10 - "React & Redux": learn to associate React and Redux.

11 - "Use the react-redux module": use this module to facilitate the association of React with Redux.

12 - "React Router": use a route manager in React.

1 – ES6 JAVASCRIPT

JavaScript, a language allowing easy interactions between a web page and the user, has undergone various changes in recent years, the most significant of which is the ES6 version (abbreviation of ECMAScript 6). This new version is particularly relevant to:
- Variables: declaration, scope, and formatting in strings;
- Functions: default settings, new form of function declaration;
- Objects and arrays: destructuring and operator "...";
- Object classes: creation and derivation;
- Promises: use of the asynchronous process;
- Modules: to better structure the JavaScript code;

React uses these new elements intensively. We study them below to write and understand more easily the React code that will be used in this tutorial.

> Which code editor to use? Any code editor can do the trick, and if you have not made your choice yet, we recommend using Visual Studio Code (free and maintained by Microsoft)

In the rest of the chapter, we will use an index.html file that will contain the JavaScript code used (using `<script>` tags). The structure of this file is as follows:

index.html file
```
<html>
<head>
</head>
<body>
</body>
<script>
// here the JavaScript code
// ...
</script>
</html>
```

This HTML file can be run either by dragging it into a browser window (from the file manager) or by typing the http://localhost/react URL, assuming you have started a server (PHP, Node.js, J2EE, etc.) and you have dropped the index.html file into the server's react directory. In this chapter, we use the first solution (sliding in the browser window).

Of course, this file is empty code for now, its execution produces a blank page on the screen.

Variables

Various keywords have been added to the JavaScript language to modify the scope of variables. The var keyword to define a local variable is still active, but its edge effects have been corrected as we will see below.

Using const

The const keyword is used to define a constant, which by definition can not be changed. In case of modification by the program, a JavaScript error is caused.

Let's write the following code in the index.html file, in the reserved part (<script> tag).

Using const
```
const name = "Trump";
console.log(name);
name = "Obama";   // error
```

Changing the name constant causes an error that can be seen in a browser, for example Chrome using its development tools (F12 key and Console tab).

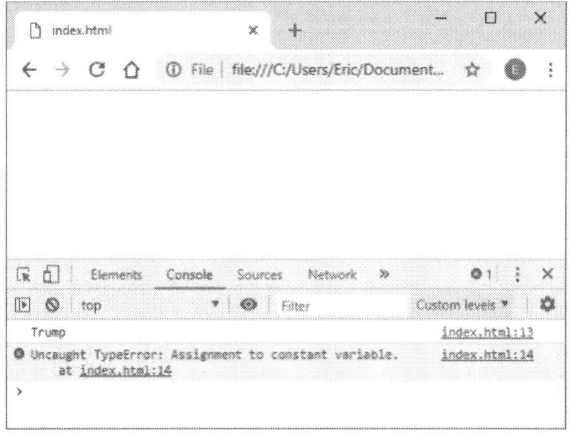

A constant (defined by `const`) can not be assigned a second time. Only the first assignment is allowed, while the following ones produce an error allowing us to correct the bug.

Using let

The `let` keyword allows you to define real local variables, which disappear when the code block in which they are defined is no longer executed. Moreover, if a variable of the same name is defined at a higher level in the code, this new variable defined with let does not overwrite the value of the higher-level variable. The behavior of `let` is very different from that of `var`.

Let's see on an example the difference between the use of `var` and that of `let`. The difference is seen when `var` or `let` is used in a code block (surrounded by braces).

With use of var in a block

```
var name = "Trump";
console.log("before block: " + name);   // "Trump"
if (true) {
  var name = "Obama";
  console.log("inside block: " + name); // "Obama"
}
console.log("after block: " + name);    // "Obama"
```

The `name` variable is defined first out of the block (at the value `"Trump"`). A variable of the same name is created in the block, assigned with a new value (`"Obama"`). This variable, declared using `var`, overwrites the variable of the same name defined before the block. Then this variable, modified, is then displayed with this new value after the block.

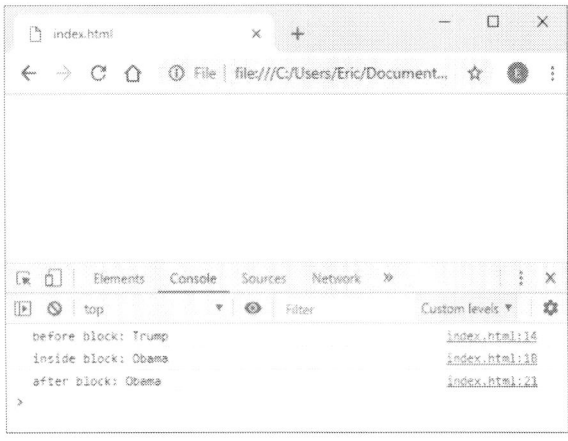

The name variable defined in the block overwrites the same variable (of the same name) defined before the block, because the variable defined in the block is not seen as being local to the block. In fact, we do not have two variables, but only one in memory.

The overwrite effect (of the variable) observed comes from the fact that the name variable defined in the block using var is not local to this block, but comes to take the same place as a possible variable of the same name defined previously.

Using let will actually create local variables in a block, without interfering with other variables of the same name defined elsewhere.

With use of let in a block

```
var name = "Trump";
console.log("before block: " + name);   // "Trump"
if (true) {
  let name = "Obama";
  console.log("inside block: " + name);   // "Obama"
}
console.log("after block: " + name);    // "Trump"
```

We now use the let keyword to define the variable in the block. The result will be very different from the previous example ...

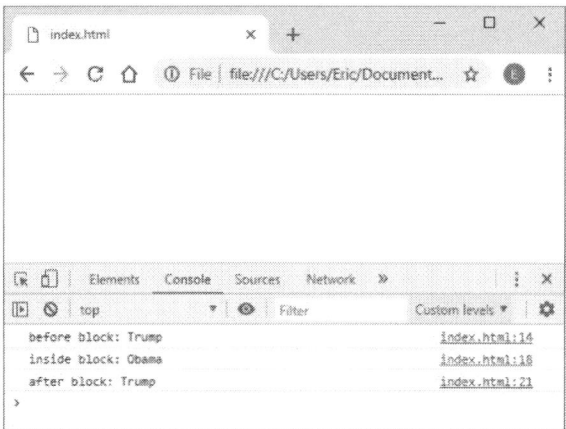

The name variable now has a different value in the block and outside of it. It is the use of let (in the block) that allows it.

We can also see the difference between var and let on a second example. In a for() loop, a variable declared by var or let affects the behavior of JavaScript code.

Let's modify the index.html file to create five <div> elements on which the click on each one is intercepted. We first use the var keyword to define the i index in the loop.

Click on the <div> elements created with a loop index defined by var in a for() loop

```
for (var i=0; i<5; i++) {  // use of var to set i in the block
  var div = document.createElement("div");
  var text = document.createTextNode("Element " + i);
  div.appendChild(text);
  document.getElementsByTagName("body")[0].appendChild(div);
  div.onclick = function() {
    console.log("Click on Element " + i);
  }
}
```

This program simply performs a loop from 0 to 4 inclusive, to create <div> elements on which an onclick event handler is set. Each click on a <div> element displays "Click on Element" followed by the index of the clicked <div> element.

The interest of this little program is not in the JavaScript code to create the <div> elements in the loop, but rather in the observation of the value displayed in the console when clicking on the different <div> elements of the page. Each click on an element produces the display of "Click on Element 5", knowing that this element 5 is not even present in the page!

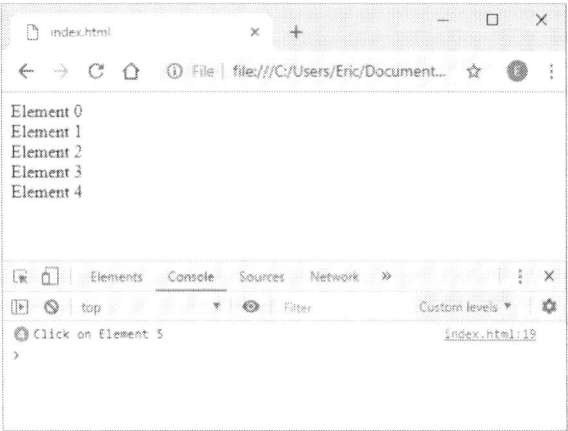

Indeed, the i variable defined by var is not local to the block in which it is defined, and thus comes to overwrite its old value. At the end of the loop, it eventually reaches the value 5, which causes the end of the loop. Subsequently, clicking on any element <div> retrieves the final value of this variable, here the value 5.

A very different behavior is visible if we use the let keyword instead of var to set the i variable in the for() loop.

Click on the <div> elements created with a loop index defined by let in a for() loop
```
for (let i=0; i<5; i++) {   // use of let to set i in the block
  var div = document.createElement("div");
  var text = document.createTextNode("Element " + i);
  div.appendChild(text);
  document.getElementsByTagName("body")[0].appendChild(div);
  div.onclick = function() {
    console.log("Click on Element " + i);
  }
}
```

The program is identical to the previous one except that let replaced var to set the i loop variable.

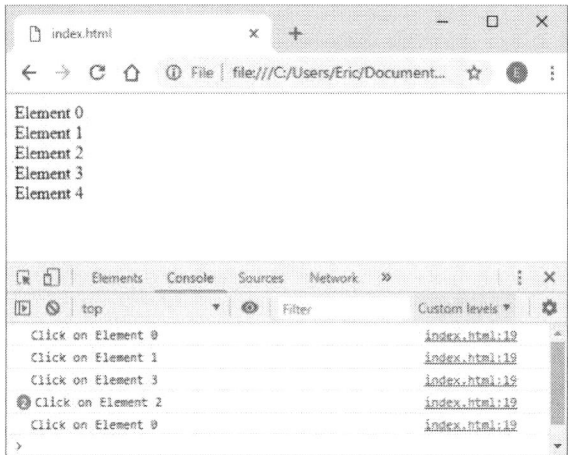

It is clear that the i variable defined by let is now local to the for() loop. And each click indicates the element on which we clicked.

Formatting strings

Using variables in a JavaScript string is a bit tedious, because you must close each string before using the variable to concatenate to that string. We often write lines of code such as these:

Concatenation of variables in strings
```
var lastname = "Trump";
var firstname = "Donald";
var txt = "Firstname is " + firstname + ", lastname is " + lastname;
console.log(txt);
```

It can be seen that the line for setting the txt variable requires closing each character string before using a variable when concatenating.

The result is the expected one.

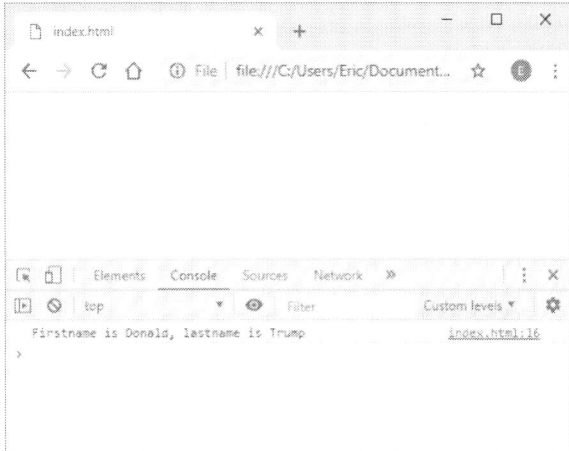

A clearer way of writing can be used in ES6, without closing the string when concatenating variables. To do this, use the inverted quote (`` ` ``) to define the character string (instead of the simple (') or double (") traditional quotation mark.) The program can then be written as:

Concatenation of variables in strings with ES6

```
var lastname = "Trump";
var firstname = "Donald";
var txt = `Firstname is ${firstname}, lastname is ${lastname}`;
console.log(txt);
```

Each variable is used in the string using ${variable}, knowing that the string is surrounded by inverted commas.

The result is identical to the previous one, but the writing is easier to read.

Functions

The declaration of functions has been improved in ES6, to make it more efficient and more concise to write.

Using default parameters

We will now be able to pass default values to function parameters, as is done in other programming languages. Just define the parameters of the function by indicating the default values they must have (for those who have them), with the = sign.

The rule is to define the default parameters at the end of the parameter declaration in the function. As soon as a default value is indicated for a parameter, all the other parameters that follow must also have a defined default value (otherwise an ambiguity is created when the function is called, and in this case it is necessary to indicate the undefined value for this argument during the call). Hence the setting of these default parameters at the end of the declaration of the function.

Using default values in functions

```
function log(lastname="Trump", firstname="Donald") {
  console.log(`${lastname} ${firstname}`);
}
log("Martin", "Gerard");    // "Martin Gerard"
log();                      // "Trump Donald"
log("Martin");              // "Martin Donald"
log(undefined, "Gerard");   // "Trump Gerard"
log(null, "Gerard");        // "null Gerard"
log("", "Gerard");          // " Gerard"
```

The log() function has two parameters with default values, and we use the function with 0, 1 or 2 arguments to see its behavior.

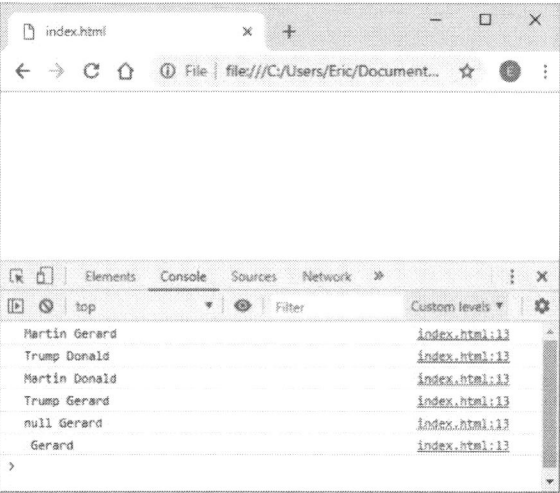

We see that when an argument is not used, it is replaced by its default value. However, as here all the arguments are optional, the undefined value must be used when calling the function if the argument is not the last one (null or "" values are not replaced by the default values).

Let's write a variant of this program, by default only the first parameter (which is not advisable because it produces ambiguities). The behavior of the program is very different.

Using a default value in the first parameter of the function

```
function log(lastname="Trump", firstname) {
  console.log(`${lastname} ${firstname}`);
}
log("Martin", "Gerard");    // "Martin Gerard"
log();               // "Trump undefined"
log("Martin");          // "Martin undefined"
log(undefined, "Gerard");   // "Trump Gerard"
log(null, "Gerard");     // "null Gerard"
log("", "Gerard");      // " Gerard"
```

The ambiguity relates here to the call to log("Martin"), for which the argument "Martin" is considered as the first parameter of the function. To remove the ambiguity, we have to mention undefined in the first argument when calling log(undefined, "Gerard"), which replaces the undefined argument with its default value.

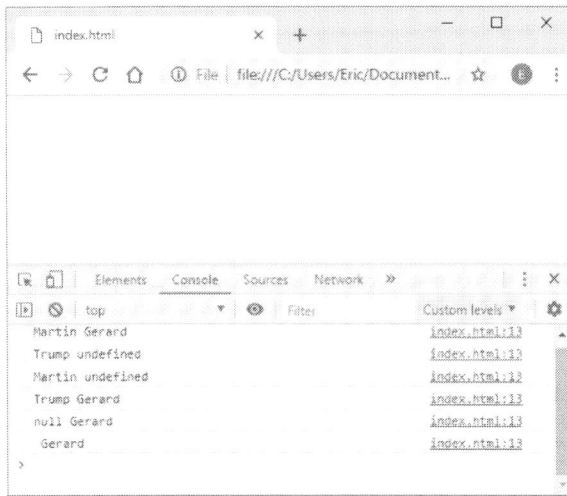

We will remember that the default settings are prioritized in the end of the list of parameters when defining functions.

New form of function declaration in ES6

Take the log(lastname, firstname) function written previously. It can be rewritten in the following form:

log() function written in ES6

```
var log = (lastname="Trump", firstname="Donald") => {
  console.log(`${lastname} ${firstname}`);
}
```

The function keyword has disappeared, replaced by the => sign. Function parameters are always written in parentheses, while the function body is always surrounded by the start and end braces.

If the function has no parameters, it is written as follows:

log() function written in ES6

```
var log = () => {
  console.log("Hello");
};
```

The call to the function is always the same as before (only the definition can be done in a different way):

Call to the log() function

```
log();           // without parameters
log("Martin");   // with parameters
```

The this object in functions

This way of defining functions in ES6 can affect the value of this object, which represents the object being used.

Consider for example the following object, in which is defined a list of names to be displayed by means of the log() function also defined in the object. We use the old form of declaration of functions (with the function keyword instead of =>).

Object with built-in log() function (not ES6)

```
var obj = {
  names : ["Trump","Obama","Bush"],
  log: function() {
    console.log(this.names);
  }
}
obj.log();  // ["Trump","Obama","Bush"]
```

The this object represents here the object in use of the log() function, so the obj object.

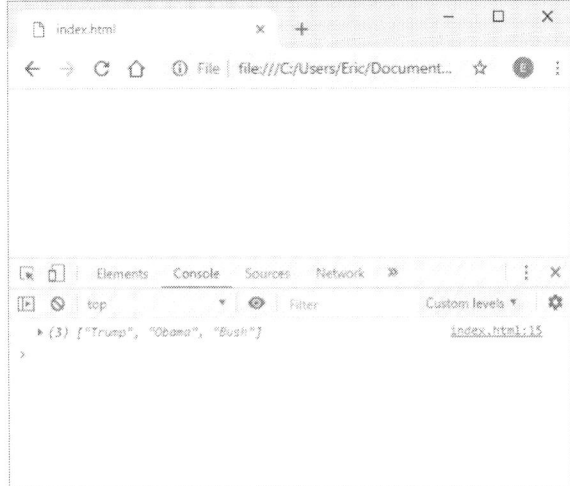

The this object provides access to names, which are displayed in the log() function. Rewrite the function taking into account the ES6 notation.

Object with built-in log() function (in ES6)
```
var obj = {
 names : ["Trump","Obama","Bush"],
 log: () => {
  console.log(this.names);
 }
}
obj.log();  // ["Trump","Obama","Bush"]
```

This is the same program written in ES6 notation. The result should be identical ...

When running this program, we observe that the result is different from the previous one!

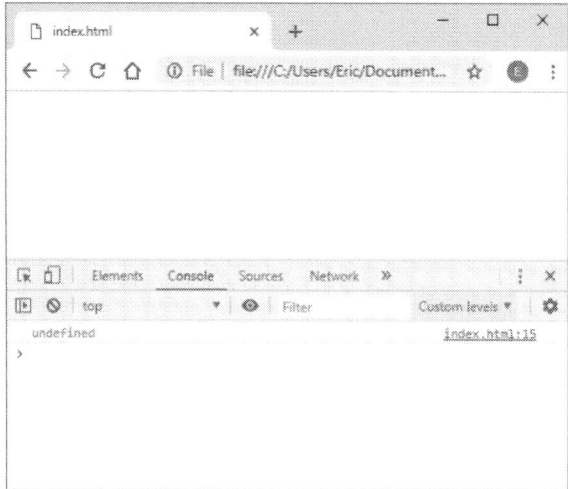

The names property of the object is no longer accessible (and is therefore undefined)!

The names object property is no longer accessible because this is now the JavaScript window object, not the obj object. To make sure, just display the value of this in the console.

Display this in the console
```
var obj = {
 names : ["Trump","Obama","Bush"],
 log: () => {
  console.log(this);  // window
 }
}
obj.log();
```

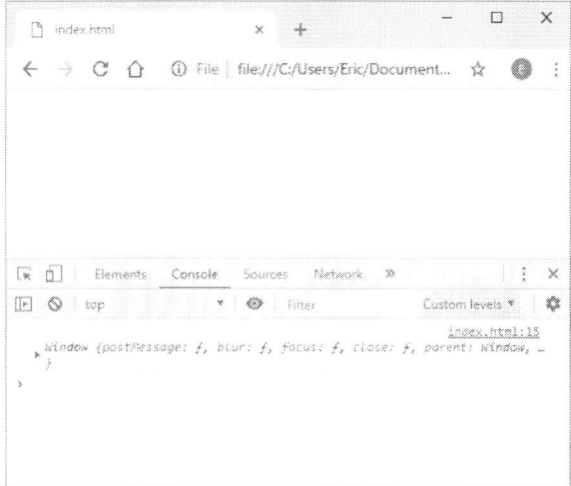

It is the window object that is referenced by this.

This observation may be of interest when using asynchronous functions, which are widely used with JavaScript.

Consider that we display the names registered in the previous obj object, after a few milliseconds, using a JavaScript timer. This timer is written using an asynchronous function defined by setTimeout().

Display names after 10 ms
```
var obj = {
 names : ["Trump","Obama","Bush"],
 log: function() {
  setTimeout(function() {
   console.log(this.names);  // undefined
  }, 10); // Execution of the timer after 10 ms
 }
}
obj.log();
```

The this object is now used in the setTimeout() function, which is itself set to the window object of the HTML page.

The this object represents the window object (that is, the object that uses the setTimeout() function, as if we had written window.setTimeout() in the code).

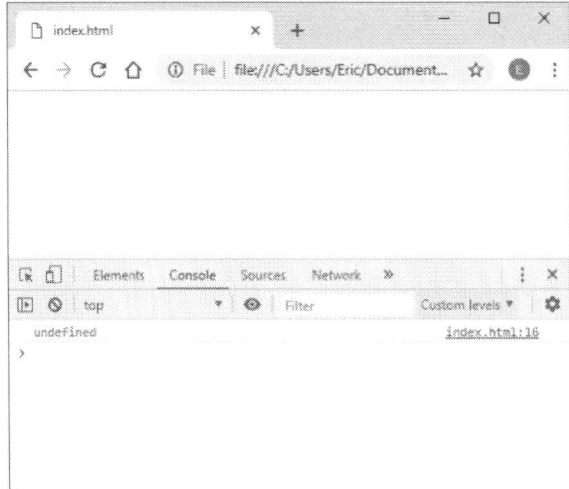

Using an asynchronous function completely changes the behavior of our program. The ES6 notation addresses this problem.

Use ES6 notation to define an asynchronous function
```
var obj = {
 names : ["Trump","Obama","Bush"],
 log: function() {
  setTimeout(() => {  // ES6 notation
   console.log(this.names);  // ["Trump","Obama","Bush"]
  }, 10);
 }
}
obj.log();
```

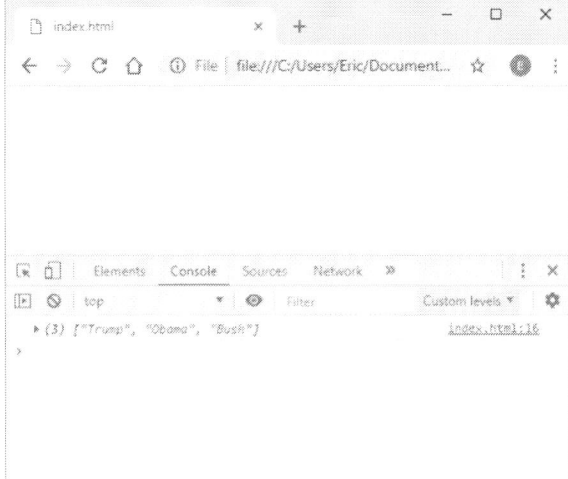

The result is now in line with our expectations.

The value of this object is well preserved and transmitted in the asynchronous function.

Objects

In order to manipulate the objects more easily, ES6 makes it possible to structure / destructure them. We discuss below what this means.

Destructuring an object

Let's start by explaining the destructuring of an object. It provides easy access to the properties that interest us of an object, without worrying about those that do not interest us in the immediate future.

Take the example of the person object, consisting of the lastname, firstname and city of this person.

person object
```
var person = {
  lastname : "Trump",
  firstname : "Donald",
  city : "Washington"
}
```

In order to access for example the lastname and firstname of the person, ES6 allows to write:

Access the lastname and firstname of the person

```
var { lastname, firstname } = person;
```

This creates lastname and firstname variables, each with the value of person.lastname and person.firstname. This is called the destructuring of an object, because one only has access to interesting properties (in this part of the program).

If only the lastname interests us, we will write:

Access only to the lastname of the person

```
var { lastname } = person;
```

> Warning: even if the notation allowing destructuring is written with braces, it does not create a new object, but only variables that correspond to the values of the properties of the object that are accessed. Here we create the lastname variable whose value is person.lastname.

This notation will be particularly useful for transmitting an object as a parameter, showing clearly which properties of the object are finally used in the function. For example, let's use this to convey the person object in the log(person) function, knowing that the log() function uses only the lastname and the firstname of the person (it is assumed here that the city property defined for the person object is not used in the log() function).

log() function defined by indicating the properties actually used in the object passed as parameters

```
var person = {
  lastname : "Trump",
  firstname : "Donald",
  city : "Washington"
}
// only lastname and firstname properties will be used in the function
var log = ({ lastname, firstname }) => {
  console.log(`${lastname} ${firstname}`);
}
// the function is called with the object in arguments
log(person);
```

A person object is passed when the log() function is called, but only the lastname and firstname are used in the log() function. Rather than indicate a person object in function parameters, we indicate the real properties that interest us in the function by indicating them in unstructured form {lastname, firstname} in the list of parameters.

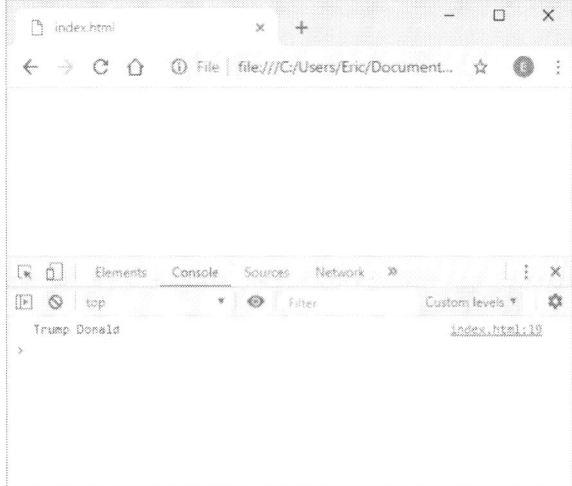

The same program, written in traditional form by not using the destructuring of objects as above, can be written:

log() function written without using the destructuring of objects
```
var person = {
 lastname : "Trump",
 firstname : "Donald",
 city : "Washington"
}
var log = (p) => {
 console.log(`${p.lastname} ${p.firstname}`);
}
log(person);
```

The log() function uses here the p parameter corresponding to a person. There is nothing in the list of parameters to indicate that what really interests us in the body of the function is the lastname and the firstname. While the use of the unstructured form makes it possible to clearly see the properties actually used in the object passed in parameters.

If the log() function has other parameters, just indicate them in the list when it is defined. Suppose we want to indicate in parameters a text that will be displayed in front of the lastname and the firstname. We will write then:

log() function with multiple parameters
```
var person = {
 lastname : "Trump",
```

```
  firstname : "Donald",
  city : "Washington"
}
var log = ({ lastname, firstname }, text) => {
  console.log(`${text} ${lastname} ${firstname}`);
}
log(person, "Here is the lastname and firstname:");
```

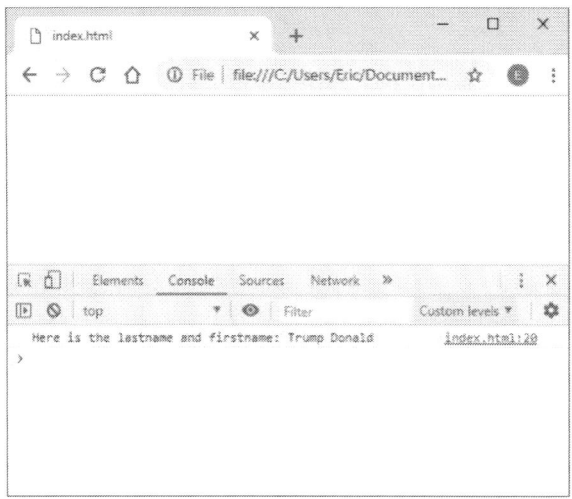

You can also use default values for the function parameters. For example, say that the displayed text has a default value (used if it is not specified when calling the function), and that the lastname is "Trump" by default if it is not indicated in the properties of the person object transmitted during the call.

<u>**Using default values in the log() function parameters**</u>

```
var person = {  // person object defined without the lastname
  firstname : "Donald",
  city : "Washington"
}
var log = ({ lastname="Trump", firstname }, text="Here is the lastname and firstname:") => {
  console.log(`${text} ${lastname} ${firstname}`);
}
log(person); // a single argument when calling
```

The person object is defined without the name property, which will have a default value when defining the log() function.

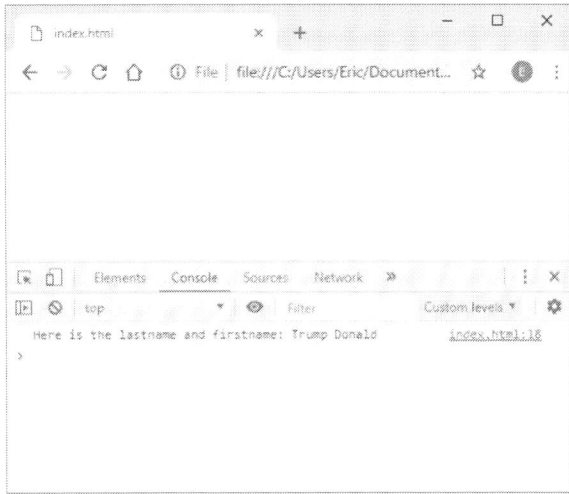

Structuring an object

The structuring of an object is the opposite of the destructuration seen previously. It allows you to create a JavaScript object from variables defined in the JavaScript code.

This was already possible with earlier versions of JavaScript, but required a more verbose syntax. To create a person object from the variables lastname, firstname and city defined in the program, we wrote for example:

Define a person object from the lastname, firstname and city variables

```
var lastname = "Trump";
var firstname = "Donald";
var city = "Washington";
var person = {
 lastname : lastname,
 firstname : firstname,
 city : city
}
console.log(person);
```

The person object has the properties lastname, firstname, and city that correspond to the same names as the variables defined in the program, hence the redundancy between the name of the property (to the left of the sign :) and its value (to the right of the sign :).

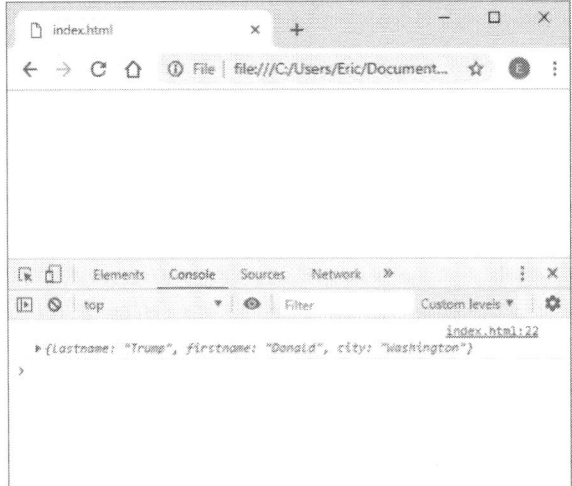

Rather than writing the person object as property: value, ES6 allows you to write only the name of the property, without the value, because it will be the value of the variable with the same name as the property. So we will write using the structuring of ES6 objects:

Define a person object in ES6 from the lastname, firstname and city variables

```
var lastname = "Trump";
var firstname = "Donald";
var city = "Washington";
var person = { // structuring the person object
  lastname,
  firstname,
  city
}
console.log(person);
```

The lastname, firstname, and city properties of the person object must match the variables defined earlier in the JavaScript code. These variables are here defined by the var keyword, but could be by the let or const keywords seen previously.

We can mix the old notation (with :) and the new one. For example, setting the city property directly in the person object without going through a city variable:

Using the two JavaScript notations

```
var lastname = "Trump";
var firstname = "Donald";
var person = {
  lastname,
```

```
  firstname,
  city : "New York"
}
console.log(person);
```

The lastname and the firstname are retrieved directly from variables of the same name, while the city property is directly assigned in the person object.

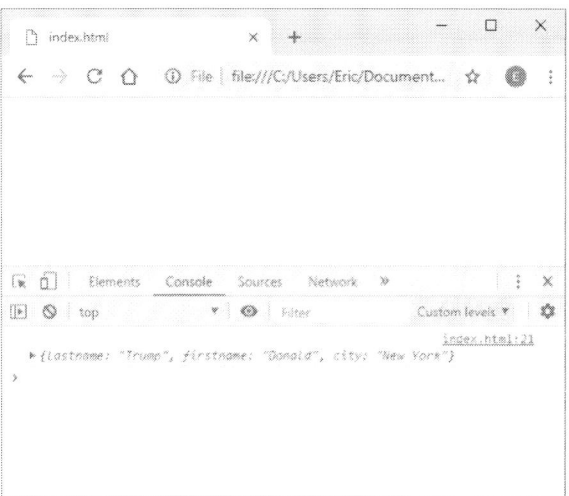

If a function is defined in the properties of the person object, it can be written as follows:

Setting the log() function in the person object

```
var lastname = "Trump";
var firstname = "Donald";
var log = function() {
  console.log(`${this.lastname} ${this.firstname}`);
}
var person = {
  lastname,
  firstname,
  log
}
person.log();
```

The log() function is set to the properties of the person object in the same way as the other properties of the object. A log variable is searched for and if it is found (which is the case here) its value is attached to this property of the object.

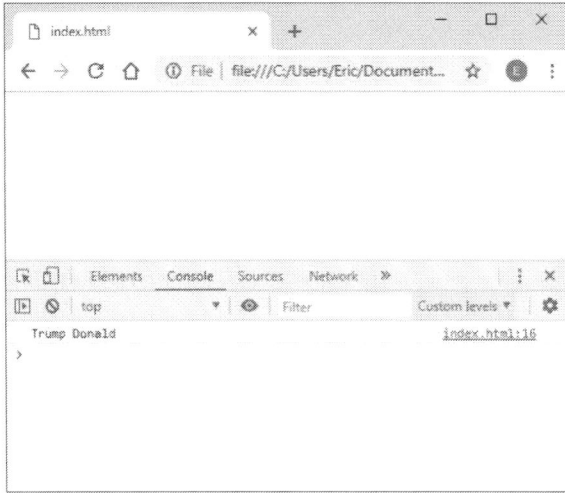

The log() function can also be defined in the following way (with the => notation):

log() function set with =>
```
var lastname = "Trump";
var firstname = "Donald";
var log = () => {
  console.log(`${this.lastname} ${this.firstname}`);
}
var person = {
  lastname,
  firstname,
  log
}
person.log();
```

But a more classic way of writing the person object is:

Definition of the person object integrating the log() function
```
var lastname = "Trump";
var firstname = "Donald";
var person = {
  lastname,
  firstname,
  log : function() {
    console.log(`${this.lastname} ${this.firstname}`);
  }
}
person.log();
```

ES6 removes the function keyword when defining the function in the object. We can then write the object as follows:

Definition of the person object in ES6
```
var lastname = "Trump";
var firstname = "Donald";
var person = {
 lastname,
 firstname,
 log() {
  console.log(`${this.lastname} ${this.firstname}`);
 }
}
person.log();
```

It is this last way of declaring the function in the object that will be used in the JavaScript code, as well as during the definition of the classes in React.

Operator ... on objects

The operator ... (called spread operator) allows to explode an object in its various properties. Let's see what this means on an example.

We want to create a new person2 object from the person object, but this new person2 object must contain (in addition) the city property (which does not exist in the person object).

Create a new object from an existing object
```
var person = {
 lastname : "Trump",
 firstname : "Donald"
}
var city = "Washington";
var person2 = {
 person,
 city
}
console.log(person2); // { person : { lastname : "Trump", firstname : "Donald" }, city : "Washington" }
```

The person object is embedded in the person2 object. But the result is not necessarily the expected one ...

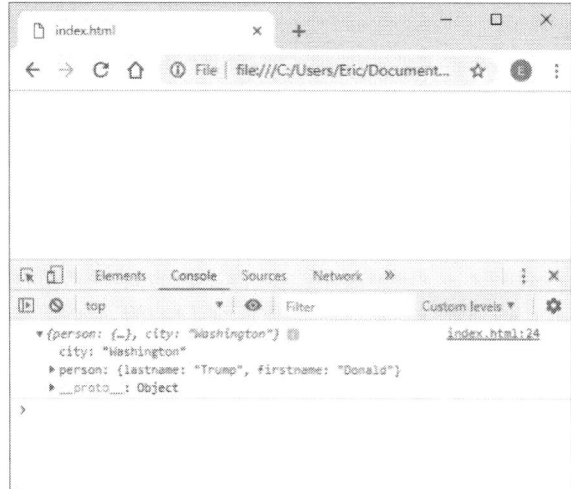

The person object, embedded in the person2 object, has become a person property of this new object. We would have rather wanted the properties of the person object to integrate directly into the new object, so that it has the properties lastname, firstname and city (instead of the person and city properties as currently).

The ... operator will help us realize the bursting of the properties of the person object by integrating them directly into the new object. Just write:

Create a new object from an existing object using the ... operator
```
var person = {
 lastname : "Trump",
 firstname : "Donald"
}
var city = "Washington";
var person2 = {
 ...person,
 city
}
console.log(person2); // { lastname : "Trump", firstname : "Donald", city : "Washington" }
```

The only difference with the previous program is the ... operator used to explode the properties of the person object by integrating them directly into the new object.

> The ... operator can only be used in a JavaScript object, as can be seen in the previous example.

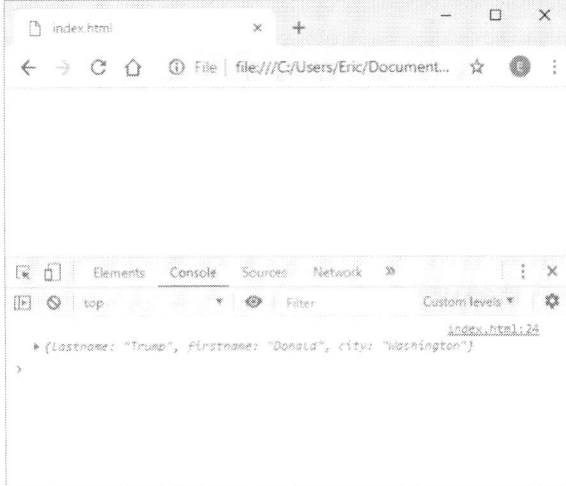

The person object has been exploded and integrated into the new object with its properties directly attached to the new object.

Several ... operators can be included in the definition of an object. If at breakup, properties have the same name in different exploded objects, only one property with that name is inserted into the new object (the last one encountered).

For example, by creating a new object from person and place objects (the place object defines the city and the postal code (postal property)).

Using multiple ... operators to define a new object

```
var person = {
 lastname : "Trump",
 firstname : "Donald"
}
var place = {
 city : "Washington",
 postal : "20001"
}
var person2 = {
 ...person,
 ...place
}
console.log(person2); // { lastname : "Trump", firstname : "Donald", city : "Washington", postal : "20001" }
```

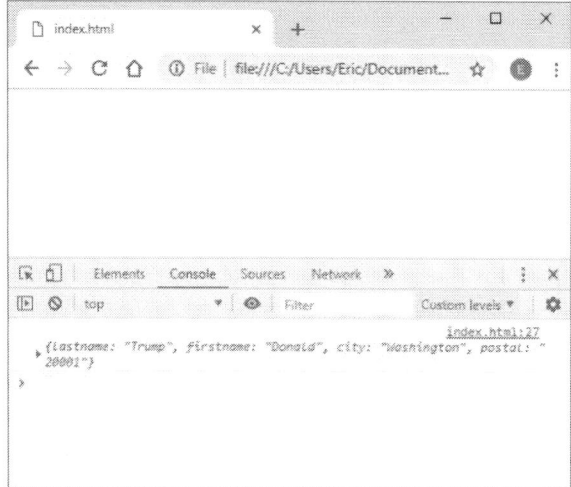

The two objects (person and place) have been exploded, and their properties are attached to the person2 object thus created.

Arrays

In the same way that we can deconstruct or structure an object, we can do the same kind of operations with the arrays.

Destructuring an array

Destructuring an array will allow you to retrieve parts of the array (as some properties of an object were retrieved).

Retrieve variables from certain elements of an array

```
var names = ["Trump", "Obama", "Bush"];
var [name1, name2, name3] = names;  // name1 = names[0], name2 = names[1], name3 = names[2]
console.log(name1, name2, name3);   // "Trump" "Obama" "Bush"
```

The elements of the names array are retrieved in the name1, name2, and name3 variables, in the order that the elements are written in the array.

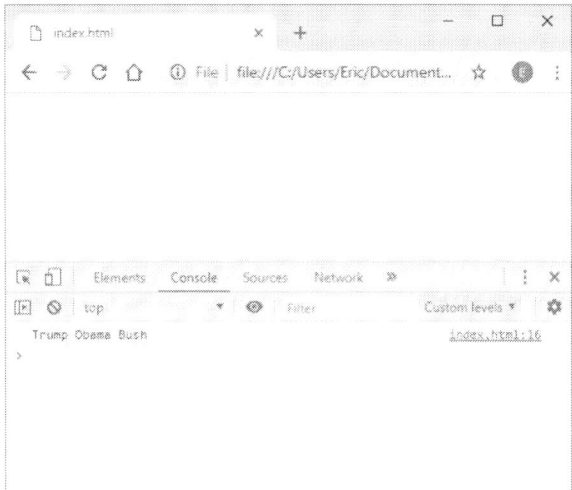

If we only want to retrieve the second element of the array, we write:

Retrieve only the second element of the array
```
var names = ["Trump", "Obama", "Bush"];
var [, name2] = names;
console.log(name2); // "Obama"
```

And to retrieve only the third element of the array:

Retrieve only the third element of the array
```
var names = ["Trump", "Obama", "Bush"];
var [,, name3] = names;
console.log(name3); // "Bush"
```

Unrecovered indexes in the array are replaced by commas.

Structuring an array

The structuring of an array is mainly done with the ... operator studied below.

Operator ... on arrays

The ... operator is the same as the one acting on the objects. It allows to explode the elements of an array, in order to access its various elements. This operator can be used in an array to create a new array.

Let's use this operator to split an array in two: the first element of the array, then everything else (which will be a new array created from the first array).

Split an array with the ... operator
```
var names = ["Trump", "Obama", "Bush"];
```

```
var [name1, ...following] = names;
console.log(name1);      // "Trump"
console.log(following);  // ["Obama", "Bush"]
```

Here we specify to create the two `name1` and `following` variables, both extracted from the `names` array. The `name1` variable corresponds to the first element of the array, while the `following` variable corresponds to the rest of the array (after the first element already extracted).

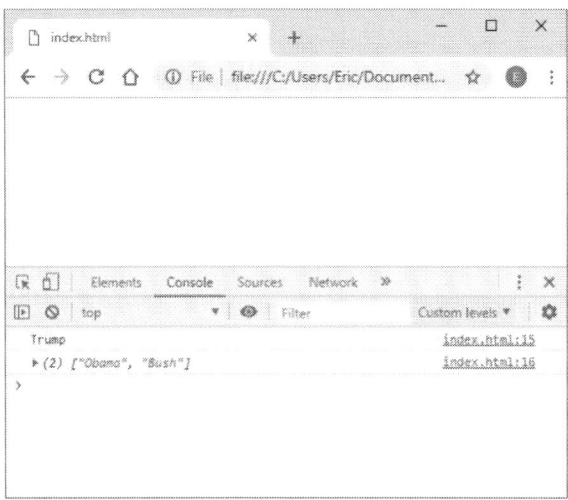

To retrieve the elements of the array from the third (instead of the second as above), simply insert an extra comma when the array is destructured.

Retrieve the elements of the array from the third
```
var names = ["Trump", "Obama", "Bush"];
var [,, ...following] = names;
console.log(following);  // ["Bush"]
```

Object classes

JavaScript allows you to create object classes, but in previous versions (before ES6), the syntax is complicated and does not look like the one used in similar object-oriented languages. ES6 offers a more classic syntax, which will be used extensively with React.

Creating a class

We use the new `class` keyword (as in many other languages). The creation of an object of this class is done using `new`.

We define below a Person class (note the capital letter on the first letter of the name of the class, because all the names of class must begin with a capital letter), then one creates a person object (here the name of the variable begins with a lowercase, unlike class names).

Creating the Person class

```
class Person {            // definition of the Person class, here empty
}
var person = new Person();    // person object of the Person class
console.log(person);
```

The Person class defined here is empty for now, it will be enriched below.

The person object (of Person class) is created using the new operator, followed by the name of the class. Here we could also have written new Person; because for the moment we do not transmit any argument during the creation of the object.

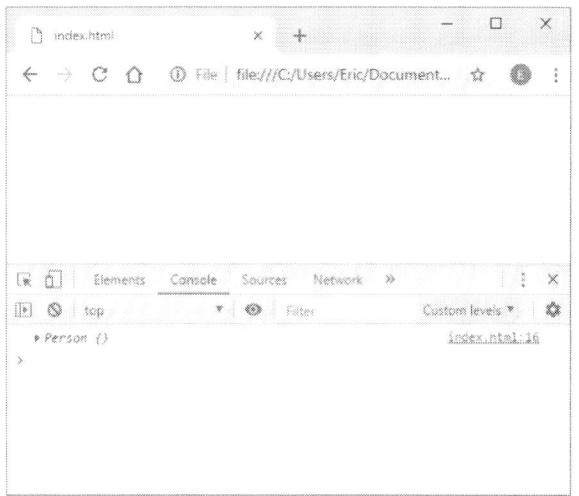

The person object displayed is of Person class, and is empty as expected since the Person class is currently empty.

A person has a firstname and a lastname. Let's add these attributes in the Person class so that the corresponding objects use them.

To define attributes in a class, it is necessary to use a method that is called as soon as an object of this class is instantiated (ie created by means of the new operator). In ES6, this build method is called constructor() and will have as parameters the elements that will be passed during the creation of the object by new. The constructor() method is present in all the classes that one creates and is called the constructor of the class.

Creating the Person class with the lastname and firstname attributes

```
class Person {
 constructor(lastname, firstname) {
  this.lastname = lastname;
  this.firstname = firstname;
 }
}
var person = new Person("Trump", "Donald"); // first created object
console.log(person);
var person2 = new Person("Obama", "Barack"); // second created object
console.log(person2);
```

The constructor() method now has the parameters that will be used when creating objects of the Person class. In order to keep them as attributes in the class (and be able to use them in methods that will be defined in this class), they are stored in the this object (using this.lastname and this.firstname).

Note that when constructing objects by new, we must now indicate in arguments the values of the used parameters, which will be passed in the constructor() method. If the constructor() method uses default parameters, the corresponding arguments may be missing when creating the associated objects.

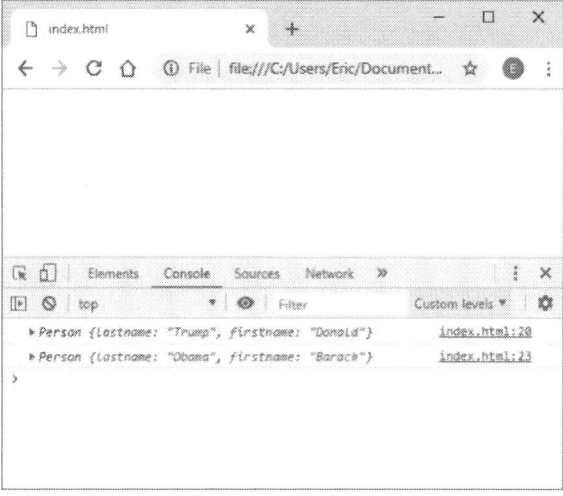

We see here the content of the two created objects, with, in brackets, the attributes created by means of this in the constructor.

A class is often enriched by means of methods, which will then be used by objects in this class. For example, you can create a log() function in the Person class that will display the lastname and firstname of objects in this class.

Creating the log() method in the Person class
```
class Person {
 constructor(lastname, firstname) {
  this.lastname = lastname;
  this.firstname = firstname;
 }
 log() {
  console.log(`Lastname : ${this.lastname}, Firstname : ${this.firstname}`);
 }
}
var person = new Person("Trump", "Donald");
console.log(person);
person.log();  // calling the log() method on the person object
var person2 = new Person("Obama", "Barack");
console.log(person2);
person2.log();  // calling the log() method on the person2 object
```

The log() method is defined in the class, without indicating the function keyword (otherwise a syntax error would occur), but using parentheses (here empty because there are no parameters to indicate during the call of the method). The body of the function follows, surrounded by braces to write the corresponding code.

The call of the log() method is then carried out on each of the objects (person and person2) for which one wishes to use it.

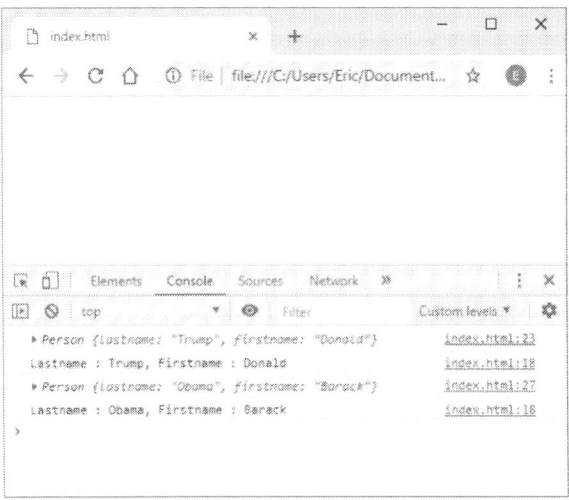

Class inheritance

Class inheritance allows you to create a new class from an already existing class. It is said that the new class is derived (inherited) from the first. This allows to enrich (enhance) an existing class without having to modify its internal code, and thus allows to reuse pieces of code already existing (ie to use other classes that have already been written and which function correctly).

To illustrate this, we want to create a new class, called Man, derived from the Person class written previously. In the same way, we can create the Woman class, also derived from the Person class, but which makes it possible to treat women persons.

To indicate that a class derives from another class, we use the extends keyword. So to indicate that the Man class derives from the Person class, one will write:

Define a Man class that derives from the Person class

```
class Man extends Person {
  // here the code of the Man class
}
```

Let's write the details of the code of the Man class.

Creation of the Man class derived from the Person class

```
class Person {
  constructor(lastname, firstname) {
    this.lastname = lastname;
    this.firstname = firstname;
  }
  log() {
    console.log(`Lastname : ${this.lastname}, Firstname : ${this.firstname}`);
  }
}
class Man extends Person {   // Man class derived from the Person class
  constructor(lastname, firstname) {
    this.sex = "M"; // all Man objects have "M" sex
  }
}
var person = new Man("Trump", "Donald");  // first created Man object
console.log(person);
person.log();
var person2 = new Man("Obama", "Barack"); // second created Man object
console.log(person2);
person2.log();
```

The Man class also has a constructor, in which we insert a new sex attribute corresponding to the sex of the person. The two created people are now using new Man() instead of new Person().

In addition, the call to the log() method defined in the Person class can be made on the objects of a derived class, here the Man class.

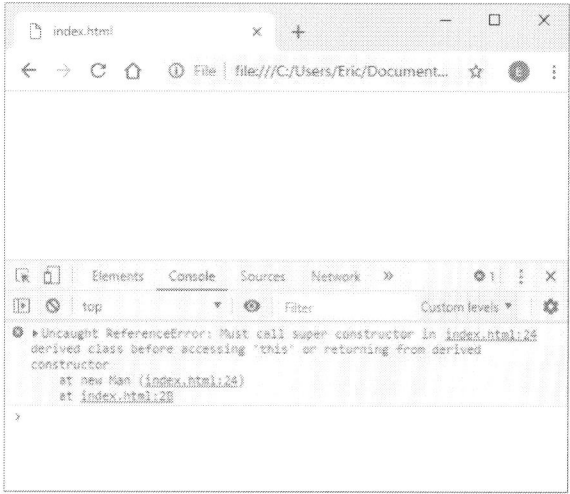

An error occurs indicating that the "super constructor" must be called in the derived class. Indeed, to create a Man object, you have to rely on the process of building a Person object (otherwise there is no point in indicating that the Man class derives from the Person class). So you need in the constructor of the Man class (derived class), also call the constructor of the Person class (parent class), which is done using the super() method to which one transmits the arguments lastname and firstname which define a Person object.

Man class using the super() method in its constructor
```
class Person {
 constructor(lastname, firstname) {
  this.lastname = lastname;
  this.firstname = firstname;
 }
 log() {
  console.log(`Lastname : ${this.lastname}, Firstname : ${this.firstname}`);
 }
}
class Man extends Person {
 constructor(lastname, firstname) {
  super(lastname, firstname); // call of the constructor of the parent class
  this.sex = "M";
 }
```

```
}
var person = new Man("Trump", "Donald");
console.log(person);
person.log();
var person2 = new Man("Obama", "Barack");
console.log(person2);
person2.log();
```

The only modification made is in the call to the super(lastname, firstname) method done in the constructor of the Man class.

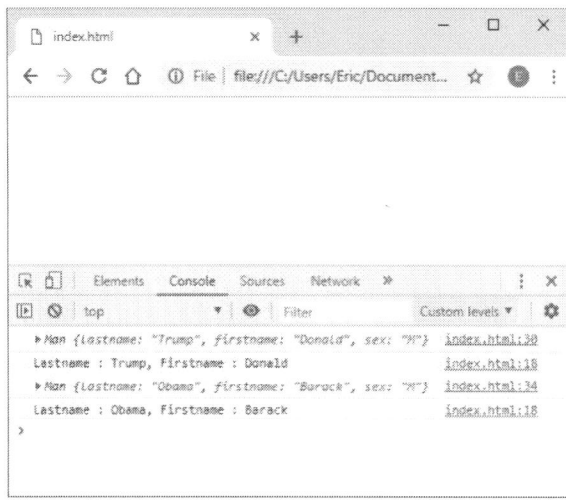

The call to the super() method in the constructor eliminates the previous error. And moreover we can also use the log() method on the Man class objects, because this method being defined in a parent class (the Person class), it is then accessible in the derived classes, here the Man class.

Suppose now that we want to modify the log() method, to make it display specific information for men. For the moment this method, being defined in the Person parent class, does not take into account the sex of the person.

ES6 allows you to redefine the methods of a parent class in a derived class. We can therefore define a new log() method in the Man class derived from the Person class.

Adding a new log() method in the Man class

```
class Person {
 constructor(lastname, firstname) {
  this.lastname = lastname;
  this.firstname = firstname;
 }
```

```
log() {
  console.log(`Lastname : ${this.lastname}, Firstname : ${this.firstname}`);
 }
}
class Man extends Person {
 constructor(lastname, firstname) {
  super(lastname, firstname);
  this.sex = "M";
 }
 log() {
  console.log("It's a man !");
 }
}
var person = new Man("Trump", "Donald");
console.log(person);
person.log();
var person2 = new Man("Obama", "Barack");
console.log(person2);
person2.log();
```

Person class objects will use the log() method defined in the Person class, while Man class objects will use the log() method defined in the Man class.

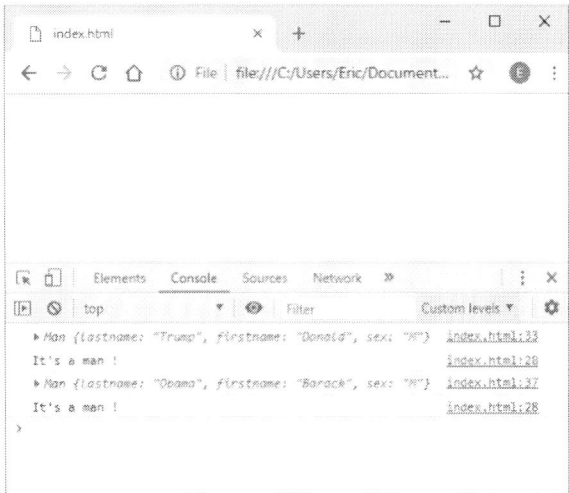

The log() method defined in the Person parent class is no longer called, because on the Man class objects, we first use the log() method defined on the objects of this class.

The question now is: how can you still call the log() method defined in the Person class from the Man class, knowing that the method has the same name in both classes?

This is possible by calling the log() method located in the parent class, using the super keyword. The super.log() statement is used to call the log() method defined in the parent class.

Call log() methods defined in a derived class and a parent class

```
class Person {
 constructor(lastname, firstname) {
  this.lastname = lastname;
  this.firstname = firstname;
 }
 log() {
  console.log(`Lastname : ${this.lastname}, Firstname : ${this.firstname}`);
 }
}
class Man extends Person {
 constructor(lastname, firstname) {
  super(lastname, firstname);
  this.sex = "M";
 }
 log() {
  super.log();  // log() call defined in the parent class
  console.log("It's a man !");
 }
}
var person = new Man("Trump", "Donald");
console.log(person);
person.log();
var person2 = new Man("Obama", "Barack");
console.log(person2);
person2.log();
```

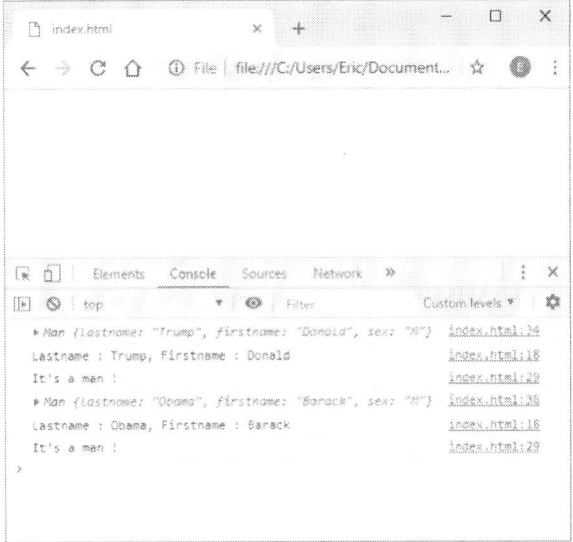

The two log() methods defined in both classes are now called.

Modules

ES6 allows you to define modules. These are JavaScript files that divide a JavaScript program into standalone files, included in the HTML page or in other modules.

A module allows you to define constants, variables, functions or classes (actually any type of data) that are by default private to the module (which means that the other modules do not have access to them unless you allows access).

To see the contribution of ES6 modules compared to traditional JavaScript files, divide the previous HTML file into various files used together.

Division of an HTML page into several files

Let's create a Person.js file to define the Person class seen previously. For now, we do not see any difference between a classic JavaScript file and an ES6 module.

Person.js file defining the Person class

```
class Person {
 constructor(lastname, firstname) {
  this.lastname = lastname;
  this.firstname = firstname;
 }
```

```
  log() {
    console.log(`Lastname : ${this.lastname}, Firstname : ${this.firstname}`);
  }
}
```

The Person class can be used in an HTML file by including the Person.js file using a classic <script> tag.

Using the Person class in an HTML file
```
<html>
<head>
<script src="./Person.js"></script>
</head>
<script>
var person = new Person("Trump", "Donald");
person.log();
</script>
</html>
```

Once the file containing the definition of the Person class included in the HTML page, we can access the class and its features.

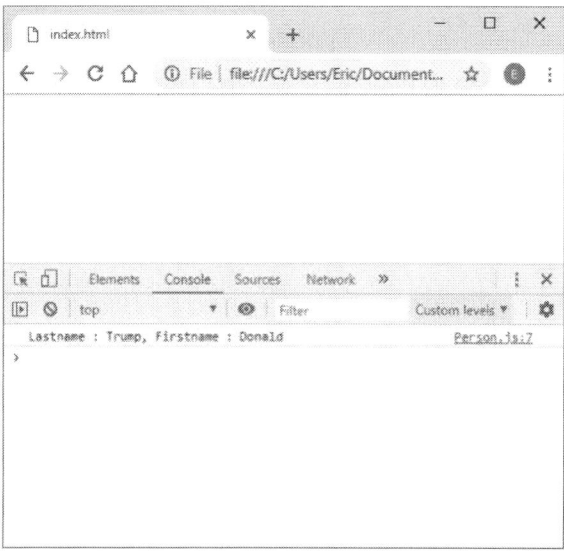

The Person class is accessible as well as the log() function defined in the class.

Let's do the same thing with the Man class, by defining it in a Man.js file which will also be included in the HTML page.

Man.js file defining the Man class
```
class Man extends Person {
```

```
  constructor(lastname, firstname) {
    super(lastname, firstname);
    this.sex = "M";
  }
  log() {
    super.log();
    console.log("It's a man !");
  }
}
```

To include this file in the HTML page, it is mandatory to include beforehand the Person.js file that defines the Person class (otherwise the Person class, used by the Man class, is unknown).

Using the Person and Man classes in an HTML file

```
<html>
<head>
<script src="./Person.js"></script>
<script src="./Man.js"></script>
</head>
<script>
var person = new Person("Trump", "Donald");
person.log();
var man = new Man("Obama", "Barack");
man.log();
</script>
</html>
```

The two JavaScript files including the Person and Man classes are included, which allows to use both classes in the script of the HTML page.

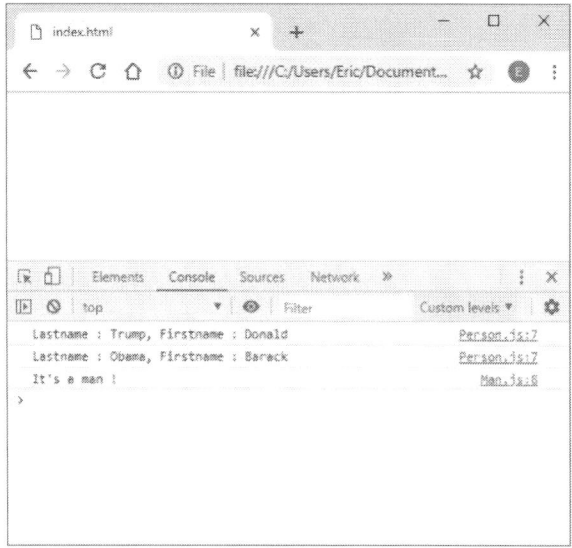

The Person class object is displayed, then the Man class object. Each class uses the log() method defined in its class.

Interest of modules

In the previous example, we did not use the modules as ES6 defines them. We simply cut a file into several files, then included in the main file.

This approach, although functional, has a major disadvantage (in the context of a development requiring a lot of files). Indeed, when including the necessary JavaScript files in the main file:

- The order of inclusion must be known: Person.js must be included before Man.js, otherwise it does not work,
- Dependencies between files must be known: the Man.js file needs to include the Person.js file, otherwise the Man class can not be created from the Person class.

So we see that having independent priori files such as Person.js and Man.js files requires information to know how to use them.

The purpose of the ES6 modules is to help use these files (here Person.js and Man.js) without having to know this information. Indeed this information will be inserted in some form in the file itself, which becomes a module.

This is the role of export and import of data, discussed below.

Data export

In each module (actually a file containing JavaScript code), we decide which data we want to make visible externally (for other modules or for an HTML page). We use for this the new JavaScript `export` keyword, which allows to export one or more data to the outside.

In our example, we want to export the `Person` and `Man` classes in order to make them accessible outside. We add the `export` keyword in each of the two files (which become modules).

Person.js module
```
class Person {
 constructor(lastname, firstname) {
  this.lastname = lastname;
  this.firstname = firstname;
 }
 log() {
  console.log(`Lastname : ${this.lastname}, Firstname : ${this.firstname}`);
 }
}
export { Person };
```

To transform a JavaScript file into a module, just add the `export` keyword specifying the exported data, separated by commas if several data are to be exported, and surrounded by braces.

In the case where only one data is exported in the module, one can also write:

Exporting a single data in the module
```
export default Person;
```

The `export default` statement is only used if only one data is exported to the module. In other cases, we use the first syntax with braces.

Using the module in the HTML file

Once the module is written, you have to see how to use it in the HTML page. Let's use the `Person.js` module in the HTML page.

Using the Person.js module in the HTML page
```
<html>
<head>
</head>
<script type="module">
```

```
import { Person } from "./Person.js";
var person = new Person("Trump", "Donald");
person.log();
</script>
</html>
```

The module's JavaScript file is included by means of the import statement, but for this statement to be understood by the browser, it must be inserted into a <script type = "module"> tag, otherwise the import statement is not recognized.

Let's run this HTML page in the browser:

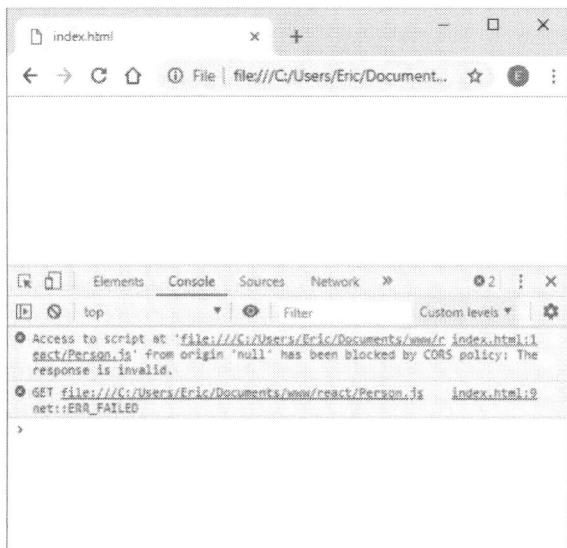

The error message indicates a problem accessing the module file. Indeed, the files associated with modules are accessible only by the http protocol, and here it is for the moment the file protocol which is used in the URL of the browser. Hence the error message ...

The error can easily be corrected by changing the access protocol to the URL of the index.html file. Just install a web server (if you have not already done so) and access the index.html file from an http URL, for example http://localhost/react, assuming the index.html file and the different modules used are deposited in the react directory of the server.

When done, the HTML page is now displayed (with the information in the console):

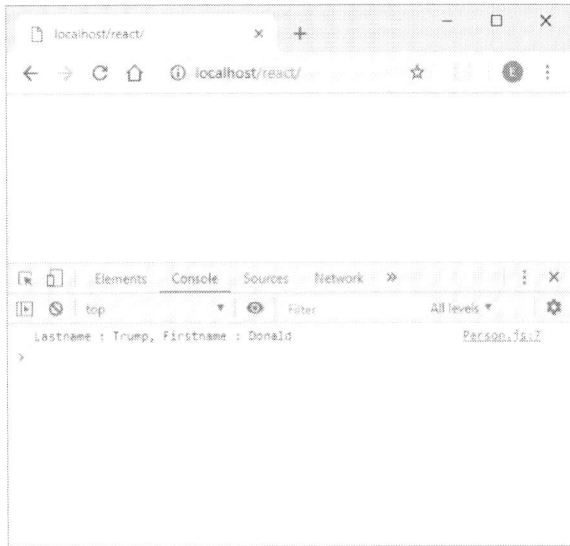

When using ES6 modules, `http` URLs are required to access the HTML page.

Data import

In the previous example we used the `import` statement so our script could use the imported module's data. The data used in the script (and imported from the module) is specified in the `import` statement.

You can only import data that has been previously exported, otherwise an error will occur. For example, you can not import the `Person` class if this class has not been exported to the module where it is defined.

Module Person.js exporting

```
export { Person };
```

If other data is to be exported in this module, it must be indicated afterwards (between braces) and separated by a comma.

Module that imports

```
import { Person } from "./Person.js";
```

If other data is to be imported from this module, it must be indicated afterwards (between braces) and separated by a comma.

In the case where a single piece of data is to be exported in a module, it can be exported using the `export default` statement.

Exporting a single piece of data in a module

```
export default Person;
```

Data exported by `export default` must then be imported like this:

Import of data exported by export default
```
import Person from "./Person.js";
```

Braces are no longer necessary (and cause an error if you put them!).

Note that the `import` and `export` statements can be used in the files describing the modules, but also in modules that use them, or in HTML files using the tag `<script type = "module">`.

Use multiple modules simultaneously

Let's apply the previous explanations in the case of our two Person.js and Man.js modules.

Person.js module
```
class Person {
 constructor(lastname, firstname) {
  this.lastname = lastname;
  this.firstname = firstname;
 }
 log() {
  console.log(`Lastname : ${this.lastname}, Firstname : ${this.firstname}`);
 }
}
export default Person;
```

Man.js module
```
import Person from "./Person.js";
class Man extends Person {
 constructor(lastname, firstname) {
  super(lastname, firstname);
  this.sex = "M";
 }
 log() {
  super.log();
  console.log("It's a man !");
 }
}
export default Man;
```

Once these two modules are defined, they can be used in two ways:
- Integration of the modules in a global module, then use of this global module

in the HTML page,
- Direct use of both modules in the HTML page.

Let's see these two possibilities.

Import modules into a global module

These two modules are integrated into a global module index.js, and it is this last module that is included in the index.html HTML page.

index.js module

```
import Person from "./Person.js";
import Man from "./Man.js";
var person = new Person("Trump", "Donald");
person.log();
var man = new Man("Obama", "Barack");
man.log();
```

Both modules are imported into the global module.

index.html file

```
<html>
<head>
</head>
<script type="module" src="./index.js"></script>
</html>
```

Note the use of the `<script type = "module">` tag to specify that the index.js file uses the module concept. If the type attribute does not have the value "module", an error occurs.

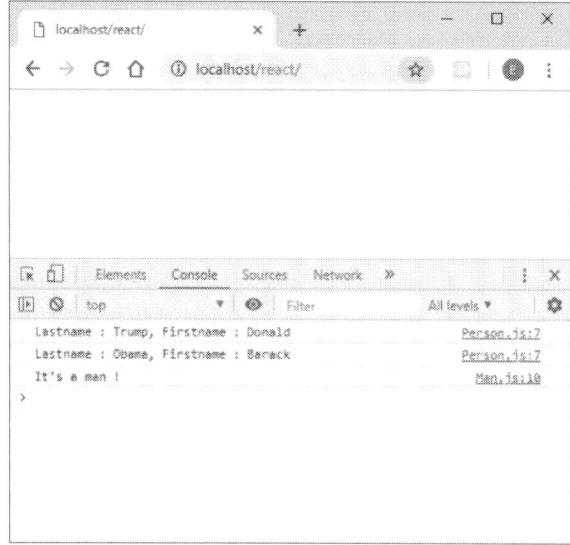

Both Person and Man objects are correctly displayed in the console.

Import modules directly into the HTML page

Rather than going through an intermediate module (here index.js), one can use the Person.js and Man.js modules directly in the HTML page. This solution is faster to write (one less file to write), but also less frequently used than the previous one.

It is nevertheless simple to write: the contents of the previous index.js file are found directly in a script of the HTML page. The script should have the attribute type = "module" to accept the import statements of the different modules.

index.html file

```
<html>
<head>
</head>
<script type="module">
import Person from "./Person.js";
import Man from "./Man.js";
var person = new Person("Trump", "Donald");
person.log();
var man = new Man("Obama", "Barack");
man.log();
</script>
</html>
```

The import statements appear directly in the JavaScript code of the HTML page, provided that this JavaScript code has been declared with the `type = "module"` attribute.

2 – HELLO REACT

In this chapter, we finally start writing React code! Our goal will be to discover the basics of React, in order to understand how it works.

React, what is it?

React is a JavaScript library developed by Facebook, which is used to create reusable display components. In the MVC model (Model View Controller) it corresponds to the View aspect of it.

To create an application with React, we will create display components (usually classes or functions) which will then be assembled to form the final application. React's interest, in addition to creating reusable components, is also to allow a quick update of the HTML page (in case of modifications in this one).

Indeed, when using libraries such as jQuery (which manipulate the HTML elements of the page, ie the DOM, directly) the performances are much lower because the manipulation of the DOM directly in JavaScript is slow during execution. React does not manipulate the DOM directly but an internal copy of it (the React objects or elements, called the virtual DOM), and produces the changes on the display only when necessary.

Finally React is not only a library for displaying on the web, but can also be used to produce native iPhone and Android applications, using a variant that is React Native (not covered in this tutorial).

A first display with React

We want to simply display the "Hello React" text in the browser, using the features of React. This text corresponds to a simple HTML paragraph, which will be inserted into the HTML page by React. React allows you to display an HTML page using React code (JavaScript code) so you do not write HTML code (used to display

HTML elements) directly in the page (except an empty `<div>` element that will contain the HTML code produced by React).

React consists of two JavaScript libraries to insert into the HTML page. These are `React` and `ReactDOM`.

- `React` is React itself, which we study in this tutorial, and which allows to create reusable display components,
- `ReactDOM` is an extension to view, in an HTML page, the components created with React. Other extensions are available, for example to display these components in an iPhone or Android application.

We can see here the distinction made by React between the creation of components (independent of the medium on which they will be displayed) and the display media (web page or iPhone / Android application for example).

As indicated on the page https://reactjs.org/docs/cdn-links.html there are two versions of each library, a version for use in development mode, and a version for use in production mode. We use here the version defined for the development mode.

Minimum basic index.html page that will contain the React code

```
<html>
<head>
<script crossorigin
  src="https://unpkg.com/react@16/umd/react.development.js"></script>
<script crossorigin
  src="https://unpkg.com/react-dom@16/umd/react-dom.development.js"></script>
</head>
<body>
  <div id="root"></div>
</body>
<script>
// here React code
</script>
</html>
```

The HTML page includes both React and ReactDOM libraries in development mode (here version 16). It is a simple copy of the code proposed on the HTML page of ReactJS.org cited above.

The `<body>` part includes a `<div>` element with the `"root"` id. This `<div>` element will be used to contain the HTML elements displayed in the page by the React code, and that is why its content is empty (only the id is useful in order to access it by JavaScript).

51

The React code is created in JavaScript, hence the <script> tag at the end of the page that will insert it. The React code is inserted here directly from the HTML page, but could have been written in a separate JavaScript file, itself included in the HTML page by means of another <script> tag.

Note that this HTML page displays a blank page in the browser, because currently no HTML element is displayed (except the <div> element without content), and no JavaScript code is executed to create HTML content.

You can view this page in a browser, either by depositing the HTML file in a browser (drag and drop from a file explorer), or by installing a server on your machine. For the moment we retain the first solution.

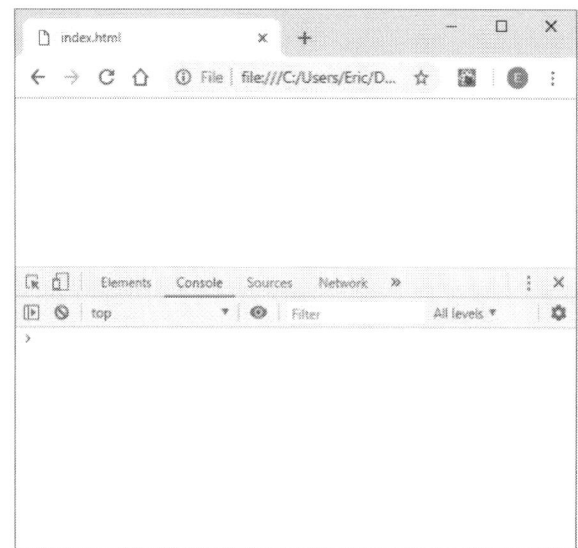

The page displayed is actually blank. The window below corresponds to the development tools available in Chrome by pressing the F12 key.

The Elements tab that appears in the window allows you to see the HTML elements displayed in the page, while the Console tab allows you to see any messages displayed (either Javascript errors, or displayed by our program by means of console.log()).

The React tab is the React Developper Tools extension that has been previously installed in Chrome. It allows to visualize the components created by React and will always be useful for the continuation.

It remains now to produce a display in this page. For this we write the React code in JavaScript, in the <script> part reserved for this purpose (at the bottom of the index.html file).

The React code below will make it possible to create an HTML paragraph (`<p>` tag) and insert it into the `<div>` element created for this purpose in the page (the one whose id is `"root"`).

Creating a paragraph and inserting it into the HTML page

```
var p = React.createElement("p", null, "Hello React");   // React element creation
console.log(p);
ReactDOM.render(p, document.getElementById("root"));    // insert in the page
```

The index.html file that contains this React code is this one:

index.html file

```
<html>
<head>
<script crossorigin
  src="https://unpkg.com/react@16/umd/react.development.js"></script>
<script crossorigin
  src="https://unpkg.com/react-dom@16/umd/react-dom.development.js"></script>
</head>
<body>
  <div id="root"></div>
</body>
<script>
var p = React.createElement("p", null, "Hello React");   // React element creation
console.log(p);
ReactDOM.render(p, document.getElementById("root"));    // insert in the page
</script>
</html>
```

Including React files in the `<head>` part of the page gives you access to React features, especially the `React` and `ReactDOM` objects used here.

The `React.createElement(element, attributes, children)` method is used to create a React object corresponding to an HTML element (here a `<p>` element, indicated in the first parameter), by indicating its attributes as an object as a second parameter (here no one therefore indicates `null`), then in third parameter its children (here the text of the paragraph).

The `React.createElement()` method creates a JavaScript object that can be used by React, but this object must be displayed in the HTML page to be visible, which allows the call to the `ReactDOM.render(React object, DOM element to display the React object)` method. The DOM element where the React object is to be displayed is retrieved by the JavaScript `document.getElementById("root")` statement, hence the utility of having an id set to this element to access it here.

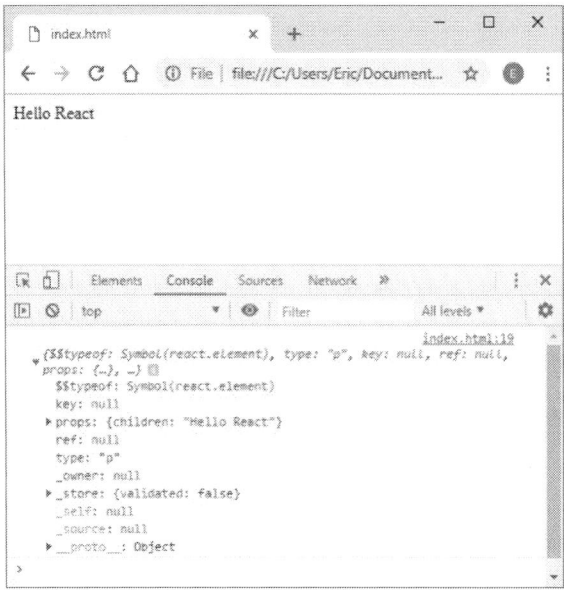

The paragraph displaying "Hello React" is displayed in the page. The window below shows the result of console.log(p), where p is the React object created by React.createElement().

If we select the React tab in this window, we see the elements created by React.

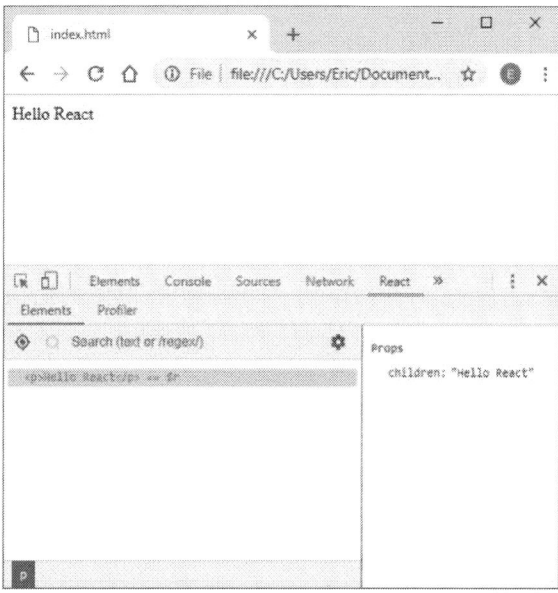

Here we display a simple React element, but this part of the window will be more interesting when the elements created will be more numerous ...

Adding attributes to an element

The paragraph shown here has no attributes at this time. For example, you could assign an id, a style, or even a CSS class.

The second parameter of the React.createElement() method is used to specify, as a JSON object, the attributes that you want to assign to the element.

Let's start by adding an id attribute to the previous paragraph.

Add an id attribute to the element

```
var p = React.createElement("p", { id : "id1" }, "Hello React");
console.log(p);
ReactDOM.render(p, document.getElementById("root"));
```

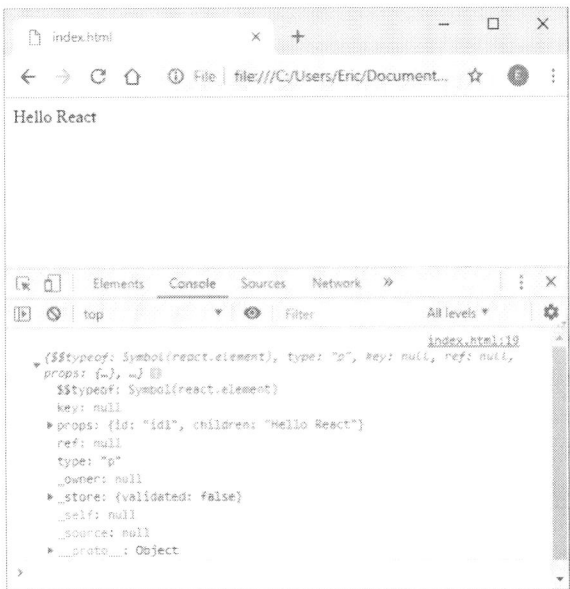

The value of the id attribute has been set in the React object associated with the paragraph (object created by React.createElement()), in its props property. The props property is added by React to all React elements created by React.createElement().

We could retrieve the id using the console.log(p.props.id) statement, which would display here "id1".

Now let's change the style of the element by assigning it the red color (CSS color property), and a black background (CSS background-color property). This is done using the HTML style attribute.

Changing the style of the element (color and background-color)
```
var p = React.createElement("p",
 { id : "id1", style : { color:"red", backgroundColor:"black" } }, "Hello React");
console.log(p);
ReactDOM.render(p, document.getElementById("root"));
```

The style attribute is described as a JSON object, not as a character string as would be done if the paragraph was written directly in HTML code. Let's not forget that the elements created by React are thanks to JavaScript code, which implies to respect the syntax of this language.

A CSS property composed of several words, such as background-color, can be used either by replacing each dash by the capitalization of the word that follows (so here backgroundColor), or by surrounding it with quotation marks (so here "background-color").

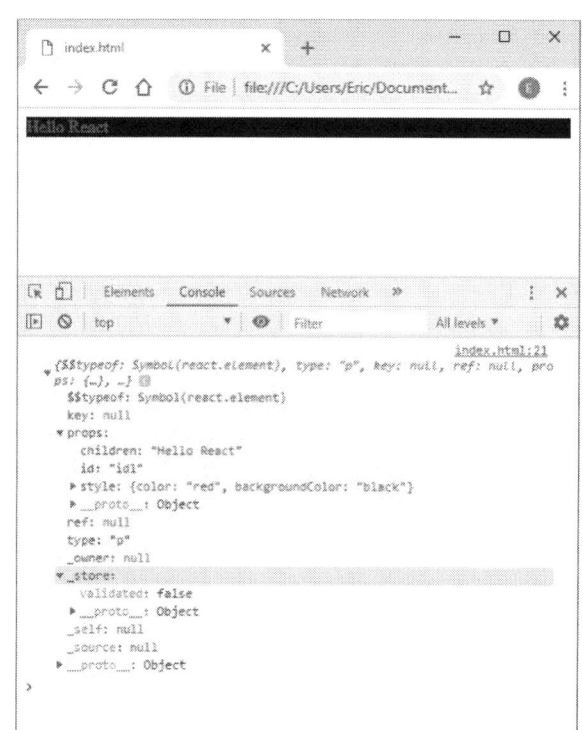

The style of the paragraph has been modified (red on a black background).

The window below shows the React object associated with this element, in particular the style object created by React in the props object.

If you select the React tab, you can see the React element in another form.

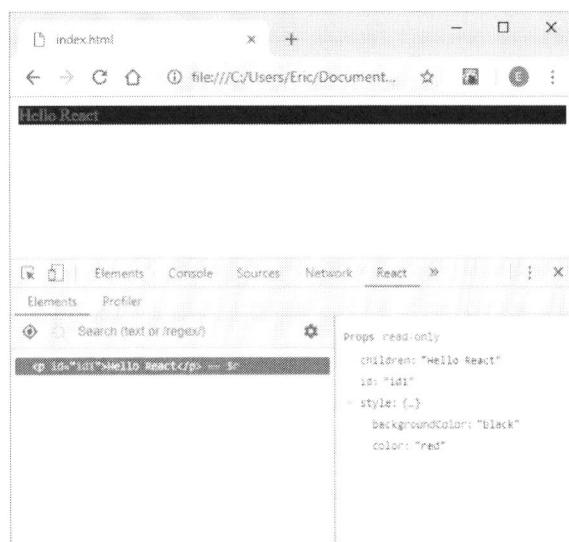

The advantage of the React tab is that it allows you to see the architecture of elements created by React without using console.log().

A special case of attribute is when using the class attribute. Indeed, this attribute can not be used directly in the JavaScript code because it would be interpreted as a JavaScript class declaration. React allows you to replace it with the className attribute as shown below.

Adding the class attribute to an element

```
<html>
<head>
<script crossorigin
  src="https://unpkg.com/react@16/umd/react.development.js"></script>
<script crossorigin
  src="https://unpkg.com/react-dom@16/umd/react-dom.development.js"></script>
<style type="text/css">
 .red { /* red CSS class definition */
   color : red;
 }
</style>
</head>
<body>
 <div id="root"></div>
</body>
```

```
<script>
var p = React.createElement("p",
 { id : "id1", className : "red" }, "Hello React");
console.log(p);
ReactDOM.render(p, document.getElementById("root"));
</script>
</html>
```

In JavaScript, the `className` property is used instead of `class`. The CSS `red` class is defined in the HTML code by means of the `<style>` tag.

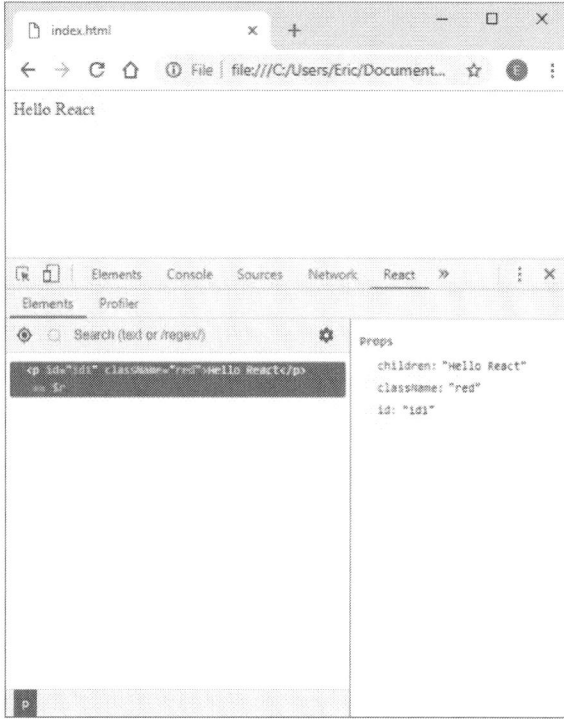

Creating children in an element

The previous paragraph has only one child that is a text element, inserting directly into the third parameter of React.createElement().

To illustrate how to create an element with multiple children, let's create a `<ul>` element with five children that are `<li>` elements in a list.

Creating a list of five elements

```
var ul = React.createElement("ul", null,          // parent element
      React.createElement("li", null, "Element1"),  // child 1
```

```
        React.createElement("li", null, "Element2"),  // child 2
        React.createElement("li", null, "Element3"),  // child 3
        React.createElement("li", null, "Element4"),  // child 4
        React.createElement("li", null, "Element5")   // child 5
    );
console.log(ul);
ReactDOM.render(ul, document.getElementById("root"));
```

The five children are created by the same method as the parent element (ie by React.createElement()) and are inserted into the last parameter of the React.createElement() method, one after the other (separated by a comma). This method can therefore contain any number of arguments, the children of the element to be created being considered as appearing from the third position of the list of arguments (or can be put in an array as we will see below).

Each of the children can also have children himself, which means that instead of having a text element like this ("Element1" for example), we could have the React.createElement() statement in place of the text element. So we see that in this way we can build any HTML fragment.

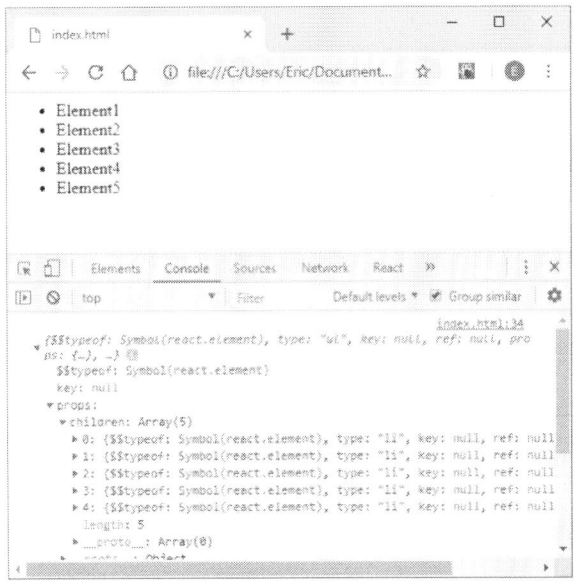

The five children of the React element are put in the children property of the props object associated with that React element, each of which is itself a React element.

By selecting the React tab in the window, you can see the tree of React elements created.

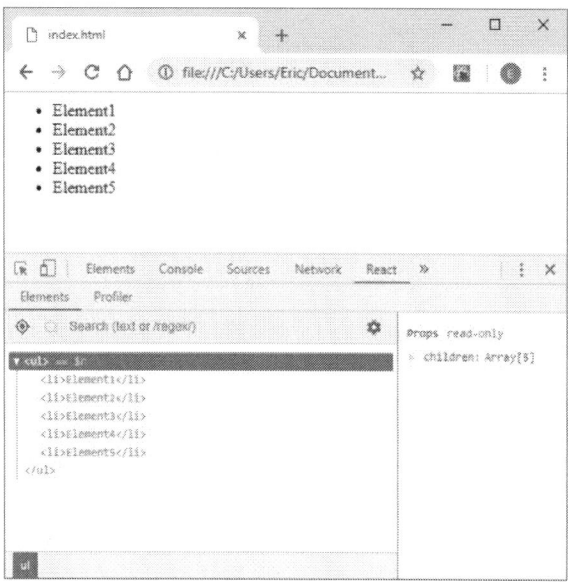

By clicking on each of the elements in the left part of the window, we can see its properties grouped in the props object.

The children of an element can be inserted in the parameter list of the React.createElement() method, starting from the third, as we did above. You can also specify them as an array, always in the third parameter of the React.createElement() method.

Insert list items as an array
```
var ul = React.createElement("ul", null,
        [ React.createElement("li", null, "Element1"),
          React.createElement("li", null, "Element2"),
          React.createElement("li", null, "Element3"),
          React.createElement("li", null, "Element4"),
      React.createElement("li", null, "Element5") ]
    );
console.log(ul);
ReactDOM.render(ul, document.getElementById("root"));
```

The <li> children of the <ul> element are now grouped into an array of elements corresponding to the third parameter of the React.createElement() method.

Even though the program is functional, an error message appears in the React tab. We see how to eliminate this error message in the next section.

Being able to group the children of an element in an array will serve us in the next section.

Dynamic insertion of elements in a list

The previously created list of five elements can have many more than five elements, and in this case it is difficult to write it as we did. The list should be created using a JavaScript program loop.

Creating the list of elements using a JavaScript loop

```
var elems = ["Element1", "Element2", "Element3", "Element4", "Element5"];
var ul = React.createElement("ul", null ,
    elems.map(function(elem, index){
      return React.createElement("li", null, elem);
    }));
ReactDOM.render(ul, document.getElementById("root"));
```

The texts of the list elements are put in an elems array. This array is traversed using the map() method (JavaScript method defined on the Array class). The map() method uses a callback function (defined as a parameter) that is called for each element of the array. For each call of this callback function, the element of the array and its index in the array are passed as parameters to the callback function (elem and index). Because the map() method returns an array of <li> React elements, this array of elements is passed as a list of children in the <ul> element.

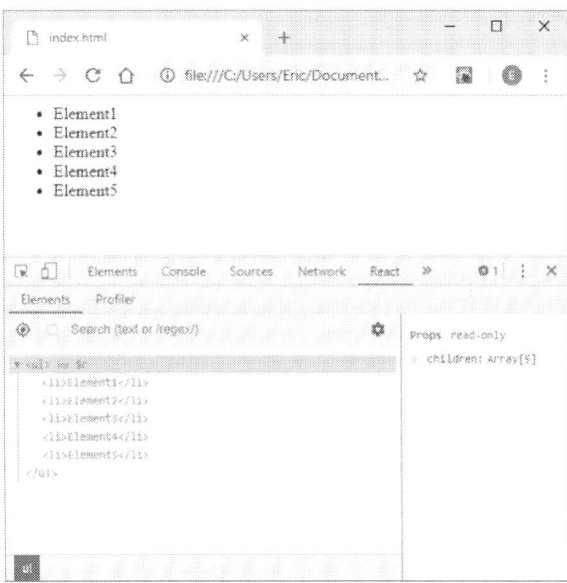

List items are actually inserted into the <ul> element. However, the React tab displays an error (red cross with the number 1 next to it). Clicking on this cross displays a message that explains the error: "Each child in an array or iterator should have a unique key prop." This error message is the same that was displayed in the previous example.

To eliminate the React error message, simply assign a key property with a different value to each inserted <li> element.

Adding the key property to each <li> element
```
var elems = ["Element1", "Element2", "Element3", "Element4", "Element5"];
var ul = React.createElement("ul", null ,
    elems.map(function(elem, index){
      return React.createElement("li", { key : index }, elem);
    }));
ReactDOM.render(ul, document.getElementById("root"));
```

The value assigned to the key property is the index of the item in the list, which is necessarily unique as requested.

The error message displayed in the React tab has now disappeared.

If we remember the improvements made to JavaScript by its ES6 version (which was the subject of the previous chapter), the function declarations can be written in a more condensed form.

Writing in ES6 of the previous program
```
var elems = ["Element1", "Element2", "Element3", "Element4", "Element5"];
var ul = React.createElement("ul", null ,
    elems.map((elem, index)=>{
      return React.createElement("li", { key : index }, elem);
    }));
ReactDOM.render(ul, document.getElementById("root"));
```

Using a function as a first parameter of the React.createElement() method

The React.createElement() method first takes a string representing the HTML element to be created (for example "ul", "li", ...). React is used to indicate, instead of the character string, a function reference (its name) that will be called to create the corresponding React element (possibly including its children).

The following example creates a list of items (like the one in the previous example) by specifying a function as the first argument of the React.createElement() method.

Create a list using a function

```
var elems = ["Element1", "Element2", "Element3", "Element4", "Element5"];
var elementsList = function() {
 return React.createElement("ul", null,
   elems.map(function(elem, index) {
    return React.createElement("li", { key : index }, elem);
   })
  );
}
var list = React.createElement(elementsList);
ReactDOM.render(list, document.getElementById("root"));
```

The elementsList() function creates the list of elements (<ul> and its <li> children). It returns a React parent element (associated with <ul>), itself composed of React children (associated with <li>).

The elementsList() function is automatically called by React because it is located as the first argument of the call to React.createElement(elementsList). Notice that the elementsList() function is not called by our program (we did not put parentheses () afterwards), but it is the React.createElement(elementsList) statement that will cause its call automatically.

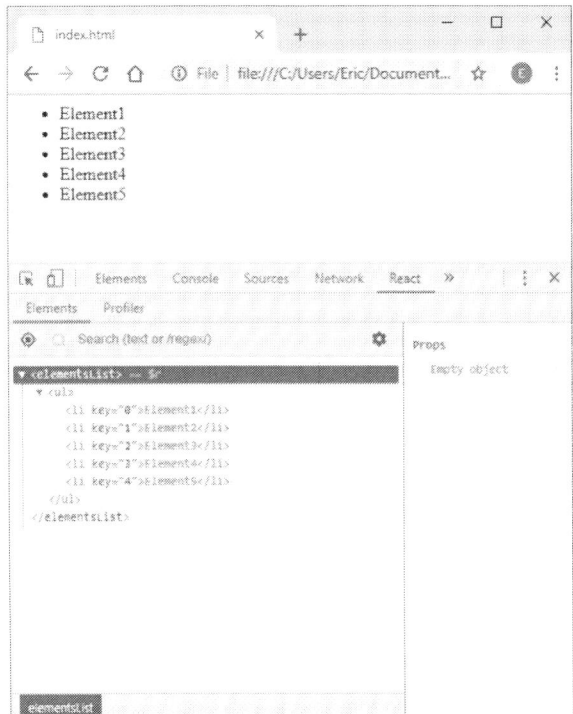

In the React tab, we see that a React element with the same name as the elementsList() function was created by React. However this element is simply an object in memory used by React, and is not visible in the HTML code of the page.

Transmitting parameters when creating a React element

The advantage of using a function to create React elements (as in the previous example) is to be able to pass parameters to the function. For example we could transmit the elems array containing the texts of the elements of the list to create.

Transmit the elems array to the elementsList(elems) function as parameters

```
var elems = ["Element1", "Element2", "Element3", "Element4", "Element5"];
var elementsList = function(elements) {
 return React.createElement("ul", null,
  elements.map(function(elem, index) {
   return React.createElement("li", { key : index }, elem);
  })
 );
}
var list = React.createElement(elementsList);
ReactDOM.render(list, document.getElementById("root"));
```

The only change is the indication of an additional parameter (elements) when declaring the elementsList (elements) function.

However, this can not work because we have to find a way for the elems array to be passed when calling the elementsList(elements) function, which is not the case at the moment.

The only place where this elems array can be passed is when using the elementsList() function, ie in the call to the React.createElements(elementsList) method. For this, remember that this React.createElements() method has a second parameter which is an object in which we can specify attributes of the element to create (id, style, className, etc. as we did in beginning of this chapter). We will insert a new attribute that will contain the list of elements texts, so the elems array. Let's call elems this new attribute for example.

Pass the elems attribute to the elementsList() function

```
var elems = ["Element1", "Element2", "Element3", "Element4", "Element5"];
var elementsList = function(props) {
 console.log(props);
 return React.createElement("ul", null,
```

```
    props.elems.map(function(elem, index) {
      return React.createElement("li", { key : index }, elem);
    })
  );
}
var list = React.createElement(elementsList, { elems : elems });
ReactDOM.render(list, document.getElementById("root"));
```

The `elementsList()` function receives as parameters the `props` object specified as the second argument of the `React.createElement(fct, props)` method. To access the `elems` attribute in the `elementsList function(props)`, just read `props.elems`.

Other values can be passed in the attributes, which will be retrieved in the same way from the `props` object, passed by React as a parameter.

In ES6, we had seen the principle of destructuring an object. Since in our `elementsList(props)` function we only use the `elems` property of the `props` object, it is more straightforward to write the program using this syntax.

Writing the program using ES6

```
var elems = ["Element1", "Element2", "Element3", "Element4", "Element5"];
var elementsList = function({ elems }) {
  console.log(elems);
  return React.createElement("ul", null,
    elems.map(function(elem, index) {
      return React.createElement("li", { key : index }, elem);
    })
  );
}
var list = React.createElement(elementsList, { elems : elems });
ReactDOM.render(list, document.getElementById("root"));
```

Since the `props` object no longer exists in the list of parameters of the `elementsList()` function, the `elems` property passed in the `props` object is accessed directly.

And rather than using the `function` keyword to define the function, one can also use the ES6 syntax with `=>`.

Writing the program using ES6

```
var elems = ["Element1", "Element2", "Element3", "Element4", "Element5"];
var elementsList = ({ elems }) => {
  return React.createElement("ul", null,
    elems.map(function(elem, index) {
      return React.createElement("li", { key : index }, elem);
    })
```

```
  );
}
var list = React.createElement(elementsList, { elems : elems });
ReactDOM.render(list, document.getElementById("root"));
```

Using the React.Component class

We have, in the previous examples, shown how to create a React element (whether or not it is composed of other React elements) by means of the React.createElement() method.

As we have seen, this method can be used in a function that returns the parent React element, but can also be used in a JavaScript class that derives from a class named React.Component defined in React. It is this new way of proceeding that we will explain now, by creating a list of elements as before.

Use React.Component to create a list of items

```
var elems = ["Element1", "Element2", "Element3", "Element4", "Element5"];
class ElementsList extends React.Component {
 constructor(props) {
  super(props);
```

```
  }
  render() {
    return React.createElement("ul", null,
      this.props.elems.map(function(elem, index) {
        return React.createElement("li", { key : index }, elem);
      })
    );
  }
}
var list = React.createElement(ElementsList, { elems : elems });
ReactDOM.render(list, document.getElementById("root"));
```

The React.createElement() method now uses as first parameter the name of a JavaScript class (here ElementsList) derived from React.Component. The second parameter of the method is used to pass the attributes of the element to be created, which are retrieved from the class using this.props.

The render() method defined in the class is a method called internally by React whenever an element of the ElementsList class is to be displayed. It is the React-DOM.render() statement that triggers the call to the render() method defined in the ElementsList class.

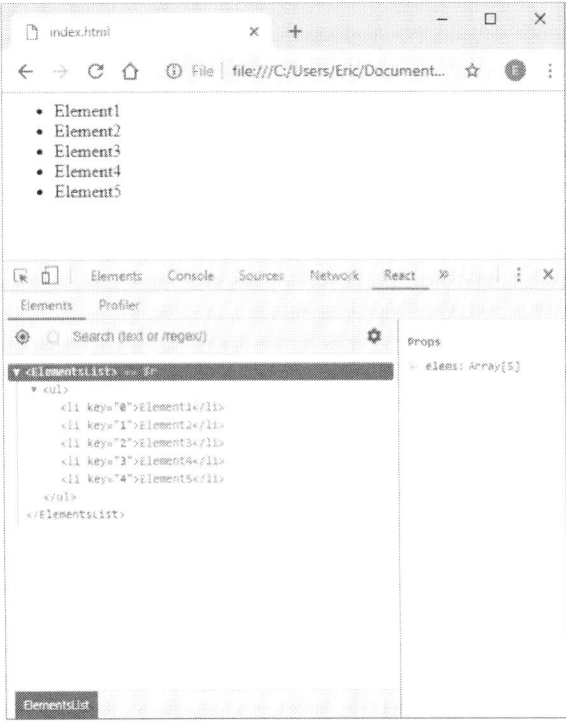

We see in the React tab that the list contains the desired HTML elements (`<ul>` and `<li>`) but also a React element with the same name as the ElementsList class.

Let's modify the program so that each list item is written in a color that is passed when the list is created (in the list of attributes). You only need to specify this style when creating the ElementsList element.

Transmit the color of list items

```
var elems = ["Element1", "Element2", "Element3", "Element4", "Element5"];
class ElementsList extends React.Component {
 constructor(props) {
  super(props);
 }
 render() {
  return React.createElement("ul", null,
    this.props.elems.map(function(elem, index) {
       return React.createElement("li", {
          key : index,
        style : this.props.style
     }, elem);
    })
  );
 }
}
var list = React.createElement(ElementsList, {
  elems : elems,
  style : { color : "red" }
});
ReactDOM.render(list, document.getElementById("root"));
```

The style attribute is added in the attributes passed when creating the ElementsList class object via the props object, and thus retrieved in the class by this.props.style.

However, the result is not the one hoped for:

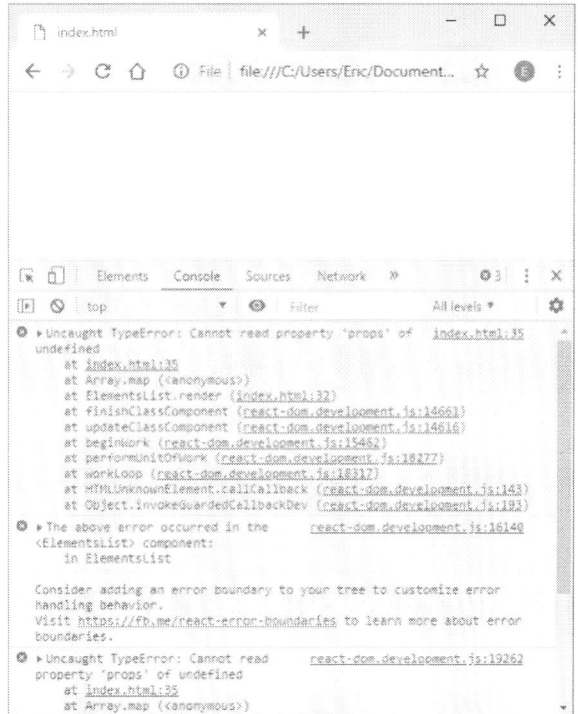

The error is visible in the Console tab of the window. It is explained that we can not access the props property of the this object (in the this.props.style statement written on the corresponding line). Yet there is no error when trying to access this.props.elems written on the top line ...

Why can we access this.props.elems and not this.props.style? The answer is that the this.props.style statement is used in a callback function, which looses the this variable, which is no longer the same in the callback function and outside of it. The this object used in this.props.elems is not the same as the one used in this.props.style.

We had already seen this problem during the study of ES6 in the previous chapter. We saw that the use of the new syntax with => to define a function could have an impact on the value of this object. Use this syntax to define the callback function used in the map() method.

Using the ES6 syntax to set the callback function

```
var elems = ["Element1", "Element2", "Element3", "Element4", "Element5"];
class ElementsList extends React.Component {
 constructor(props) {
  super(props);
```

```
}
render() {
  return React.createElement("ul", null,
    this.props.elems.map((elem, index) => {
        return React.createElement("li", {
          key : index,
          style : this.props.style
      }, elem);
    })
  );
}
}
var list = React.createElement(ElementsList, {
  elems : elems,
  style : { color : "red" }
});
ReactDOM.render(list, document.getElementById("root"));
```

The only difference with the previous program is the use of the syntax with => instead of the function keyword when defining the callback function in the map() method.

The list items are now red, as indicated in the attributes when creating the list. The `this` variable is now the same in and out of the callback function, thanks to the use of the ES6 syntax for function definitions.

Use a function or class instead to create React elements?

In the previous examples, we saw that the `React.createElement()` method could take as first parameter:
- either a string representing the HTML element to be created (for example `"ul"`, `"li"`, etc.),
- either a function name that will be used to create the tree of the elements to be created,
- a class name that allows the same thing as calling the function.

The class allows to define methods and internal variables, which the function does not allow. So depending on the complexity of the React element to create, we will use the function if it is enough, and we will use the class in case the creation becomes more complex.

3 – REACT & JSX

We saw in the previous chapter how to create React elements and display them in the HTML page. The base of the whole mechanism is the React.createElement() method to create the React elements, then the ReactDOM.render() method to display them in the HTML page.

However, the construction of a React element tree by means of React.createElement() is not easy, and moreover does not make it possible to visualize well the tree which will be actually built (because of the mixture of JavaScript statements with HTML in the middle).

The designers of React have therefore looked for a way to lighten the writing and their choice has focused on the use of JSX (JavaScript eXtension). JSX is a form of writing React elements, easier to read and write than the React.createElement() statements. This syntax is therefore used extensively in React programs.

Hello React with JSX

JSX is therefore a new form of writing React elements. For example, here is a paragraph containing "Hello React" in its text.

A paragraph containing "Hello React" in JSX
```
var p = <p>Hello React</p>;   // JSX code
```

It looks like a string, but it's not surrounded by single or double quotation marks symbolizing the string. In fact we have here written a React element, in JSX.

Be careful not to put quotation marks when writing JSX code, otherwise it's no longer JSX code, but a string!

However, if we write this piece of program in our HTML page, it will not be correctly interpreted as can be seen in the error message below.

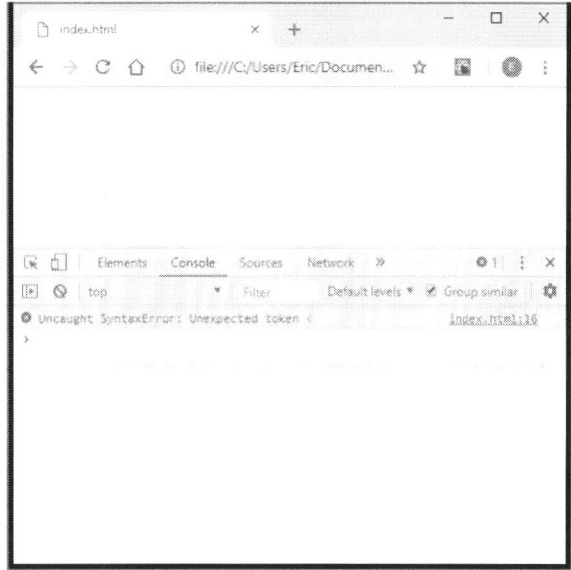

This error message (Unexpected token <) is normal because you can not write HTML in the middle of the JavaScript code. It should have put quotes around the JSX code, but if you do it is no longer the JSX code that you write, it's a string of characters.

To solve the problem and eliminate the error message, it is necessary that the JSX code that one writes is previously translated into real JavaScript code, here in React elements. We use a tool called Babel, which allows to interpret the JSX code and transform it internally into JavaScript code understandable by the browser. Other tools exist, but for now use Babel as proposed.

The HTML page using Babel is written in the following way, integrating our JSX code.

index.html file using Babel to interpret the JSX code

```
<html>
<head>
<script crossorigin
  src="https://unpkg.com/react@16/umd/react.development.js"></script>
<script crossorigin
  src="https://unpkg.com/react-dom@16/umd/react-dom.development.js"></script>
<script src="https://unpkg.com/babel-standalone@6/babel.min.js"></script>
</head>
<body>
  <div id="root"></div>
</body>
```

```
<script type="text/babel">
var p = <p>Hello React</p>;   // JSX code
console.log(p);               // display of the React element in the console
ReactDOM.render(p, document.getElementById("root"));
</script>
</html>
```

We include the JavaScript file of Babel by means of the `<script src="...">` tag (this corresponds to the interpreter which will translate the JSX code into JavaScript code), then we indicate which part of the JavaScript code is to be interpreted by Babel. For this, we include the `type="text/babel"` attribute in the `<script>` tag containing our JavaScript code (and JSX).

The JavaScript code for creating React elements is written in JSX (and will be translated into pure JavaScript by Babel), while the React elements created in this way will be inserted in the HTML page by means of the `ReactDOM.render()` statement (like it was done in the previous chapter).

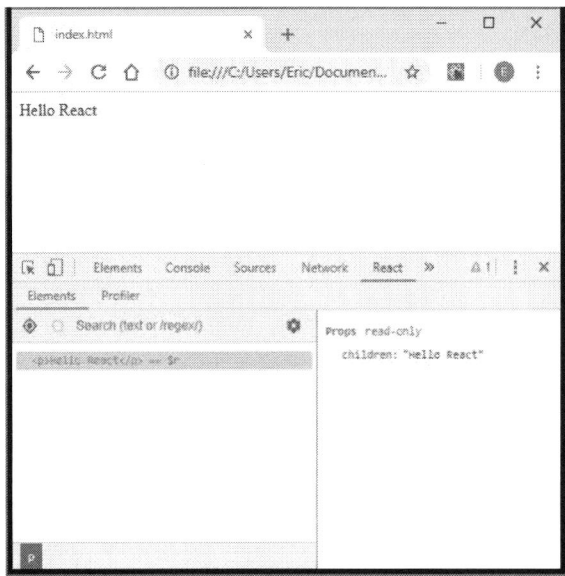

The display corresponds to the paragraph containing "Hello React", while the React tab in the window shows the React element created following the transformation of the JSX code by Babel.

Note that the inclusion of Babel to interpret the JSX code slows down the program, since a translation step is required before running the JavaScript code. So the use of Babel can be viable only in the context of writing the program (in development mode) but can not be used as part of a deployment (production mode). In the latter case, we will use other tools such as Webpack to create a more compact package.

Use Babel to interpret the JSX code

To see the translation process done by Babel, just go to the site https://babeljs.io/ corresponding to Babel, then go to the `Try it out` tab of this site (tab to see the JavaScript code generated by Babel). An example program is proposed to us, it is enough to modify it slightly in order to introduce the following code (allowing to display a paragraph containing `"Hello React"` in the `<body>` element of the page).

Code to display a paragraph on the Babel website
```
import React from "react";
import ReactDOM from "react-dom";
var p = <p>Hello React</p>;
ReactDOM.render(p, document.body);
```

The code generated by Babel is displayed on the right side of the Babel website window. It is reproduced below.

Code generated by Babel (using React code)
```
"use strict";
var _react = require("react");
var _react2 = _interopRequireDefault(_react);
var _reactDom = require("react-dom");
var _reactDom2 = _interopRequireDefault(_reactDom);
function _interopRequireDefault(obj) {
   return obj && obj.__esModule ? obj : { default: obj };
}
var p = _react2.default.createElement(
 "p",
 null,
 "Hello React"
);
_reactDom2.default.render(p, document.body);
```

We can see the `createElement()` statement generated by Babel, corresponding to the JavaScript translation of the JSX code.

Babel is an interpreter that transforms, on the fly, JSX code into JavaScript code, which can then be executed directly by the browser.

Create an item tree with JSX

Rather than just the previous paragraph, use JSX to display a list of five items.

The basic HTML file, which will contain the JSX and JavaScript code, is as follows.

Basic index.html file containing JSX code and JavaScript

```html
<html>
<head>
<script crossorigin
  src="https://unpkg.com/react@16/umd/react.development.js"></script>
<script crossorigin
  src="https://unpkg.com/react-dom@16/umd/react-dom.development.js"></script>
<script src="https://unpkg.com/babel-standalone@6/babel.min.js"></script>
</head>
<body>
  <div id="root"></div>
</body>
<script type="text/babel">
// here the JSX code and the JavaScript code
</script>
</html>
```

As previously seen, we include the file of Babel, and we indicate the `type="text/babel"` attribute in the `<script>` tag so that the JSX code is translated into JavaScript code.

All we have to do is add our JSX code in the `<script>` part reserved for this purpose (at the bottom of the file).

Create a list of five elements in JSX

```
var list = <ul>
        <li> Element1 </li>
        <li> Element2 </li>
        <li> Element3 </li>
        <li> Element4 </li>
        <li> Element5 </li>
    </ul>;
ReactDOM.render(list, document.getElementById("root"));
```

The JSX code is easy to read and write. It is written as HTML, but is written in the JavaScript code part (in the `<script>` tag). It can be written on several lines for the same instruction, but must include an opening tag at the beginning, associated with the same closing tag at the end (here `<ul>` and `</ul>`).

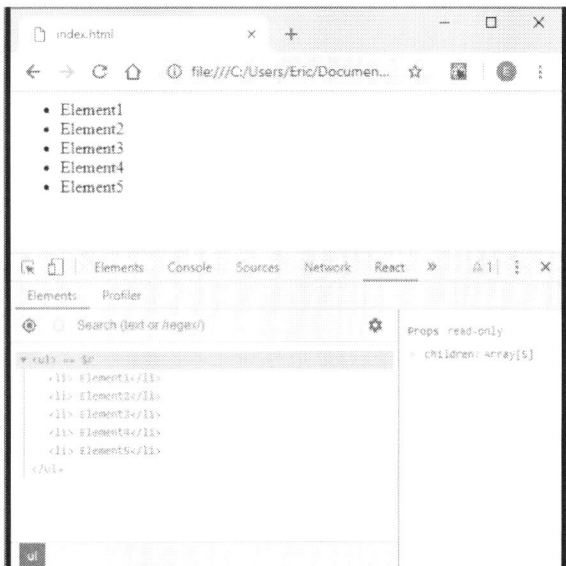

Add attributes in the JSX code

The JSX code contains the elements that will be displayed in the HTML page. These elements can have attributes, such as id, style, or className (the class attribute is replaced by the className attribute).

Adding id and className attributes to JSX

Let's start by adding the id and className attributes. For this we define the red CSS class in the <style> tag of the page.

Definition of the red class
```
<style type="text/css">
 .red {
   color : red;
 }
</style>
```

The <style> tag should be inserted in the <head> part of the page, as it was done in the previous chapter.

The program that inserts the JSX code using the id and className attributes is as follows.

Set the id and className attributes in the JSX code
```
var list = <ul id="list1" className="red">
```

```
        <li> Element1 </li>
        <li> Element2 </li>
        <li> Element3 </li>
        <li> Element4 </li>
        <li> Element5 </li>
    </ul>;
ReactDOM.render(list, document.getElementById("root"));
```

The id and className attributes are inserted into the JSX code as a string.

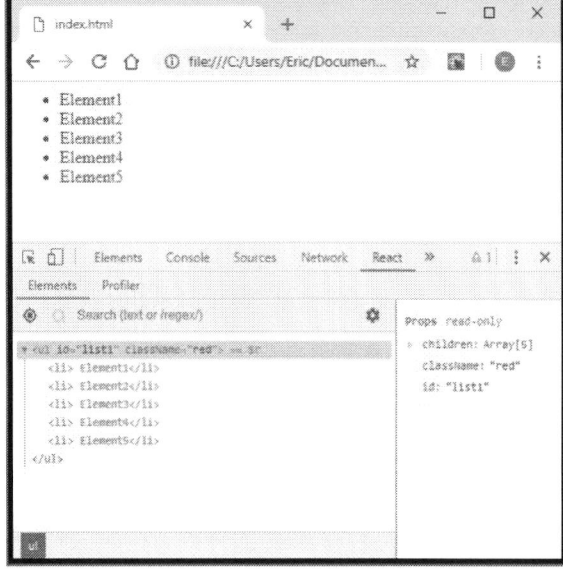

The list defined by <ul> has the "list1" id, while the CSS red class is well defined on the list (the list items are red).

Adding the style attribute to JSX

The syntax to use to insert the style attribute is slightly different. We now want to set the list-style-type CSS property to "none" in the style of the list (<ul> element), which means that list items have no points in front of each one.. The color property will also be set to "red" in the style (it is assumed that the previously used className attribute is removed so that the color of list items is not defined in two places).

Set the style attribute in the JSX code
```
var list = <ul id="list1" style={{listStyleType:"none", color:"red"}}>
        <li> Element1 </li>
        <li> Element2 </li>
        <li> Element3 </li>
```

```
        <li> Element4 </li>
        <li> Element5 </li>
    </ul>;
ReactDOM.render(list, document.getElementById("root"));
```

The list-style-type property is written in the JavaScript code in the listStyleType form, replacing as usual every dash and the letter that follows it with a capital letter.

The style attribute is defined using {{ and }}, which is two opening braces and two closing braces. The outer braces indicate that the expression inside is a JavaScript expression. Moreover the style must in this case, be defined by means of a JavaScript object (here in JSON notation, so with another pair of interior braces to define it).

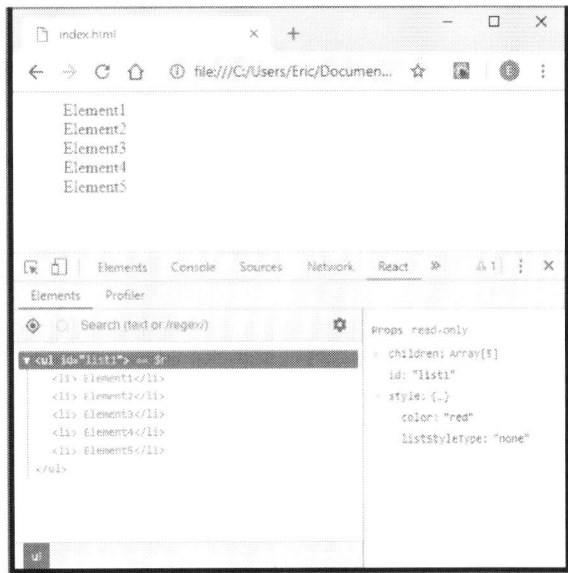

The style of the list has been modified.

Using JavaScript statements in JSX code

You can use JavaScript statements in JSX code, as long as you surround the JavaScript statements with braces. Each statement surrounded by braces is evaluated by the browser, and its result is inserted in place of the evaluated JavaScript statement. This makes it possible to create JSX code that adapts to the conditions defined in the program.

Suppose the previous style is actually calculated by the program, using different instructions in it.

Define JavaScript statements that calculate the style of the element in JSX

```
var color = "red";
var listStyle = { listStyleType:"none", color:color };
var list = <ul id="list1" style={listStyle}>
        <li> Element1 </li>
        <li> Element2 </li>
        <li> Element3 </li>
        <li> Element4 </li>
        <li> Element5 </li>
    </ul>;
ReactDOM.render(list, document.getElementById("root"));
```

The JavaScript statement {listStyle} specifies to calculate the value of the listStyle expression, and then assign that value to the style of the element in the JSX code.

We can improve our code by inserting the elements of list by means of a block of JavaScript code. The elements of the list are put in an elems array which is then traversed by the JavaScript code and JSX.

Insert list items defined in an elems array

```
var color = "red";
var listStyle = { listStyleType:"none", color:color };
var elems = ["Element1", "Element2", "Element3", "Element4", "Element5"];
var list = <ul id="list1" style={listStyle}>
        {
          elems.map(function(elem, index) {
            return <li key={index}>{elem}</li>
          })
        }
    </ul>;
ReactDOM.render(list, document.getElementById("root"));
```

JavaScript statements in a JSX code block must be surrounded by braces, especially the elems.map() statement. Similarly, in every JSX statement, any JavaScript expression must be surrounded by braces, hence their presence in {listStyle} and {index}.

The key attribute is similar to that used in the previous chapter and avoids a warning when executing the code (message "Each child in an array or iterator should have a unique key prop.").

And using the notation with => (available in ES6) to define the callback function, we can write more simply:

Use ES6 notation to define the function

```
var color = "red";
var listStyle = { listStyleType:"none", color:color };
var elems = ["Element1", "Element2", "Element3", "Element4", "Element5"];
var list = <ul id="list1" style={listStyle}>
        {
          elems.map((elem, index) => {
            return <li key={index}>{elem}</li>
          })
        }
        </ul>;
ReactDOM.render(list, document.getElementById("root"));
```

This can also be written even more shorthand (braces and the return statement in the callback function are not necessary if only one statement is present in braces):

Use ES6 notation with no braces or return statement in the callback function

```
var color = "red";
var listStyle = { listStyleType:"none", color:color };
var elems = ["Element1", "Element2", "Element3", "Element4", "Element5"];
var list = <ul id="list1" style={listStyle}>
        {
          elems.map((elem, index) =>
            <li key={index}>{elem}</li> // no return or braces
          )
        }
        </ul>;
ReactDOM.render(list, document.getElementById("root"));
```

Create a JSX element with a function

The interest of JSX is that it is possible to create its own HTML elements, which will be seen as React elements (written in JSX). We will learn how to create the `<ElementsList>` element which will represent the `<ul>` list containing the `<li>` elements.

Create a function that returns JSX code

Let's improve the previous program to make it a function that returns the JSX code needed to create the list. In the previous chapter, we performed a similar function, but returned the list using the `React.createElement()` statements. Here we do not use these instructions but rather the JSX code.

Create a function that returns the JSX code

```
var elems = ["Element1", "Element2", "Element3", "Element4", "Element5"];
var ElementsList = function() {
 return <ul>
     {
       elems.map(function(elem, index) {
         return <li key={index}>{elem}</li>;
       })
     }
     </ul>
}
ReactDOM.render(<ElementsList/>, document.getElementById("root"));
```

The ReactDOM.render() method takes here as first argument, a React element defined in JSX (<ElementsList />). This element corresponds to a function of the same name that creates and returns React elements also defined in JSX.

Note that an element defined in JSX, such as <ElementsList />, must start with a capital letter, otherwise React produces an error. The corresponding associated function must therefore also begin with a capital letter. The only JSX elements that can begin with a lowercase are those corresponding to HTML tags, such as <ul>, <li>, and so on.

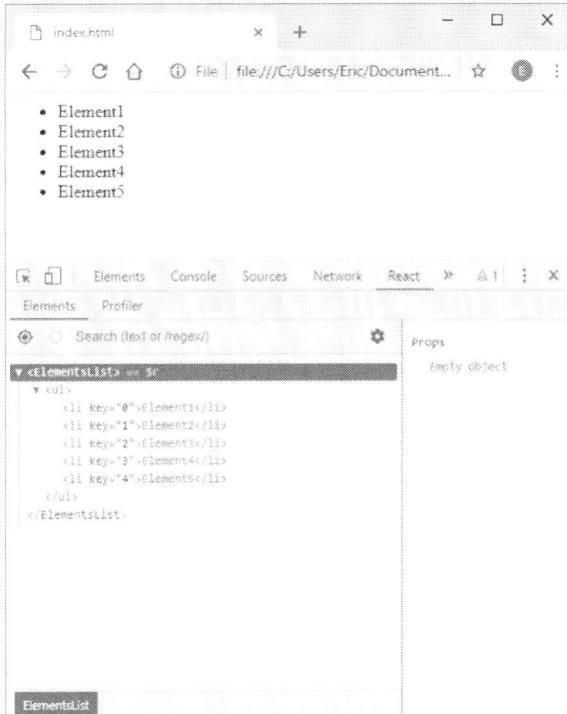

We see in the React tab that a React element named <ElementsList> was created by React, and this element contains the list defined by <ul>.

Another form of writing the program could be the following. Rather than returning the <ul> element in the function, it is indicated as an argument to the ReactDOM.render() method.

Return only <li> elements in the function (without the <ul> element)

```
var elems = ["Element1", "Element2", "Element3", "Element4", "Element5"];
var ElementsList = function() {
 return elems.map(function(elem, index) {
      return <li key={index}>{elem}</li>;
    })
}
ReactDOM.render(<ul><ElementsList/></ul>, document.getElementById("root"));
```

The function no longer returns the <ul> element, so the braces that used to indicate the JavaScript code inside the JSX code are no longer needed here (and if you keep them, they cause an error).

However, the ReactDOM.render() method must return the complete JSX code, including the `<ul>` element.

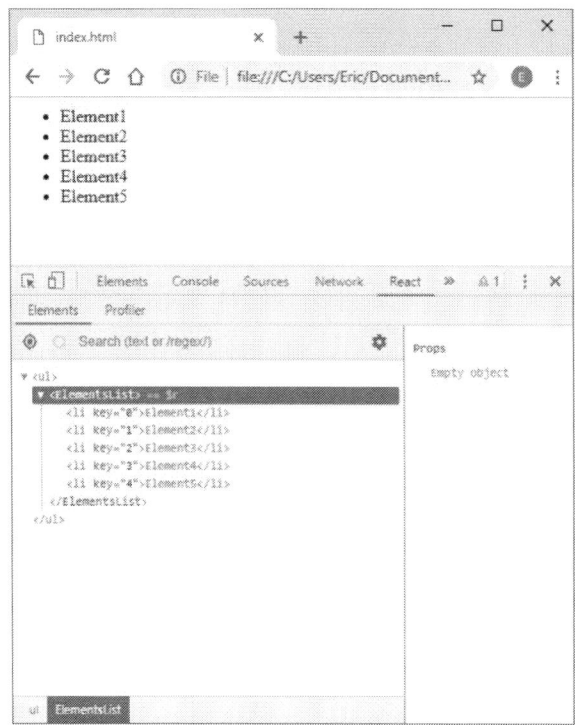

Even if the display of the list is identical to the previous one, one sees here that the `<ul>` and `<ElementsList>` React elements were reversed in the tree structure.

Pass attributes in a JSX element

As we saw in the previous chapter, we can transmit attributes to React elements defined here in JSX. For example, the elems array could be passed in the elems attribute of the JSX element. We can create the attributes we want in a JSX element, these attributes will be passed as parameters for the processing function in the props object.

Transmission of the elems attribute in the JSX element
```
var elems = ["Element1", "Element2", "Element3", "Element4", "Element5"];
var ElementsList = function(props) {
  return <ul>
    {
      props.elems.map(function(elem, index) {
        return <li key={index}>{elem}</li>;
      })
```

```
    }
  </ul>
}
ReactDOM.render(<ElementsList elems={elems}/>, document.getElementById("root"));
```

The `elems` attribute is set when writing the JSX element `<ElementsList elems={elems} />`. The attributes of an element defined by a function are passed into the `props` object as a parameter of the function. So to access the `elems` attribute in the function, we use `props.elems`.

Now let's pass the `style` attribute in the JSX element. The specified style will be assigned to `<li>` elements in the list.

Transmitting the style attribute in the JSX element

```
var elems = ["Element1", "Element2", "Element3", "Element4", "Element5"];
var ElementsList = function(props) {
  return <ul>
      {
        props.elems.map(function(elem, index) {
          return <li key={index} style={props.style}>{elem}</li>;
        })
      }
    </ul>
}
ReactDOM.render(<ElementsList elems={elems} style={{color:"red"}} />,
        document.getElementById("root"));
```

The style is indicated as usual as a JSON object (here `{color: "red"}`), and since it's a JavaScript statement, it must be surrounded by braces, hence the double braces that the can be seen here in the JSX element.

This style is retrieved from the function using the `props` parameter, and is accessed using `props.style` in the JSX element defining each `<li>`.

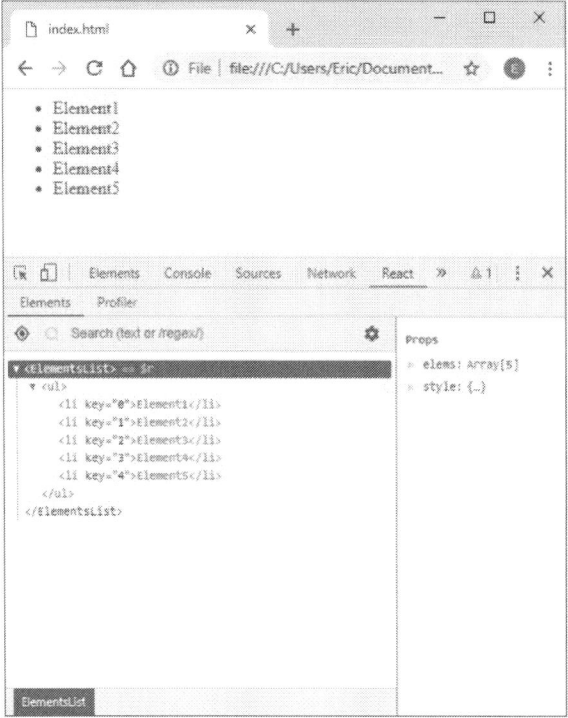

Let's modify this program to pass not the style attribute in the JSX element, but directly the color property, which will have to be positioned in the style of each <li> list element.

Pass the color property in the attributes of the JSX element
```
var elems = ["Element1", "Element2", "Element3", "Element4", "Element5"];
var ElementsList = function(props) {
  return <ul>
    {
      props.elems.map(function(elem, index) {
        return <li key={index} style={{color:props.color}}>{elem}</li>;
      })
    }
    </ul>
}
ReactDOM.render(<ElementsList elems={elems} color="red" />,
        document.getElementById("root"));
```

The color attribute is set in the JSX element, and is retrieved into the function using props.color. This value must be set in an object defining the style (here {color: props.color}), and since this is a JavaScript statement in JSX code, it must be wrapped around braces for evaluation. Hence the double braces used to define the style in the function.

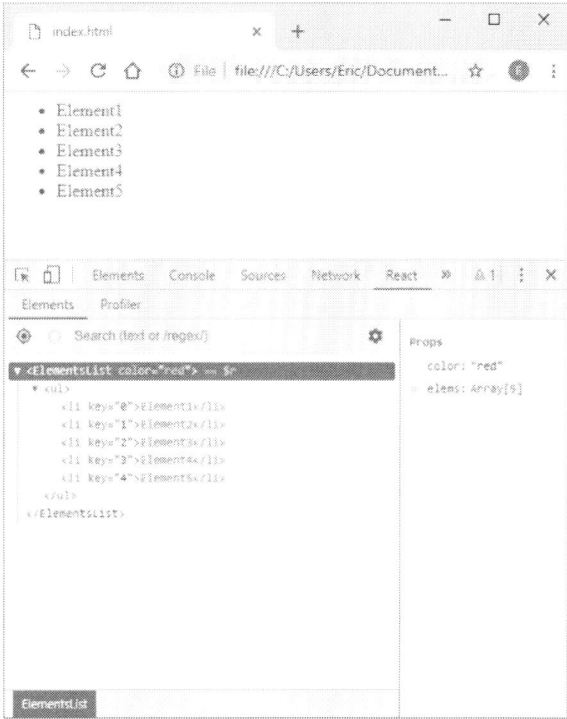

The React tab shows that the color attribute is passed to the <ElementsList> element, and that the CSS color property is then assigned to the style of each <li> list element.

Let us now use the destructuring of objects allowed by ES6 to no longer indicate the props object in parameter, but rather its elems and color properties used here.

Writing the program by destructuring the props object (in ES6)

```
var elems = ["Element1", "Element2", "Element3", "Element4", "Element5"];
var ElementsList = function({elems, color}) {
  return <ul>
    {
      elems.map(function(elem, index) {
        return <li key={index} style={{color:color}}>{elem}</li>;
      })
    }
    </ul>
}
ReactDOM.render(<ElementsList elems={elems} color="red" />,
      document.getElementById("root"));
```

We now access directly the elems and color variables previously defined as properties in the props object.

Create the list by means of components

A JSX element created by our program is also called a React component. Here the component is <ElementsList> which represents the list of elements to be displayed as a list.

However, React encourages us to go further and create as many components as possible in our React programs. Indeed, the goal is to write independent components that can be used in various parts of the program or in other programs. This allows modularity and reuse of code through components.

In our program, it is not difficult to find a new component to write, it would be called <Element> and correspond to an element of the list. This corresponds to React's philosophy of architecting the code into components that are used with each other. The main component <ElementsList> is composed of several <Element> components.

Let's write the <Element> component used by the <ElementsList> component.

Using the <Element> and <ListElements> components

```
var elems = ["Element1", "Element2", "Element3", "Element4", "Element5"];
var Element = function({color, elem}) {
 return <li style={{color:color}}>{elem}</li>;
}
var ElementsList = function({elems, color}) {
  return <ul>
      {
        elems.map(function(elem, index) {
          return <Element key={index} elem={elem} color={color} />
        })
      }
    </ul>
}
ReactDOM.render(<ElementsList elems={elems} color="red" />,
        document.getElementById("root"));
```

The <Element> component is also created with a function in which the index, color and elem attributes are passed as parameters in the props object (here used in unstructured form). The key attribute is used to avoid the classic React error indicating that this attribute is mandatory. However it only serves to put a different key on the elements resulting from an iteration function, so it is used in the writing of the `<Element>` element (written in an iteration loop) but not in the parameters of the `Element()` function.

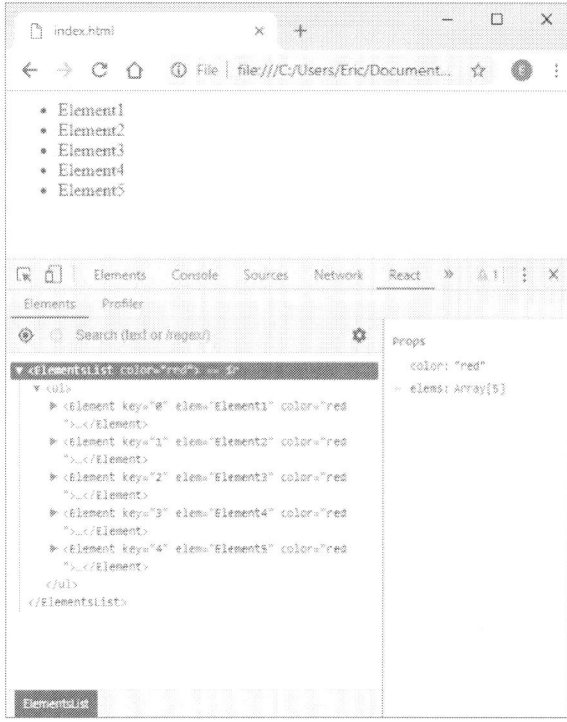

In the `React` tab, we see that the `<ElementsList>` component contains the `<Element>` components as requested.

Create a JSX element with a class

The previous section showed how to create a JSX element from a function. But we know that we can also create React elements (and JSX) from a class derived from the `React.Component` class (see the previous chapter).

Let's now create two classes corresponding to the two previously used components (`<Element>` and `<ElementsList>`). These two classes derive from the `React.Component` class.

Create the classes associated with the `<Element>` and `<ElementsList>` components

```
var elems = ["Element1", "Element2", "Element3", "Element4", "Element5"];
class Element extends React.Component {
  constructor(props) {
```

```
    super(props);
  }
  render() {
    return <li style={{color:this.props.color}}>{this.props.elem}</li>
  }
}
class ElementsList extends React.Component {
  constructor(props) {
    super(props);
  }
  render() {
    return <ul>
        {
          this.props.elems.map((elem, index) => {
            return <Element key={index} elem={elem}
                    color={this.props.color} />
          })
        }
        </ul>
  }
}
ReactDOM.render(<ElementsList elems={elems} color="red" />,
        document.getElementById("root"));
```

The `ReactDOM.render()` statement is the same as the one used in the previous section. In the `ElementsList` class, we pass the `elems` and `color` attributes used in the class via the `this.props` object that contains them.

Note that the callback function used in the `map()` method is defined via the notation ES6 (with `=>` instead of `function`), in order not to lose the value of the `this` object in the callback function (and therefore that `this.props` is accessible in the callback function so that one uses its `color` property).

In the `Element` class, notice the use of double braces to define the style: the first pair of braces is used to indicate a JavaScript statement, the second is used to write the object as JSON.

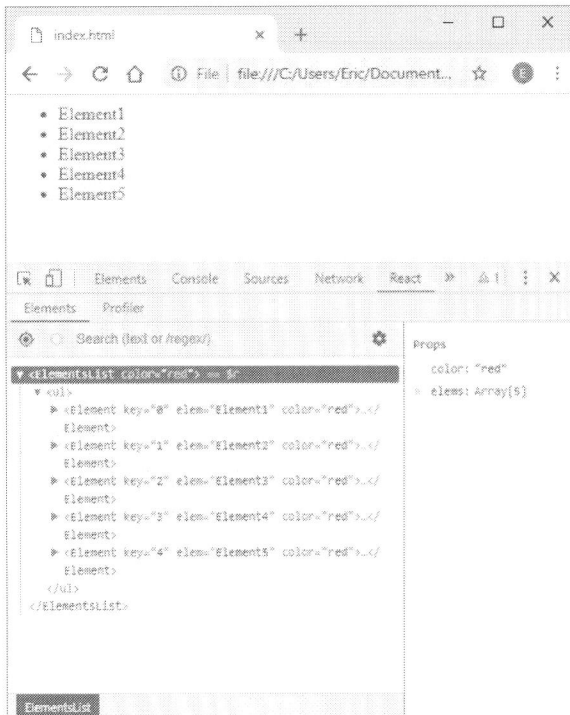

We see on the previous example the utility of the notation of the functions in ES6 (with =>) which avoids to lose the value of this in a callback function. However, one can write the program slightly differently and not lose the value of this while using the function keyword for the callback function.

To do this, simply memorize the value of the color attribute that is used via this.props.color, outside the callback function, before the value of this is lost.

Remember the value of the attributes before using them in the callback function

```
var elems = ["Element1", "Element2", "Element3", "Element4", "Element5"];
class Element extends React.Component {
 constructor(props) {
  super(props);
 }
 render() {
  return <li style={{color:this.props.color}}>{this.props.elem}</li>
 }
}
class ElementsList extends React.Component {
 constructor(props) {
```

```
  super(props);
}
render() {
  var { elems, color } = this.props;  // elems = this.props.elems
                        // color = this.props.color
  return <ul>
      {
        elems.map(function(elem, index) {
          return <Element key={index} elem={elem} color={color} />
        })
      }
      </ul>
  }
}
ReactDOM.render(<ElementsList elems={elems} color="red" />,
      document.getElementById("root"));
```

We recover (here thanks to the destructuration of the ES6 objects) the values of the elems and color attributes (initially stored by React in this.props), then we use these elems and color values in the rest of the render() method of the ElementsList class. Even if the value of this has been changed in the callback function, it does not cause any problems since it is no longer used now ...

Use a function or class to create components in JSX?

This question arises because the two ways seen above are similar and obviously lead to the same results.

As when asked about creating functions or classes with React elements (by React.createElement() in the previous chapter), the answer is similar:

- we will use a function if we do not need to create properties or methods to facilitate treatments,
- and we will use a class instead if properties or methods are needed for the treatments.

In fact, a very important property of a component will be the state property, making it possible to manage the state of the component (this is studied in the next chapter). The observed rule is that if the component has a state, we will use a class to define it (it is even mandatory in this case), otherwise a function will be sufficient.

JSX code writing rules

Here we show some rules for writing the JSX code.

Only one parent element can be returned

Several JSX elements of the same level can not be returned simultaneously, it is mandatory that they be encapsulated in a parent element, which will be the one returned (to be unique), the other elements being its children. In general, we use a `<div>` element that encompasses the set, but React also proposes to use a `<React.Fragment>` component that plays this role.

Note that this rule is also valid if you use the `React.createElement()` method, with which you must also return a single parent React element.

Use a fragment with the <React.Fragment> component

Adding a parent, such as a `<div>` element, works when you want to wrap multiple returned elements in one. The disadvantage of this solution is that it adds an additional `<div>` element in the JSX code, without this being really necessary for the React application (except to avoid the error produced by React).

For that, React proposes a specific component called `<React.Fragment>` which one can use for these cases there.

Let's use the `<React.Fragment>` component to encompass a set of three `<div>` elements without parents. The `<React.Fragment>` element will become the parent of the three `<div>` elements, without appearing in the React element tree.

Use a <React.Fragment> component

```
function ElementsList(props) {
  return <React.Fragment>
      <div>Element1</div>
      <div>Element2</div>
      <div>Element3</div>
    </React.Fragment>
}

ReactDOM.render(<ElementsList />, document.getElementById("root"));
```

We return a single parent element which is the `<React.Fragment>` element defined in React.

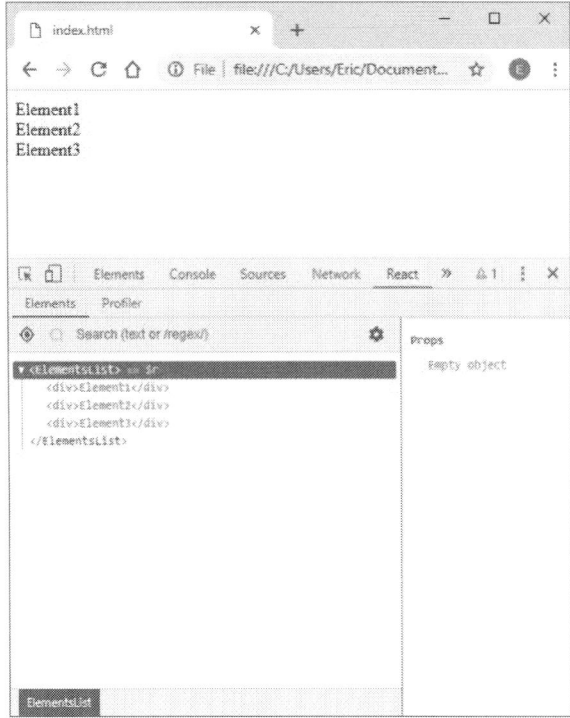

The `<React.Fragment>` element allows you to return a single parent, avoiding the addition of a new unnecessary parent element.

Note that React does not view the `<React.Fragment>` element in the React elements tree.

Use parentheses at the beginning and end of the JSX code

When returning a JSX code on several lines (for example an `<ul>` element followed by several `<li>` elements), the return statement must contain, on the same line, the first JSX element returned, otherwise an error occurs. This makes it necessary to shift the JSX code of the first returned element to the right. For example :

View a list of items without using parentheses
```
function ElementsList(props) {
 return <ul>
     <li>Element1</li>
     <li>Element2</li>
     <li>Element3</li>
     <li>Element4</li>
     <li>Element5</li>
```

```
    </ul>
}
ReactDOM.render(<ElementsList />, document.getElementById("root"));
```

The list of `<li>` elements is shifted to the right to visually show the nesting in the `<ul>` element.

Using parentheses at the beginning and end of the returned JSX code, writing the JSX code becomes more readable because less shifted to the right.

View a list of items using parentheses
```
function ElementsList(props) {
 return (
  <ul>
   <li>Element1</li>
   <li>Element2</li>
   <li>Element3</li>
   <li>Element4</li>
   <li>Element5</li>
  </ul>
 )
}
ReactDOM.render(<ElementsList />, document.getElementById("root"));
```

Without the parenthesis following the return statement, a syntax error would occur.

Comments in JSX code

We use the /* and */ comments to indicate respectively the beginning and the end of the JSX code to comment, provided to surround the set with braces { and }.

❚ Comments with // do not work with JSX code ...

For example, let's comment on `"Element2"` and `"Element3"` from the previous list.

Use comments in JSX elements
```
function ElementsList(props) {
 return (
  <ul>
   <li>Element1</li>
   {/* <li>Element2</li>
   <li>Element3</li>*/}
   <li>Element4</li>
```

```
    <li>Element5</li>
  </ul>
 )
}
ReactDOM.render(<ElementsList />, document.getElementById("root"));
```

Both lines are commented simultaneously, but it is possible to do it line by line (see below).

One can also write in the following form, commenting line by line:

Use line-by-line comments
```
function ElementsList(props) {
 return (
  <ul>
   <li>Element1</li>
   {/* <li>Element2</li>*/}
   {/* <li>Element3</li>*/}
   <li>Element4</li>
   <li>Element5</li>
  </ul>
 )
}
ReactDOM.render(<ElementsList />, document.getElementById("root"));
```

In both program examples, commented items do not appear in the display:

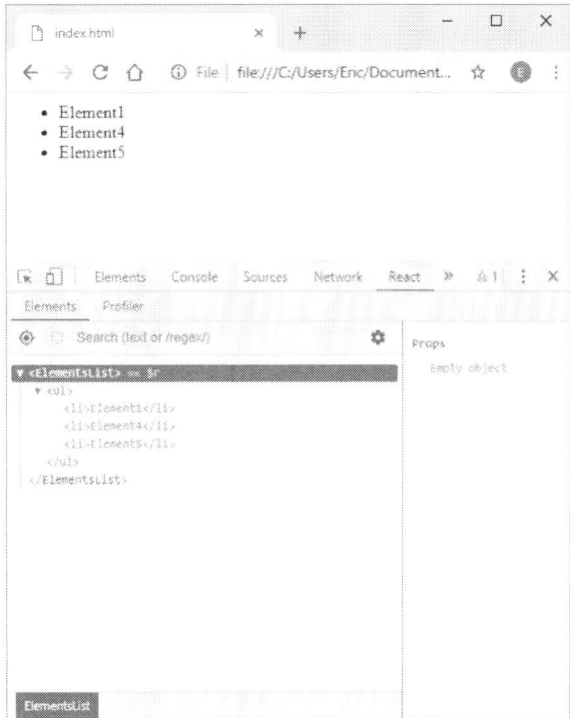

`"Element2"` and `"Element3"` elements are not displayed.

Use conditional expressions in JSX code

It is possible to use conditional expressions with ? and : in the JSX code, as long as you enclose the set with braces { and } (because this corresponds to a JavaScript expression that is evaluated).

Suppose we have an attribute in the `<ElementsList>` component to indicate whether or not to hide the first item in the list. The attribute will be named `hideFirstItem` and is `true` if you want to hide this element, `false` otherwise.

Hide or not the first item on the list
```
function ElementsList(props) {
  return (
    <ul>
      { props.hideFirstItem ? null : <li>Element1</li> }
      <li>Element2</li>
      <li>Element3</li>
      <li>Element4</li>
      <li>Element5</li>
```

```
  </ul>
 )
}
ReactDOM.render(<ElementsList hideFirstItem={true} />,
        document.getElementById("root"));
```

If no element is to be displayed, you must specify null, otherwise you specify the list element in JSX. This line can also be written even more concisely:

Hide or not the first item on the list
```
{ !props.hideFirstItem && <li>Element1</li> }
```

In case we want to hide the first list element (hideFirstItem set to true):

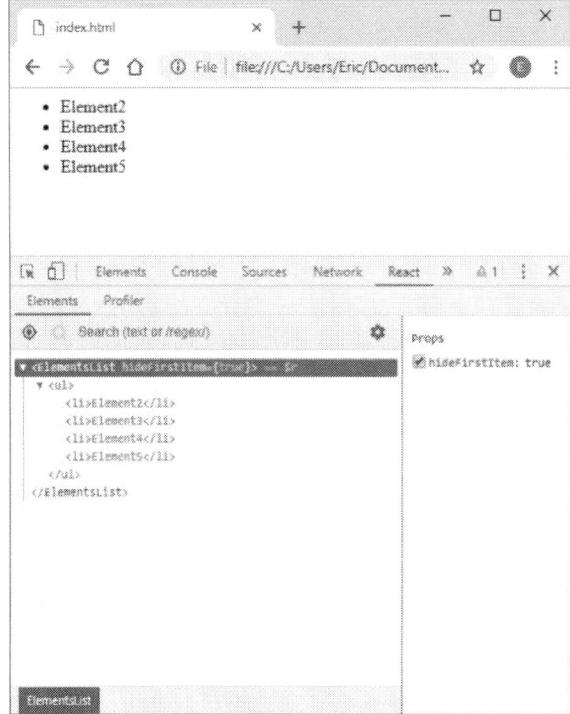

The first item in the list does not appear.

4 – STATE OBJECT

The state object is an object associated with a React component, which can be created (for each component) in the constructor of a class derived from React.Component. This state object is used only in components created with a class, and is not used for components created with functions.

This state object makes it possible to indicate the state of the component (with properties that are defined internally in the class), knowing that if this state is modified (via the modification of one or more of its properties), the component is redisplayed (its render() method is then called again). This is the only way to cause the component to display (outside of its creation).

So to modify the display of a React component, it will be necessary to modify its state object. And to modify the state object (actually this.state, this represents the object associated with the component), the associated component must be created via a class, not a function.

> Note that if a component is redisplayed, all the internal components of the component are re-displayed as well, whether they have been created as a class or a function.

Use the state object to update a component

To explain the state object, consider that we wanted to write a Timer component that allows to count down the remaining time to 0. The initial time would for example be set to 01:00 (or 1 minute) and decrease from one second to every second elapsed until you reach 00:00.

Timer component initialized at 01:00 (1 minute)
```
class Timer extends React.Component {
 constructor(props) {
  super(props);
 }
 render() {
```

```
  return <div>01:00</div>
 }
}
ReactDOM.render(<Timer/>, document.getElementById("root"));
```

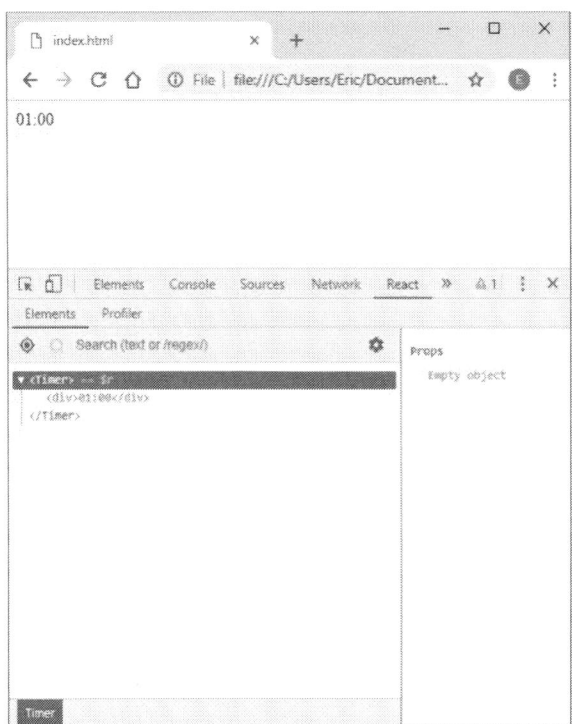

The Timer component is displayed at its initial value (01:00), but the problem is immediately apparent. How to decrement the display every second? In fact it would be necessary to be able to modify the display when one wishes it. This is the role of the state object.

As the remaining time varies (with each second), it must not be frozen as here at 01:00, but must be put in a variable that will be changed every second. We set the remaining time in the state object, and we decrement that remaining time every second through a timer set in the class constructor, using JavaScript's setInterval() function.

Use this.state in the component

```
function decrTime({min, sec}) {
  // decreases sec by 1 second, decreasing min if needed
  // 01:10 => 01:09
  // 01:00 => 00:59
```

```
    sec = sec - 1;
    if (sec < 0) {
     min = min - 1;
     if (min < 0) {
      min = 0;
      sec = 0;
     }
     else {
      sec = 59;
     }
    }
    return { min, sec };
 }
 function formatTime({min, sec}) {
    // format the time in the mm:ss form
    if (min < 10) min = "0" + min;  // 9 => "09"
    if (sec < 10) sec = "0" + sec;  // 9 => "09"
    return `${min}:${sec}`;   // => "10:08"
 }
 class Timer extends React.Component {
    constructor(props) {
     super(props);
     this.state = { min : 1, sec : 0 }; // create the state object in the component
     setInterval(() => {
      this.state = decrTime(this.state); // decrement by 1 second
      console.log(this.state);  // display the state in the console
     }, 1000);  // 1000 milliseconds = 1 second
    }
    render() {
     return <div>{formatTime(this.state)}</div>
    }
 }
 ReactDOM.render(<Timer/>, document.getElementById("root"));
```

The this.state object is created in the constructor of the class, and initialized with the {min: 1, sec: 0} object corresponding to a timer of 1 minute.

The timer is set right after by setInterval(), and decrements (every second) the {min, sec} values of the state object by 1 second.

The callback function used in setInterval() is written in the ES6 notation, in order to keep the value of this (which otherwise becomes equal to the window object in the callback function).

The decrTime() and formatTime() methods are utility methods that can respectively decrease the time by 1 second, and display the time as mm:ss.

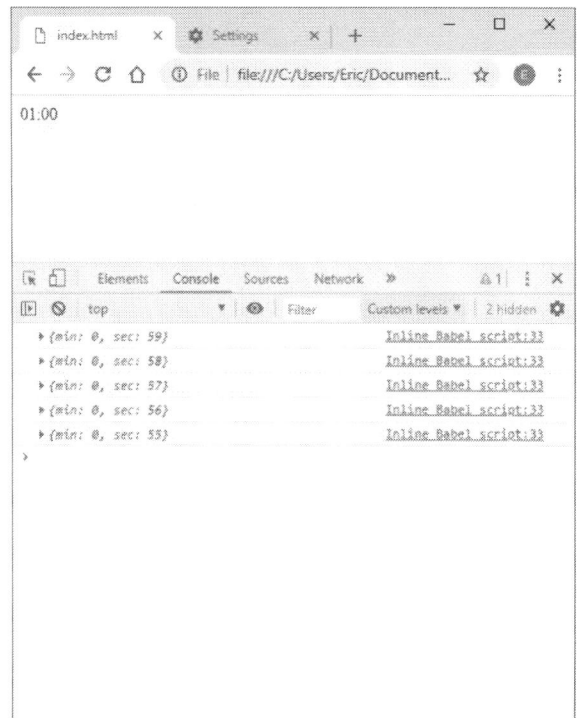

We can see that the time decreases in the console, but not in the display in the HTML page! In fact, although the state is updated, it still lacks an instruction that would refresh the component.

Indeed, after the state object has been updated, you must tell React that the state has been modified (which will cause a new call to the render() method). For this, we use the this.setState(newState) method, where newState is an object that indicates the values of the modified properties in the state object. Here it would be necessary to indicate an object {min, sec} with the new values.

If only the sec property is specified in the newState during the this.setState(newState) statement, the minutes display will never be changed and only the seconds will be decremented back to 59 after reaching 0. This shows that for change the display, you must indicate in the newState object all properties that have been changed in it.

The state object should never be changed directly except when created. It can only be modified with this.setState(newState), which modifies the properties of this.state with those specified in newState (properties not indicated or not modified in newState are left as they are in this.state).

So an instruction like this.state = decrTime(this.state) should never be written because the state object should never be modified directly. We must always go through the statement this.setState(newState).

Now use the statement this.setState(newState) in our program:

Use the this.setState(newState) statement
```
class Timer extends React.Component {
 constructor(props) {
  super(props);
  this.state = { min : 1, sec : 0 };
  setInterval(() => {
   var newState = decrTime(this.state);
   console.log(newState);
   this.setState({min : newState.min, sec : newState.sec });
  }, 1000);
 }
 render() {
  return <div>{formatTime(this.state)}</div>
 }
}
ReactDOM.render(<Timer/>, document.getElementById("root"));
```

The this.setState() statement takes the min and sec values of the newState object as arguments. We could also write the statement as this.setState(newState) because newState contains the min and sec properties.

After a few seconds the display becomes:

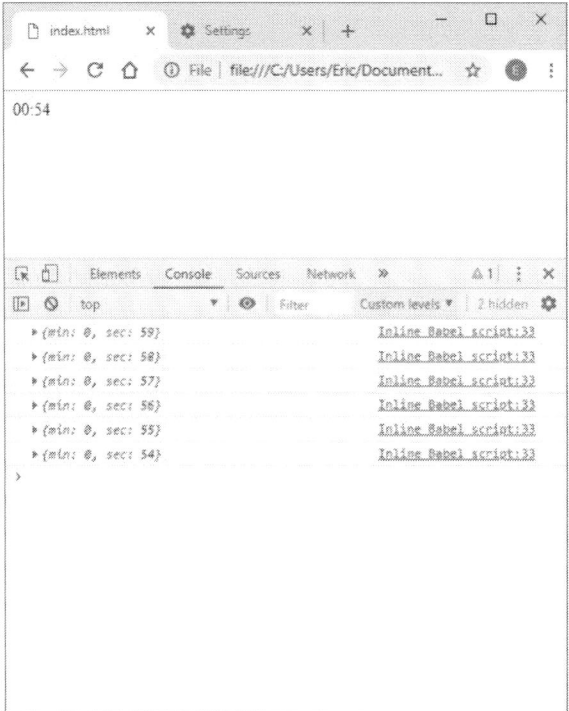

Calling the this.setState() method causes the display (and the component) to update.

Use the props object with the state object

The delay of the timer is initialized in the Timer component's constructor, which does not allow a great flexibility, and does not allow to use several different timers. It would be better to set the timer so that you can write:

Using the Timer component by setting the minutes and seconds in the attributes
```
<Timer min={1} sec={0}/>
```

The min and sec values are now shown in the attributes of the Timer component, which must use them to start counting.

> Notice the use of braces around numeric attributes. Indeed the value of an attribute in JSX must be specified either as JavaScript expressions (thus surrounded by braces like here), or in the form of string (thus surrounded by single or double quotes).

Let's write the new Timer component that uses these attributes. These attributes will be passed into the props object used in the component's constructor (as seen in the previous chapter).

Timer component using min and sec attributes
```
class Timer extends React.Component {
 constructor(props) {
  super(props);
  this.state = { min : props.min, sec : props.sec };
  setInterval(() => {
   var newState = decrTime(this.state);
   console.log(newState);
   this.setState({min : newState.min, sec : newState.sec });
  }, 1000);
 }
 render() {
  return <div>{formatTime(this.state)}</div>
 }
}
ReactDOM.render(<Timer min={1} sec={0}/>, document.getElementById("root"));
```

The state object is updated from the props object, containing the min and sec attributes used in the component.

Stop the timer when it's 00:00

You will notice that when the timer has reached 0, it is continuously displayed at 00:00, and the timer continues to run (even if the display is no longer modified, the console window displays the this.state object value every second). It would be desirable to stop the timer when it arrived at 0, then to display a message indicating that the alarm is triggered.

Stop the timer when it is 0 and display a stop message
```
class Timer extends React.Component {
 constructor(props) {
  super(props);
  this.state = { min : props.min, sec : props.sec };
  this.timer = setInterval(() => {
   var newState = decrTime(this.state);
   console.log(newState);
   this.setState({min : newState.min, sec : newState.sec });
  }, 1000);
 }
 render() {
  if (this.state.min == 0 && this.state.sec == 0) {
```

```
    clearInterval(this.timer);
    return <div>End of Timer</div>
   }
   return <div>{formatTime(this.state)}</div>
  }
 }
ReactDOM.render(<Timer min={0} sec={5}/>, document.getElementById("root"));
```

When the timer is 0 (min and sec are 0 in this.state), it is stopped by means of clearInterval(this.timer), this.timer being stored when the timer is set by setInterval().

In this case (timer at 0), we return a different JSX code from the one where the timer is still running.

Let's check that it works correctly (the timer is here for 5 seconds):

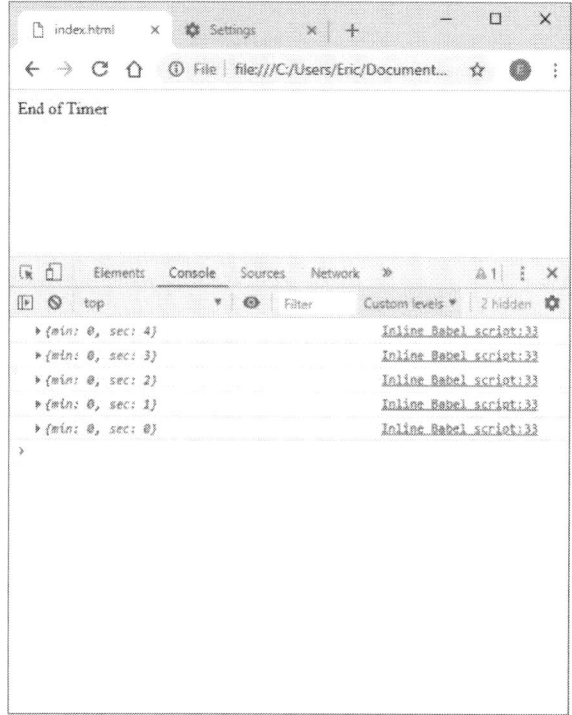

After 5 seconds, the message "End of Timer" is displayed instead of the counter.

Lifecycle of a component

When a React component is created (here using a class derived from React.Component), some methods internal to the class are automatically called by React. These methods can be overloaded in the component's class to perform specific processes during that component's lifecycle.

The lifecycle of a React component has three basic steps:
- The creation of the component
- The component update
- The destruction of the component

Let's look at React's methods in each of the stages of a component's lifecycle.

> These methods are available only if the component is created as a class, not a JavaScript function.

Methods called when a component is created

When creating a component, the following methods are called in the order below. They are called only once (during the creation of the component) except the `render()` method which is called at each update.

- `constructor(props)`: constructor of the class, to which are passed the properties (`props` object, also accessible via `this.props`) that correspond to the attributes passed in the React element (created via `React.createElement()` or via JSX). The `this.state` object is created (if needed) here.

- `render()`: method that is called when the component is displayed (or when updated by `this.setState()`)

- `componentDidMount()`: once the component is rendered (`render()` method) after its creation, the `componentDidMount()` method is called. The DOM tree has been updated.

Methods called when a component is updated

At each update of the component by `this.setState(newState)`, or when the component is used again (by a second call to `reactDOM.render()`), the following methods are also called.

- `shouldComponentUpdate(nextProps, nextState)`: If this method returns `false`, the methods described below are not called (and the component is not updated). The `nextProps` and `nextState` objects indicate the next properties and the next state, which we can possibly compare to the current ones in `this.props` and `this.state`, and possibly decide to return `false` if needed.

- `render()`: Method that is called for the component update (only if `shouldComponentUpdate()` does not return `false`).

- componentDidUpdate(prevProps, prevState): Once the component is updated, this method is called. The component is updated either because the state has been updated (by this.setState()), or because new props have been passed to it. The prevProps and prevState parameters indicate the previous properties and the previous state, to be compared possibly with the new ones (registered in this.props and this.state). As before, this method is called provided that shouldComponentUpdate() did not return false.

Methods called when a component is destroyed

The destruction of a React component is done by calling the ReactDOM.unmountComponentAtNode(DOMelement), where DOMelement is the DOM element in which the React component was inserted by ReactDOM.render(component, DOMelement).

The following method is called in this case:

- componentWillUnmount(): Before destroying the React element (and removing it from the HTML page), the componentWillUnmount() method is called. It will finalize the destruction of the element, for example stop timers positioned.

Using the lifecycle in a HelloReact component

Let's create a component to simply display "Hello React" in order to visualize the lifecycle methods previously seen.

The methods listed above are inserted into the HelloReact class, with a display in the console each time one of them is called.

HelloReact class containing lifecycle methods

```
class HelloReact extends React.Component {
 constructor(props) {
  console.log(`constructor(props=${JSON.stringify(props)})`);
  super(props);
 }
 render() {
  console.log("render()");
  return <div>Hello React</div>
 }
 componentDidMount() {
  console.log("componentDidMount()");
 }
 shouldComponentUpdate(nextProps, nextState) {
```

```
    nextProps = JSON.stringify(nextProps);
    nextState = JSON.stringify(nextState);
    var props = JSON.stringify(this.props);
    var state = JSON.stringify(this.state);
      console.log(`shouldComponentUpdate(nextProps=${nextProps},
                nextState=${nextState})`);
      console.log(`shouldComponentUpdate() : this.props=${props},
                  this.state=${state}`);
    return true;   // to continue the component update
  }
  componentDidUpdate(prevProps, prevState) {
    prevProps = JSON.stringify(prevProps);
    prevState = JSON.stringify(prevState);
    var props = JSON.stringify(this.props);
    var state = JSON.stringify(this.state);
      console.log(`componentDidUpdate(prevProps=${prevProps},
                prevState=${prevState})`);
      console.log(`componentDidUpdate() : this.props=${props},
                  this.state=${state}`);
  }
  componentWillUnmount() {
    console.log("componentWillUnmount()");
  }
}
ReactDOM.render(<HelloReact a="1"/>, document.getElementById("root"));
```

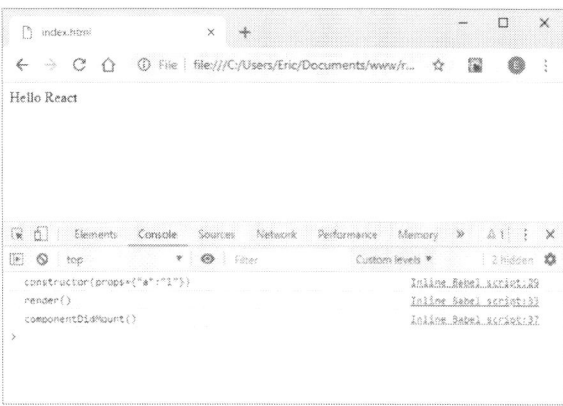

When `ReactDOM.render()` of the `<HelloReact>` component is done in the "root" id element, the methods for creating the component are called, as well as the `render()` display method.

The update or destruction methods are of course not called here.

Let's add a second call to ReactDOM.render() of the <HelloReact> component made in the "root" id element. The component will then be considered, during this second call, as updated.

Adding a second call to ReactDOM.render()

```
ReactDOM.render(<HelloReact a="1"/>, document.getElementById("root")); // 1st
ReactDOM.render(<HelloReact a="2"/>, document.getElementById("root")); // 2nd
```

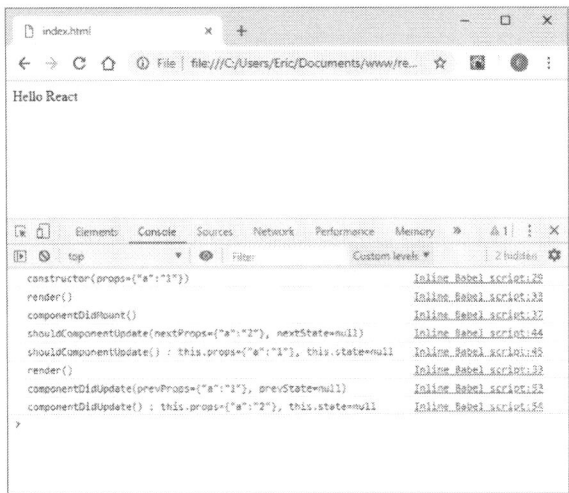

As a result of the component creation methods (which are called only once, for the first display), we can see the update methods (they use the new props).

> Note the call to the componentDidUpdate() method following the transmission of new props to the component.

Rather than update the same component in the same DOM element, let's create a second DOM element <div id="root2"> that we use to do the second ReactDOM.render().

Use a second DOM element to perform the second ReactDOM.render()

```
<body>
 <div id="root"></div>
 <div id="root2"></div>
</body>
<script type="text/babel">
// ...
ReactDOM.render(<HelloReact a="1"/>, document.getElementById("root"));
ReactDOM.render(<HelloReact a="2"/>, document.getElementById("root2"));
</script>
```

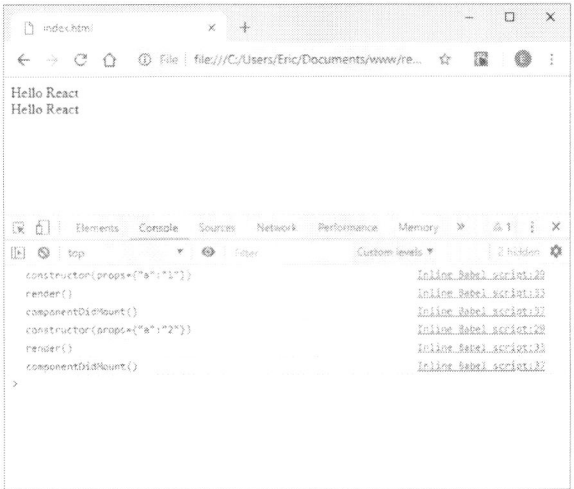

Two `<HelloReact>` components are displayed on the page, each being created independently of the other (because they are associated with different DOM elements). Finally if we destroy the component after creating it:

Destruction of the React component after creation

```
ReactDOM.render(<HelloReact a="1"/>, document.getElementById("root")); // creation
ReactDOM.unmountComponentAtNode(document.getElementById("root"));  // destruction
```

The `ReactDOM.unmountComponentAtNode()` method is used to destroy the component.

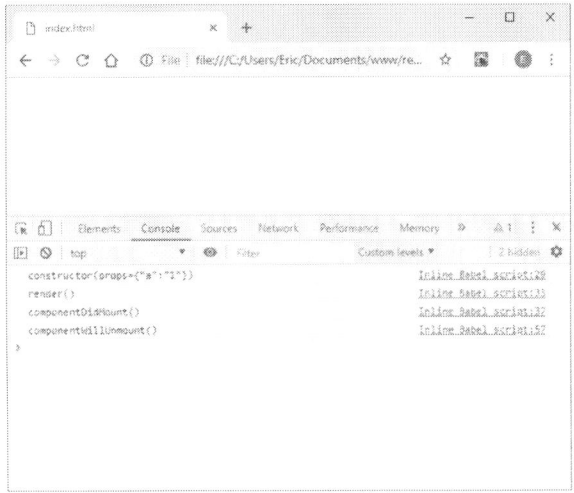

The `componentWillUnmount()` method is called, and the component is removed

Update the component with new props

A component can be updated with new props (that is, with the attributes that are passed to it when it is created).

For this, consider that we want to reset the alarm when it has expired. In our example, the first alarm is set to 5 seconds (00:05), after which a second alarm of 2 minutes (02:00) is set. Just reuse the `<Timer>` component once the first component has expired.

Reset the timer as soon as the previous one has expired

```
// timer on 5 seconds
ReactDOM.render(<Timer min={0} sec={5}/>, document.getElementById("root"));
setTimeout(function() {
  // timer on 2 minutes at the end of the first timer
  ReactDOM.render(<Timer min={2} sec={0}/>, document.getElementById("root"));
}, 5000); // 5 seconds
```

The first timer is programmed for a duration of 5 seconds, and when it expires, it is repositioned for a duration of 2 minutes.

The complete program is as follows:

Using 2 timers on the same DOM element

```
function decrTime({min, sec}) {
  // decreases sec by 1 second, decreasing min if needed
  // 01:10 => 01:09
  // 01:00 => 00:59
  sec = sec - 1;
  if (sec < 0) {
    min = min - 1;
    if (min < 0) {
      min = 0;
      sec = 0;
    }
    else {
      sec = 59;
    }
  }
  return { min, sec };
}
function formatTime({min, sec}) {
```

```
// format the time in the mm:ss form
  if (min < 10) min = "0" + min;  // 9 => "09"
  if (sec < 10) sec = "0" + sec;  // 9 => "09"
  return `${min}:${sec}`;  // => "10:08"
}
class Timer extends React.Component {
  constructor(props) {
    super(props);
    this.state = { min : props.min, sec : props.sec };
    this.timer = setInterval(() => {
      var newState = decrTime(this.state);
      console.log(newState);
      this.setState({min : newState.min, sec : newState.sec });
    }, 1000);
  }
  render() {
    if (this.state.min == 0 && this.state.sec == 0) {
      clearInterval(this.timer);
      return <div>End of Timer</div>
    }
    return <div>{formatTime(this.state)}</div>
  }
}
// timer on 5 seconds
ReactDOM.render(<Timer min={0} sec={5}/>, document.getElementById("root"));
setTimeout(function() {
  // timer on 2 minutes at the end of the first timer
  ReactDOM.render(<Timer min={2} sec={0}/>, document.getElementById("root"));
}, 5000); // 5 seconds
```

Let's run the program:

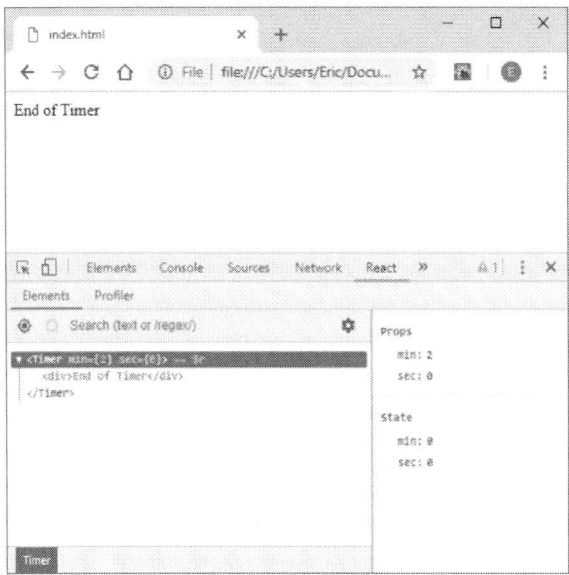

Once the 5 seconds of the first timer have elapsed, the second timer is positioned (we see it in the props object that is updated), but this timer does not start for as long (at least the display does not show because it remains stuck on "End of Timer").

The problem we observe comes from the lifecycle that we previously studied. In effect, the this.setState() statement that triggers the component's render() is only done in the class's constructor. But this constructor is no longer called when displaying the second <Timer> component, because we use the same DOM element to display the two components (in both cases we use the DOM element whose id is "root"). For this to work, it would be necessary to put the second <Timer> component in a new DOM element, for example by writing:

Insert the second <Timer> component into a DOM element whose id is "root2"

```
ReactDOM.render(<Timer min={0} sec={5}/>, document.getElementById("root"));
setTimeout(function() {
  ReactDOM.render(<Timer min={2} sec={0}/>, document.getElementById("root2"));
}, 5000);
```

The second <Timer> component is positioned in a <div id="root2"> element.

While the first <Timer> component remains positioned in a <div id="root"> element.

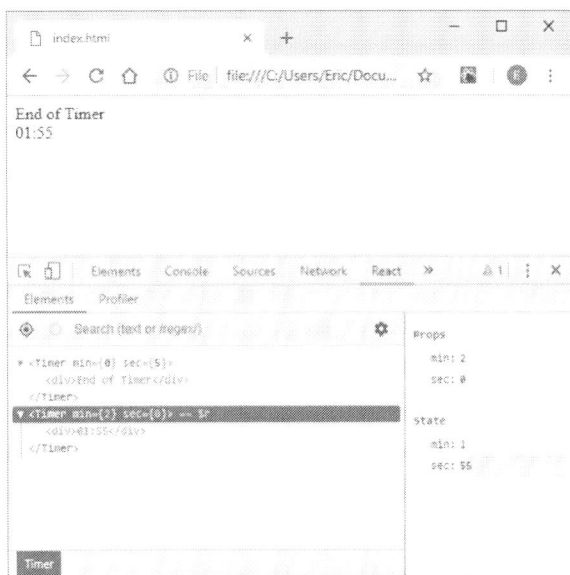

It works, but we now have two components displayed, which is not what we really want ...

In order not to have two <Timer> components displayed and to keep only the first one, you have to use the componentDidUpdate() method. In fact, this method, unlike component mounting methods that are called only once (which is problematic here), is called each time the component receives properties (modified or not, compared to the old ones). So in this componentDidUpdate() method, you just need to make the call to this.setState() to request a new render() now using the new passed properties.

Use the componentDidUpdate() method to redisplay the component

```
function decrTime({min, sec}) {
// decreases sec by 1 second, decreasing min if needed
// 01:10 => 01:09
// 01:00 => 00:59
sec = sec - 1;
if (sec < 0) {
  min = min - 1;
  if (min < 0) {
    min = 0;
    sec = 0;
  }
  else {
```

```
    sec = 59;
   }
  }
  return { min, sec };
}
function formatTime({min, sec}) {
  // format the time in the mm:ss form
  if (min < 10) min = "0" + min;  // 9 => "09"
  if (sec < 10) sec = "0" + sec;  // 9 => "09"
  return `${min}:${sec}`;  // => "10:08"
}
class Timer extends React.Component {
  constructor(props) {
   super(props);
   this.state = { min : props.min, sec : props.sec };
   this.timer = setInterval(() => {
     var newState = decrTime(this.state);
     console.log(newState);
     this.setState({min : newState.min, sec : newState.sec });
   }, 1000);
  }
  render() {
   if (this.state.min == 0 && this.state.sec == 0) {
     clearInterval(this.timer);
     return <div>End of Timer</div>
   }
   return <div>{formatTime(this.state)}</div>
  }
  componentDidUpdate(prevProps, prevState) {
   if (prevState.min == this.state.min && prevState.sec == this.state.sec) {
     // the state is not modified, so the props have been modified
     this.setState({min : this.props.min, sec : this.props.sec });
     this.timer = setInterval(() => {
       var newState = decrTime(this.state);
       console.log(newState);
       this.setState({min : newState.min, sec : newState.sec });
     }, 1000);
   }
  }
}
// timer on 5 seconds
ReactDOM.render(<Timer min={0} sec={5}/>, document.getElementById("root"));
```

```
setTimeout(function() {
  // timer on 2 minutes at the end of the first timer
  ReactDOM.render(<Timer min={2} sec={0}/>, document.getElementById("root"));
}, 5000); // 5 seconds
```

When the new properties are received, they are set in the state, and the timer that was previously stopped is reset.

To find out if new properties have been received in componentDidUpdate(), just look at whether the state has been modified. If the state has not been modified, new props have been passed (the componentDidUpdate() method is called only if the state or props have been modified).

Why do not we test that the props have been modified (rather than testing the non-modification of the state)? Because it is possible that the second call of the <Timer> component is done using the same values of props as for the first, and React would not see the change of props.

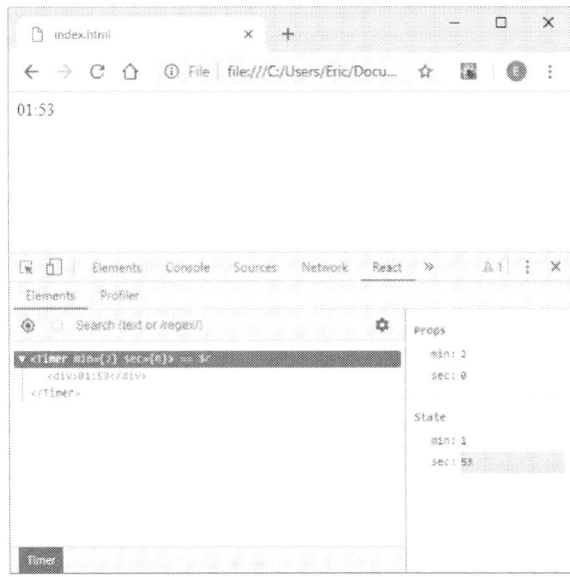

The second timer replaces the first timer as soon as the first timer expires.

5 – INTERACTIONS IN REACT COMPONENTS

We have built React components for the moment, but we have not yet seen how to handle the interaction with them. For example, how to handle the click on a list item, or button? This is the purpose of this chapter.

Manage the click of a button

Let's start with the simplest, namely to perform a treatment when clicking on a very simple element like a button. We want here simply to display a button, then a message in the console each time the button is clicked.

The component can be created by means of a function or a class, the principle is the same. Let's look at these two possibilities below.

The component is created via a function

We create the `ButtonMessage` function which allows to create a `<button>` HTML element and to manage the click on this one. Click processing is done in the `onClick` attribute associated with the button. The name of the attribute is the same as the one used in HTML, but using the camelcase notation (capitalization of the first letter of each word except the first). The `onclick` attribute used in HTML thus becomes `onClick` in the properties (attributes) of the React element.

Manage the click on the button defined in a function

```
const ButtonMessage = function(props) {
 return (
   <button onClick={console.log("click on button")}>Click here</button>
 )
}
ReactDOM.render(<ButtonMessage/>, document.getElementById("root"));
```

The instruction to execute when clicking is enclosed in braces as it is a JavaScript statement. Only one statement can appear in the expression, and moreover it should not be terminated by a semicolon (unlike the attribute if it was set to HTML) otherwise an error occurs.

Let's show this page in the browser, without at the moment click on the button:

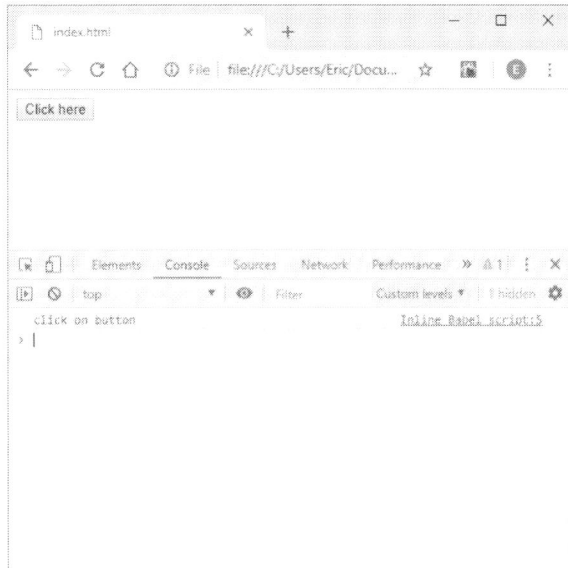

We see that the button is displayed correctly, but that clicking on the button produces no effect.

Moreover a click seems to be done (display of the message in the console) while we have simply displayed the component, without clicking anywhere. In short, nothing works!

This simple program helps to understand some important things in React's operation. Indeed, when you write an expression between braces (as here with {console.log(...)}, this expression is executed directly when the component is displayed, hence the display of the message directly in the console.

In order not to cause it to be executed, the instruction must not be a function call like this (here we call the `console.log()` function with a text argument), but a function reference (that is, the name of the function without the parentheses that follow, and which cause the call of this function). So it would be better to write {console.log} which is the reference of the requested function, without the parentheses.

But if you simply write {console.log} in the value of the `onClick` attribute of the React element, the message "click on button" will not be displayed. The only solution is to go through an intermediate function that will perform for us the call to console.log("click on button"). Let's call handlerClick() this intermediate function.

Manage click on the button via an intermediate function (callback function)

```
const ButtonMessage = function(props) {
  function handlerClick() {
    console.log("click on button");
  }
  return (
    <button onClick={handlerClick}>Click here</button>
  )
}
ReactDOM.render(<ButtonMessage/>, document.getElementById("root"));
```

The handlerClick() function can be defined directly in the component creation function because JavaScript allows nested functions. But it can also be defined outside of it, even if defining it inside the function makes it possible to locate the treatment.

This function is now referenced in the onClick attribute, and no longer called as before (we only indicate its name ie its reference, without putting parentheses that would cause its immediate call). This function is a callback function (called during event processing).

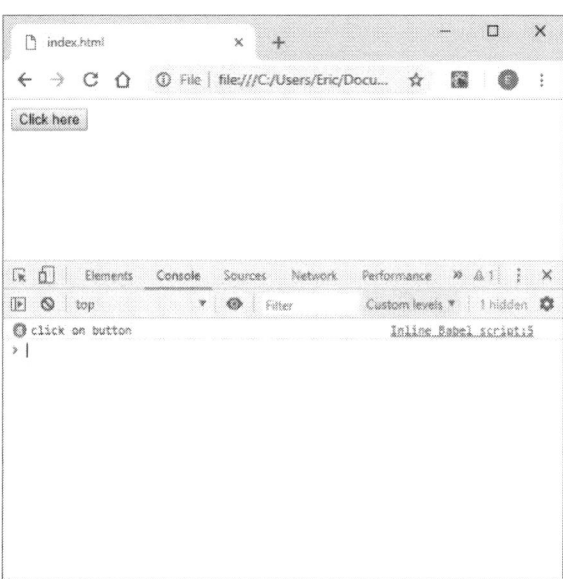

After several clicks on the button, the message appears as many times in the console.

In addition, no message is now displayed when displaying the component (unlike the previous version). Which is of course what we want!

Another form of writing, although not very easy to read or write, would be the following. The processing function is defined in the value of the attribute (between braces indicating the value of the attribute).

Define the processing function in the value of the attribute

```
const ButtonMessage = function(props) {
 return (
  <button onClick={function() {console.log("click on button");}}>
   Click here
  </button>
 )
}
ReactDOM.render(<ButtonMessage/>, document.getElementById("root"));
```

The function, here anonymous (without name), is defined directly in the value of the attribute. We use an anonymous function because its name is not used anywhere, does not need to be indicated.

In this example, we can see that the value of the onClick attribute is a callback function that will be called when the event is triggered.

The component is created via a class

Let's turn the ButtonMessage() function into the ButtonMessage class.

Manage the click on the button defined in a class

```
class ButtonMessage extends React.Component {
 constructor(props) {
  super(props);
 }
 render() {
  return (
   <button onClick={console.log("click on button")}>Click here</button>
  )
 }
}
ReactDOM.render(<ButtonMessage/>, document.getElementById("root"));
```

The button is defined in JSX in the render() method of the class. The onClick attribute is also used, as when defining the component as a function.

However, the remarks made in the previous section still apply. The statement defined in the onClick attribute is executed when the component is displayed, and the click on the button is not taken into account.

We must also go through an intermediate function, and indicate its reference in the onClick attribute. This intermediate function is called handlerClick() as before.

Manage click on the button via an intermediate function (callback function)

```
function handlerClick() {
 console.log("click on button");
}
class ButtonMessage extends React.Component {
 constructor(props) {
  super(props);
 }
 render() {
  return (
    <button onClick={handlerClick}>Click here</button>
  )
 }
}
ReactDOM.render(<ButtonMessage/>, document.getElementById("root"));
```

The click processing function is here defined outside the class, but it would be better to define it inside the class.

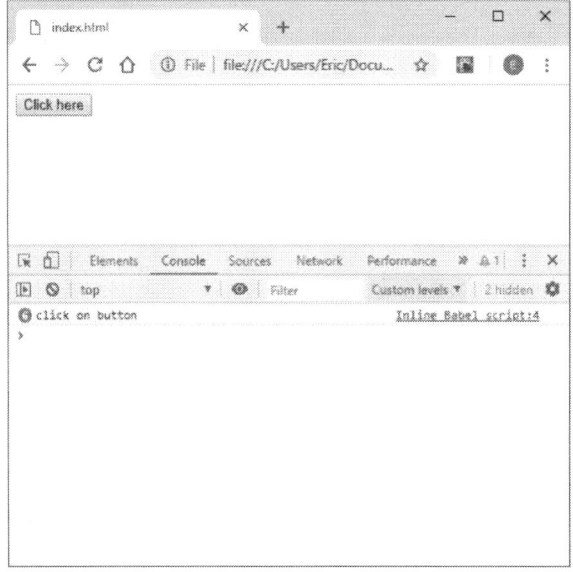

The click on the button is well taken into account.

Let's improve the previous program so that the processing function is defined inside the class, not outside.

Set the click processing function in the component class

```
class ButtonMessage extends React.Component {
 constructor(props) {
  super(props);
 }
 handlerClick() {
  console.log("click on button");
 }
 render() {
  return (
   <button onClick={this.handlerClick}>Click here</button>
  )
 }
}
ReactDOM.render(<ButtonMessage/>, document.getElementById("root"));
```

Access to the class's internal `handlerClick()` method is via the `this` object, hence the use of the `this.handlerClick` statement in the `onClick` attribute.

Access to the this object from a processing function

Consider the previous example in which the component is defined as a class, and the `handlerClick()` processing function is a class-internal method.

We now want to display, with each click, the content of the `props` object defined by React in each component. This object can be accessed in the methods of the class using `this.props`, `this` being the object associated with the React component that is created here.

Display the contents of the props object when you click the button

```
class ButtonMessage extends React.Component {
 constructor(props) {
  super(props);
 }
 handlerClick() {
  console.log(this.props); // display this.props
 }
 render() {
  return (
```

```
    <button onClick={this.handlerClick}>Click here</button>
  )
 }
}
ReactDOM.render(<ButtonMessage/>, document.getElementById("root"));
```

Compared to the previous program, we just replaced the text of the message to be displayed with the content of the this.props object.

After clicking on the button, the result is really not the one expected:

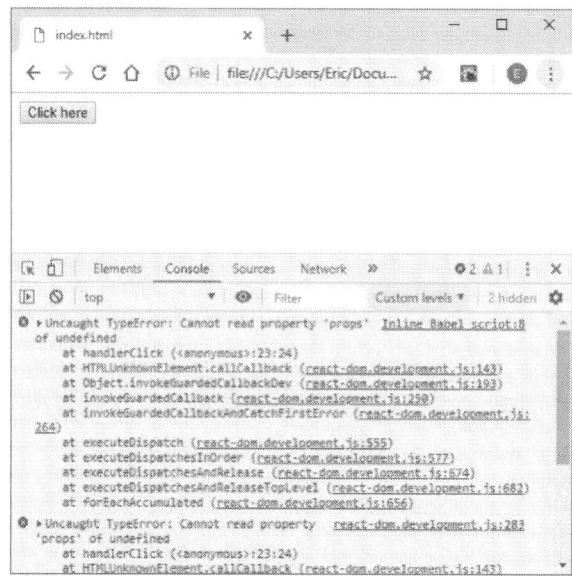

The error message indicates that we are trying to access the props property of a variable that has the undefined value. This means that the object that one tries to access in the handlerClick() processing function is undefined.

However, the handlerClick() method is a method that is internal to the component class, so this should be defined and not undefined. This would be the case if this method was not a callback function (called after an event), which makes it lose the value of this.

So we have to find a solution that would keep the value of this in the handlerClick() method, which must match the value of the instantiated <ButtonMessage> JSX element. For this, we have different possible solutions, discussed below.

Keep the value of this using the bind(this) method when calling

The bind() method defined in JavaScript allows you to specify the value of this that will be associated with a method (the method on which bind() is used).

Associate the value of this when calling the handlerClick() function
```
handlerClick.bind(this);
```

When the handlerClick() function defined above is triggered, the this value that will be used by it will be the one defined in the bind() method arguments. If this matches a JSX <ButtonMessage> element, it will be perfect!

Using this concept in the ButtonMessage class, we write:

Use bind(this) when calling
```
class ButtonMessage extends React.Component {
  constructor(props) {
    super(props);
  }
  handlerClick() {
    console.log(this.props);
  }
  render() {
    return (
      <button onClick={this.handlerClick.bind(this)}>Click here</button>
    )
  }
}
ReactDOM.render(<ButtonMessage/>, document.getElementById("root"));
```

The value of the onClick attribute is always the handlerClick() callback function, but it is indicated by bind(this) that the this to use in this one is that of the ButtonMessage class.

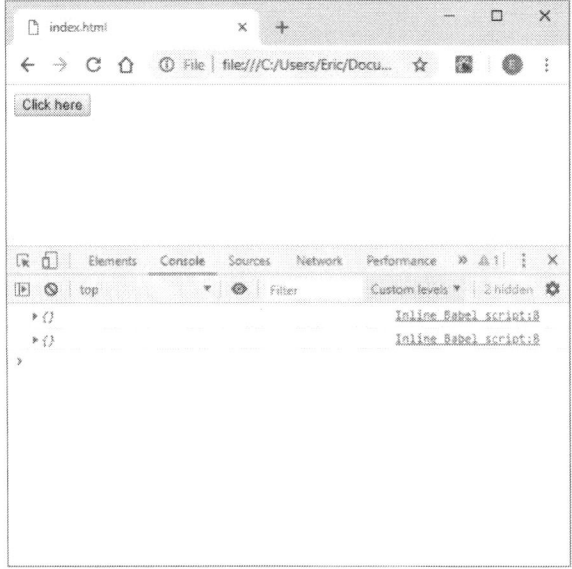

As soon as you click on the button, the content of the props object associated with the <ButtonMessage> React element is displayed (here an empty object because no props are transmitted by this element).

Keep the value of this by using the bind() method in the constructor

Rather than using the bind(this) method when calling the handlerClick() method (in the attributes of the React element), we write the bind(this) method in the constructor. This centralizes all future calls by associating them with the correct one (we will not forget to write it in an attribute value).

<u>Use bind(this) in the constructor</u>

```
class ButtonMessage extends React.Component {
 constructor(props) {
  super(props);
  this.handlerClick = this.handlerClick.bind(this);
 }
 handlerClick() {
  console.log(this.props);
 }
 render() {
  return (
   <button onClick={this.handlerClick}>Click here</button>
```

```
  )
 }
}
ReactDOM.render(<ButtonMessage msg="Hello"/>, document.getElementById("root"));
```

The `bind(this)` statement has been deported to the constructor. It will be executed for each `<ButtonMessage>` element creation.

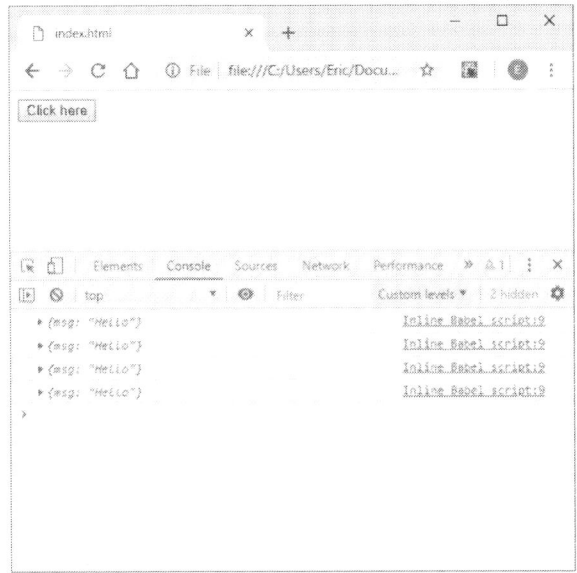

A `msg="Hello"` attribute has been added to `<ButtonMessage>` for display in `this.props`.

Retain the value of this using the new function definition during the call

Remember that the new definition of functions with `=>` also allowed to not block the value of `this`. It can be used here when writing the value of the `onClick` attribute.

Use the definition of the functions with => during the call

```
class ButtonMessage extends React.Component {
 constructor(props) {
  super(props);
 }
 render() {
  return (
   <button onClick={() => {console.log(this.props);}}>Click here</button>
  )
 }
```

```
}
ReactDOM.render(<ButtonMessage msg="Hello"/>, document.getElementById("root"));
```

The handlerClick() method no longer exists because its content is directly written in the value of the onClick attribute (using the notation with =>).

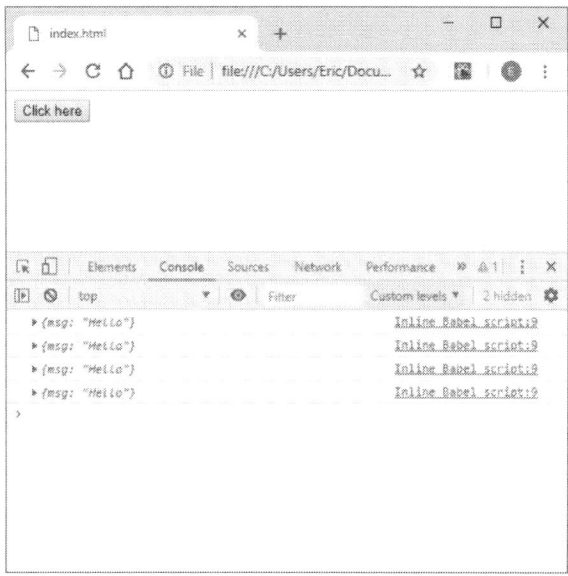

The value of this is no longer lost thanks to the new definition of the functions with =>.

Retain the value of this using the new function definition in a class

The new definition of functions with => can be used also in the definition of the functions of the class. This keeps the value of this in the method that uses this form of definition.

Use the definition of functions with => when defining the function

```
class ButtonMessage extends React.Component {
 constructor(props) {
  super(props);
 }
 handlerClick = () => {
  console.log(this.props);
 }
 render() {
  return (
```

```
    <button onClick={this.handlerClick}>Click here</button>
  )
 }
}
ReactDOM.render(<ButtonMessage msg="Hello"/>, document.getElementById("root"));
```

The handlerClick() method is now defined using the new notation with =>.

The bind() method is no longer needed and has disappeared.

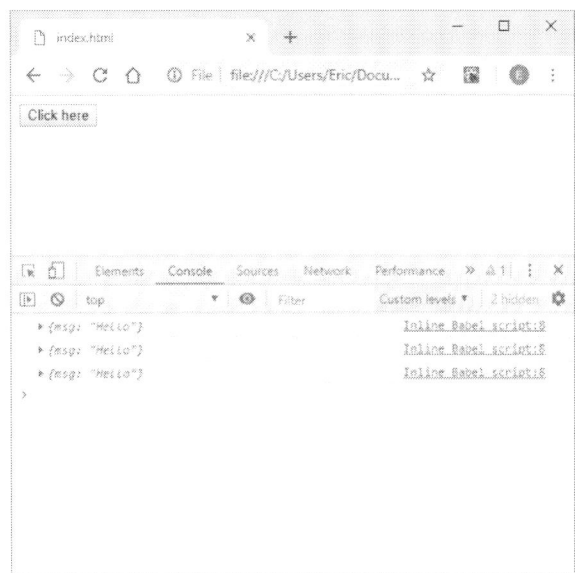

Using the definition of methods of a class with => preserves the value of this in the callback function.

What solution to choose to keep this in a callback function?

We have shown four possible solutions for keeping the value of this in the processing functions when it was lost. Among these four solutions:
- The first that has bind(this) in the value of the attribute,
- And the second one that uses bind(this) in the constructor,

are the most used ones.

Other solutions, although functional, are however less used. For our part, the first solution is our favorite because it is the least verbose of the two and it avoids duplicating the name of the method in two places (during the call and in the constructor).

6 – MANAGE THE ELEMENTS OF A LIST

Thanks to a small example, we want to show how to use React to modify a list of elements. This will consist in allowing to perform the following actions:
- Inserting an element in the list: each inserted element is labeled according to its position in the list ("Element1", then "Element2", etc.). The list is empty at the beginning.
- Deleting an item from the list: To allow the deletion of an item, a Remove button is added after the item's text. Clicking this button removes the corresponding item.
- Modification of an element in the list: following the double click on the text of an element, an input field is displayed, containing the text of the element. The text displayed in the input field can be modified, and must be validated by pressing the Enter key. The input field is then replaced by the text entered in the field.

Now let's look at these different actions.

Insert an item in the list

An Insert button is used to insert an item in the list, empty at the start. The inserted element has the label "Element1" for the first, "Element2" for the second, and so on.

To achieve this, we will use three React components:
- An App component managing the application as a whole: displaying the Insert button and the list of inserted elements.
- An ElementsList component displaying the list of items in the list. It is passed the elems property (array of elements to display) in the props object.

- An `Element` component displaying an element of the list. It is passed the `txt` property (text of the element to be displayed) in the `props` object.

The list of elements that can be modified at any time, will be put in the state (`this.state.elems`). The state will be updated each time the `Insert` button is clicked. The state is managed at the `App` component, to be accessible when clicking the `Insert` button (the button is also at the `App` component).

In addition, let's not forget that the goal is also to allow the deletion and modification of inserted elements. For this, it is best to use a unique identifier for each inserted element, which will be assigned via a `getUniqueKey()` method defined in the `App` class. This identifier will be used to indicate the element to be modified or deleted. The `getUniqueKey()` method is to return a random number between 0 and 1, using JavaScript's `Math.random()` method.

> Note that we can not use the index of the element in the list as a unique key, because depending on the insertions and deletions, this index can vary (and its update would be more complex than defining a unique key like here).

Let's start by seeing how to insert an item into the list.

Insert an item in the list

```
<html>
<head>
<script crossorigin
  src="https://unpkg.com/react@16/umd/react.development.js"></script>
<script crossorigin
  src="https://unpkg.com/react-dom@16/umd/react-dom.development.js"></script>
<script src="https://unpkg.com/babel-standalone@6/babel.min.js"></script>
</head>
<body>
 <div id="root"></div>
</body>
<script type="text/babel">
class Element extends React.Component {
 constructor(props) {
  super(props);
  this.ukey = props.ukey;
 }
 render() {
  return (
    <li>{this.props.txt}</li>
  )
 }
```

```
}
class ElementsList extends React.Component {
 constructor(props) {
  super(props);
 }
 render() {
  return (
   <ul>
     {
     this.props.elems.map((elem, index) => {
       var { ukey, txt } = elem;
       return <Element key={ukey} ukey={ukey} txt={txt} />
     })
     }
   </ul>
  )
 }
}
class App extends React.Component {
 constructor(props) {
  super(props);
  this.state = { elems : [] }; // array of objects { txt, ukey }
 }
 getUniqueKey() {  // return a unique key
  var key = Math.random() + "";  // return a string
  return key;
 }
 insertElem() {
  var elems = this.state.elems;
  var txt = "Element" + (elems.length + 1);
  var ukey = this.getUniqueKey();  // unique key associated with the element
  var elem = { txt : txt, ukey : ukey };
  elems.push(elem);
  this.setState({ elems : elems });
 }
 render() {
  return (
   <div>
     <button onClick={this.insertElem.bind(this)}>Insert</button>
     <ElementsList elems={this.state.elems} />
   </div>
  )
```

```
    }
}
ReactDOM.render(<App />, document.getElementById("root"));
</script>
</html>
```

Once we know what are the components to write, the properties to use for each component (via their props object), and the state that will be used (and in which component to put it), writing the components is more easy!

Note that this.state.elems is an array of inserted elements, each element being identified by its text (txt property) and its unique key (ukey property). The unique key in each element will be used to identify the element in the state.

The <Element> component inserted into the <ElementsList> component has both the key and ukey properties with the same value: key is used internally by React (otherwise an error occurs as explained in previous chapters), while ukey is the unique key used by our program. Our program can not use key directly (outside of its initialization) otherwise React produces an error, hence the use of the ukey property.

Notice the use of bind(this) on the insertElem() method, so that this method can access this.state as seen in the previous chapter.

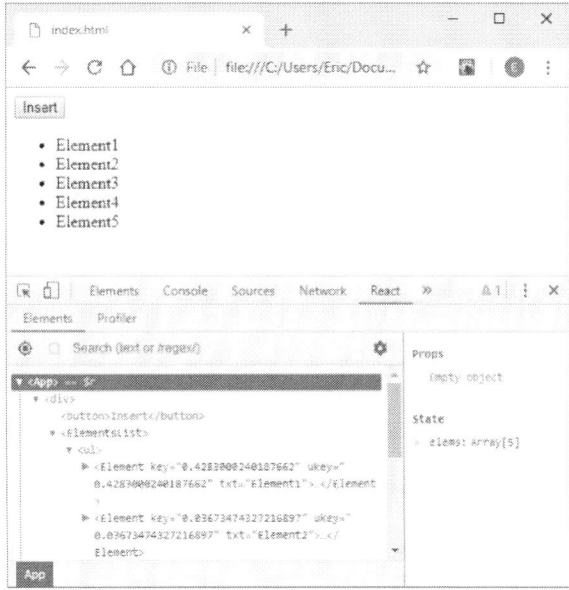

Each click on the Insert button adds an item to the list (here five elements inserted).

Styling list items when moving the mouse

The previous list does not allow any interaction (for now) with the user. Let's start by showing on which element the mouse is positioned, by putting this element in italics and in red color.

Just modify the Element component, which displays each of the elements in the list.

Since we have to deal with the events related to the mouse, we use the onMouseOver and onMouseOut properties to know if the mouse enters an element (onMouseOver) or leaves it (onMouseOut). The style of the element to be modified (color and italic), this style will be put in the state associated with each of the elements of list. The state will be changed in both events related to the mouse.

So we'll have the global state associated with the App component (containing the list of list items in this.state.elems, this here referring to the App component), and a state for each list item (containing the style of each element in this.state.style, this here referring to the Element component).

This gives the Element component an additional property called style, which will tell you what style to display for that list item.

Element component modifying the style of the element when moving the mouse

```
class Element extends React.Component {
 constructor(props) {
  super(props);
  this.ukey = props.ukey;
  this.state = { style : {} };
 }
 mouseOver() {
  var style = { color : "red", fontStyle : "italic" };
  this.setState({style : style });
 }
 mouseOut() {
  var style = { color : "", fontStyle : "" };
  this.setState({style : style });
 }
 render() {
  return (
   <li style={this.state.style}
       onMouseOver={this.mouseOver.bind(this)}
     onMouseOut={this.mouseOut.bind(this)} >
```

```
    {this.props.txt}
  </li>
 )
 }
}
```

The style of the element is initialized in the state, and corresponds when initializing to an empty object {}. The state is changed in the mouseOver() and mouseOut() methods called during onMouseOver and onMouseOut events that are positioned on the React <li> element.

The other App and ListElements components are not modified.

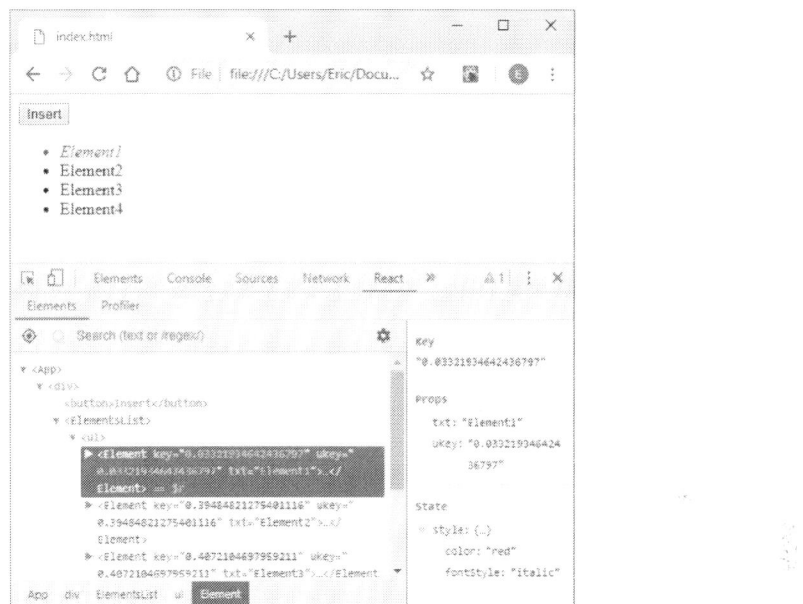

The mouse is here positioned on the first inserted element, which is in italic and red color.

Deleting an item from the list (first version)

In order to remove an item from the list, a Remove button is placed after each item in the list. Clicking on a Remove button must delete the corresponding item.

To do this, we modify the state of each element of the list, ie we add the removed property in the state object associated with the Element class. This removed property is initially false, indicating that the item is not deleted. When you click the Remove button associated with a list item, the removed property is set to true in the state, so you do not want to display this element when you render().

The Element component is modified to allow the deletion of each list element.

Deleting an item from the list

```
class Element extends React.Component {
 constructor(props) {
  super(props);
  this.ukey = props.ukey;
  this.state = { style : {}, removed : false };
 }
 mouseOver() {
  var style = { color : "red", fontStyle : "italic" };
  this.setState({style : style });
 }
 mouseOut() {
  var style = { color : "", fontStyle : "" };
  this.setState({style : style });
 }
 removeElem() {
  this.setState({removed : true });
 }
 render() {
  return (
   this.state.removed ? null :
    <li style={this.state.style}
       onMouseOver={this.mouseOver.bind(this)}
      onMouseOut={this.mouseOut.bind(this)} >
     <span>{this.props.txt}</span>
     <button style={{margin:"10px", fontSize:"10px"}}
         onClick={this.removeElem.bind(this)}>
      Remove
     </button>
    </li>
  )
 }
}
```

A Remove button has been added to each list item, which activates the removeElem() method defined in the class. This method modifies the state by setting the removed property of the state to true, which causes the component to refresh.

In the case where this.state.removed is true, the render() method does not display React elements because it returns null (so that the deleted item is not displayed).

After several insertions and deletions in the list, we have for example the following display:

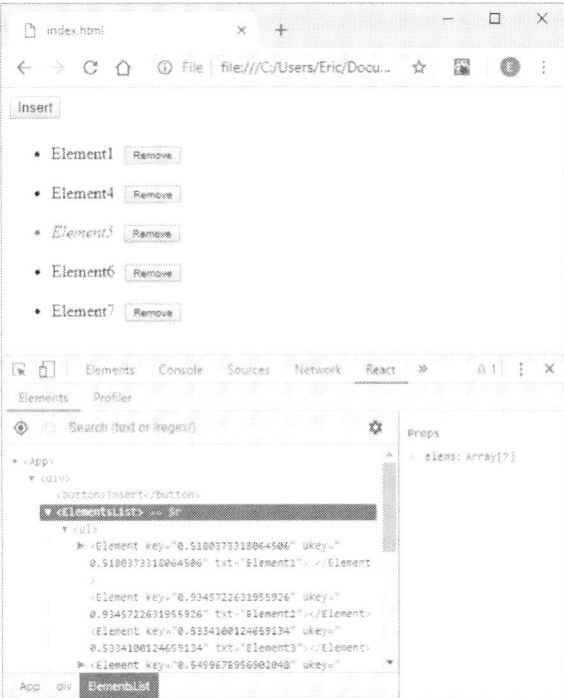

We see that the deleted list items are actually no longer displayed in the HTML page, but the React elements are still present as can be seen in the React tab. Hence the second version studied below to refresh the list of elements in the global state located in the `<App>` component.

Deleting an item from the list (second version)

The removal of an element from the list, previously performed, is visually performed (the element was visually removed from the displayed list), but the list of React elements is not changed in the state (in `this.state.elems` of the `App` component). We write here a new version of the program that allows the update of this property of the state.

The interest here is mainly to show how to update the state (`this.state.elems`) of a parent component (here `App`) from a child component (here `Element`). Indeed, we know for the moment to update the state of the component in which we are (by `this.setState()`), but not the state of a parent component …

The principle will be to allow the Element class (here considered as child) to have access to the App class (here considered as parent). By having access to the App class, the Element class will also have access to the state of the App class (and other methods of the App class).

How to allow a child component such as Element to access the instance of a parent component such as App? The answer is in the props object, which is passed by React automatically from a parent component to a child. All you have to do is create a property, called app, from the App component that will be passed to the child components (ElementsList and then Element), so that the Element component uses it.

Let's implement this solution. All the components are here modified, so we indicate the code of these integrally. For now, to allow a good understanding of the code to write, we are limited to writing traces with console.log() in the various methods implemented.

Deleting an item from the list (using the parent's state)

```
class Element extends React.Component {
 constructor(props) {
  super(props);
  this.ukey = props.ukey;
  this.state = { style : {}, removed : false };
 }
 mouseOver() {
  var style = { color : "red", fontStyle : "italic" };
  this.setState({style : style });
 }
 mouseOut() {
  var style = { color : "", fontStyle : "" };
  this.setState({style : style });
 }
 render() {
  return (
   this.state.removed ? null :
     <li style={this.state.style}
        onMouseOver={this.mouseOver.bind(this)}
      onMouseOut={this.mouseOut.bind(this)} >
     <span>{this.props.txt}</span>
     <button style={{margin:"10px", fontSize:"10px"}}
        onClick={this.props.app.removeElem}
     >
     Remove
```

```
      </button>
    </li>
  )
 }
}
class ElementsList extends React.Component {
 constructor(props) {
  super(props);
 }
 render() {
  return (
    <ul>
      {
      this.props.elems.map((elem, index) => {
        var { ukey, txt } = elem;
        return <Element key={ukey} ukey={ukey} txt={txt} app={this.props.app} />
      })
      }
    </ul>
  )
 }
}
class App extends React.Component {
 constructor(props) {
  super(props);
  this.state = { elems : [] };  // array of objects { txt, ukey }
 }
 getUniqueKey() {
  var key = Math.random() + "";
  return key;
 }
 insertElem() {
  var elems = this.state.elems;
  var txt = "Element" + (elems.length + 1);
  var ukey = this.getUniqueKey();
  var elem = { txt : txt, ukey : ukey };
  elems.push(elem);
  this.setState({ elems : elems });
 }
 removeElem() {
  console.log("removeElem");  // item to delete
 }
```

```
render() {
  return (
    <div>
      <button onClick={this.insertElem.bind(this)}>Insert</button>
      <ElementsList elems={this.state.elems} app={this} />
    </div>
  )
 }
}
ReactDOM.render(<App />, document.getElementById("root"));
```

The main change comes from passing the app property (which is this value in the App component) to the ElementsList and Element components (in these last two components, this property is accessible via this.props.app).

When you click the Remove button in the Element class, you write onClick={this.props.app.removeElem}, which allows you to run the removeElem() method defined in the App class.

Let's see what it says by clicking the Insert button and then Remove:

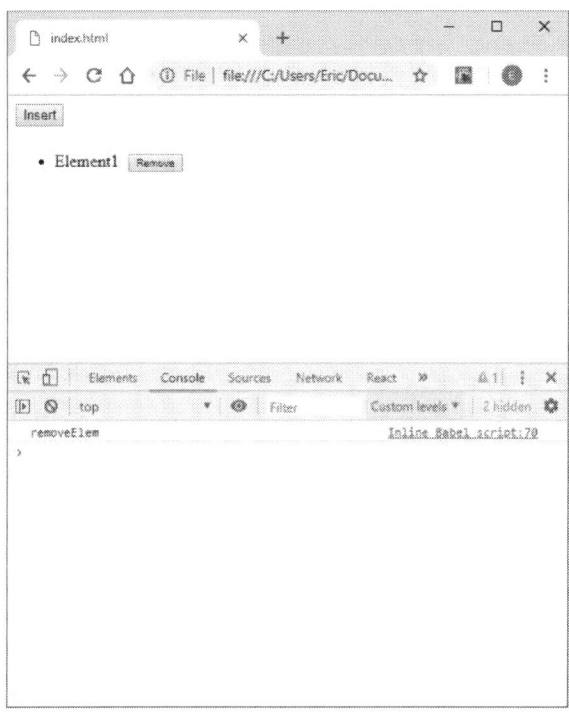

When the Remove button is clicked, the removeElem() method defined in the App component is called from the Element component. But how to indicate what is the element to delete (because for the moment we are only displaying text …)?

The goal now is to indicate the element of the list to be deleted, so that the removeElem() method removes it.

The first reflex that one could have would be to indicate the element to be deleted (here this) in parameters of the method removeElem(). One would be tempted to write something that would look like this:

Indicate the item to delete when calling removeElem()

```
class Element extends React.Component {
 constructor(props) {
  super(props);
  this.ukey = props.ukey;
  this.state = { style : {}, removed : false };
 }
 mouseOver() {
  var style = { color : "red", fontStyle : "italic" };
  this.setState({style : style });
 }
 mouseOut() {
  var style = { color : "", fontStyle : "" };
  this.setState({style : style });
 }
 render() {
  return (
   this.state.removed ? null :
     <li style={this.state.style}
         onMouseOver={this.mouseOver.bind(this)}
      onMouseOut={this.mouseOut.bind(this)} >
     <span>{this.props.txt}</span>
     <button style={{margin:"10px", fontSize:"10px"}}
         onClick={this.props.app.removeElem(this)}
     >
      Remove
     </button>
    </li>
   )
  }
}
```

The element to be deleted (this in this case, because we are in the Element class) is indicated in parameters when the removeElem() method is called when clicking.

However, this can not work because you can not specify a function call when defining an event in properties like onClick, because React causes the direct call of this function (as we saw in the previous chapter when we wrote onClick={console.log ("...")}).

So the only way to pass to removeElem() the element to be deleted is to tell it via a bind() when defining onClick in the Element class.

So let's write the element's button definition in the following form, using bind() to specify the this to use:

Setting the delete button in the Element class
```
<button style={{margin:"10px", fontSize:"10px"}}
    onClick={this.props.app.removeElem.bind(this)}
>
```

The bind(this) method here specifies that removeElem() (defined in App because we specify this.props.app in front of the call) must use the this specified in the bind(), ie the Element class object in which we are currently located.

This new definition with bind(this) when writing the method makes it unnecessary to specify a parameter to the removeElem() method (this parameter would of course be the element to be deleted) because it can use the this he was told here.

Let's now write the removeElem() method by displaying the this object associated with it:

removeElem () method that displays the this object
```
removeElem() {
  console.log(this);  // item to delete
}
```

The this object used in the removeElem() method is the one defined when writing the onClick attribute of the button in the Element class, thanks to the bind(this) performed.

Let's run this program by inserting and removing some elements:

Three elements were inserted, and two were removed as can be seen in the console. In addition, Element objects are retrieved with the this object in the removeElem() method.

At this point, one might think that the solution has been found! Unfortunately, this is not (yet) the case!

Indeed, let's not forget that the purpose of all this is to allow access to the state of the App component, from the removeElem() method defined in this same component (to access this.state.elems and update it). But this is no longer possible because this.state refers to the state defined in the Element class (which is normal because this has the value of an Element class object because of the bind() done previously) and it would need here (in the removeElem() method defined in the App component) we access the state defined in the App class (which defines this.state.elems). But it's impossible (the this must be the Element class object, and at the same time the App class object)...

Nevertheless, the solution is not so far away! It is enough that in the definition of the onClick property written in the button, one does not make the bind() there (the bind() at this location leads to a situation without solution as we have just seen).

For this, we use an intermediate method (here called handlerRemoveElem(), the handler prefix meaning it is intermediate) defined in the Element class (class that uses the <button> component) which will be the one that will call the removeElem() method. defined in the App class, by indicating in parameter the element to be removed (here the this object of Element class).

We indicate the entire component code in order to clearly visualize the changes made.

Using the intermediate handlerRemoveElem() method to remove the item from the list

```
class Element extends React.Component {
 constructor(props) {
  super(props);
  this.ukey = props.ukey;
  this.state = { style : {}, removed : false };
 }
 mouseOver() {
  var style = { color : "red", fontStyle : "italic" };
  this.setState({style : style });
 }
 mouseOut() {
  var style = { color : "", fontStyle : "" };
  this.setState({style : style });
 }
 handlerRemoveElem() {
  this.props.app.removeElem(this);   // this : Element class object
 }
 render() {
  return (
   this.state.removed ? null :
     <li style={this.state.style}
         onMouseOver={this.mouseOver.bind(this)}
      onMouseOut={this.mouseOut.bind(this)} >
     <span>{this.props.txt}</span>
     <button style={{margin:"10px", fontSize:"10px"}}
         onClick={this.handlerRemoveElem.bind(this)}
      >
      Remove
     </button>
    </li>
   )
  }
 }
```

```
class ElementsList extends React.Component {
 constructor(props) {
  super(props);
 }
 render() {
  return (
   <ul>
    {
    this.props.elems.map((elem, index) => {
     var { ukey, txt } = elem;
     return <Element key={ukey} ukey={ukey} txt={txt} app={this.props.app} />
    })
    }
   </ul>
  )
 }
}
class App extends React.Component {
 constructor(props) {
  super(props);
  this.state = { elems : [] };
 }
 getUniqueKey() {
  var key = Math.random() + "";
  return key;
 }
 insertElem() {
  var elems = this.state.elems;
  var txt = "Element" + (elems.length + 1);
  var ukey = this.getUniqueKey();
  var elem = { txt : txt, ukey : ukey };
  elems.push(elem);
  this.setState({ elems : elems });
 }
 removeElem(objElem) {   // Element class object
  console.log(objElem);  // item to delete
 }
 render() {
  return (
   <div>
    <button onClick={this.insertElem.bind(this)}>Insert</button>
    <ElementsList elems={this.state.elems} app={this} />
```

```
      </div>
    )
  }
}
ReactDOM.render(<App />, document.getElementById("root"));
```

The handlerRemoveElem() method is now the one that calls the removeElem() method defined in the App class.

The removeElem() method now has an objElem parameter indicating the element to delete (here an Element class object).

Element class objects are displayed in the console following clicks on the corresponding Remove buttons. So the operation is correct.

It now remains to implement state management in the App class, in order to remove the item from the list when the Remove button is clicked. The filter() method of JavaScript's Array class allows (via a callback function) to return a new array from an initial array. It is enough to indicate for each element of the original array if it is preserved (the callback function must return true in this case) or if one removes it (to return nothing or return false).

The removeElem(objElem) method of the App component is written as:

removeElem(objElem) method updating the state (this.state.elems)

```
removeElem(objElem) {    // Element class object
  var elems = this.state.elems;
  elems = elems.filter(function(elem) {
    if (objElem.ukey != elem.ukey) return true;  // keep the element
  });
  this.setState({ elems : elems });
}
```

The element to be deleted is filtered via the unique key (ukey property). We keep all the elements except the one with the same key to delete (transmitted in parameters).

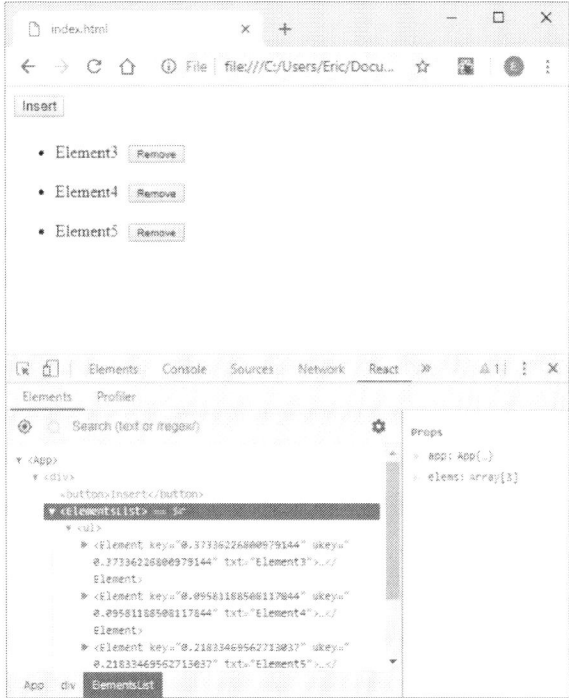

After inserting and removing a few items from the list, we can see that the this.state.elems object is updated (and the list view takes into account it thanks to React which updates the display according to of the state).

The purpose of this example was to show how to update the state of a parent component, which is a common case when using React. We pass the parent component (actually its instance corresponding to the React object) via the props object, then we implement in the child component a handlerXXX() method that calls the parent component's XXX() method.

Edit an item in the list

We now want to be able to modify the text of each element in the list. The inserted elements are always put in the form "Element1", "Element2", etc. but if you double click on an element, it is now transformed into an input field that can be modified. Pressing the Enter key validates the entry and returns to viewing mode.

To achieve this, let's proceed in stages:
- The first step will be to display an input field when double clicking on an element of the list, the input field will be initialized with the value of the element that was clicked,
- Then we will see how to take into account the entry in the field,
- Finally we will finish by confirming the entry when pressing the Enter key.

Taking double click into account and transforming the element into an input field

React provides us with the onDoubleClick property that allows you to perform a process when you double-click an element. The operating principle is the same as for a single click.

How to transform a frozen text element (here a <span> element) into an <input> element to enter new information? As usual, you have to change the state of the displayed element. We thus introduce in the state of the Element class (which allows to display a list element) a field indicating if the element is being modified (in this case it will be displayed as <input>) or not (in this case it will be displayed as <span>, which has been done so far).

Call modifyOn the state's property that handles this state. By default, it is set to false (to display as <span> at the beginning). This property changes to true when double-clicking the list item, causing the list item to refresh (which then becomes an <input> element). If this state's modifyOn property were set to true, this would cause the list to be initially displayed as input fields instead of traditional frozen elements.

The Element class is modified to take into account these novelties.

Transforming a text element into an input field

```
class Element extends React.Component {
  constructor(props) {
```

```
  super(props);
  this.ukey = props.ukey;
  this.state = { style : {}, removed : false, modifyOn : false };
}
mouseOver() {
  var style = { color : "red", fontStyle : "italic" };
  this.setState({style : style });
}
mouseOut() {
  var style = { color : "", fontStyle : "" };
  this.setState({style : style });
}
handlerRemoveElem() {
  this.props.app.removeElem(this);
}
modifyElem() {
  this.setState({ modifyOn : true });
}
render() {
  return (
    this.state.removed ? null :
      <li style={this.state.style}
          onMouseOver={this.mouseOver.bind(this)}
          onMouseOut={this.mouseOut.bind(this)}
      onDoubleClick={this.modifyElem.bind(this)} >
    { this.state.modifyOn ?
      <input type="text" value={this.props.txt}/> :
          <span>{this.props.txt}</span>
    }
    <button style={{margin:"10px", fontSize:"10px"}}
        onClick={this.handlerRemoveElem.bind(this)}
    >
      Remove
    </button>
    </li>
  )
}
}
```

An onDoubleClick event is taken into account on the <li> element, which will call the modifyElem() method that sets the modifyOn state's property to true.

In addition, when displaying the list element (render() method), we test the value of modifyOn in order to know if we display the element as <input> (if this.state.

modifyOn is to true) or as <span> (if this.state.modifyOn is false).

After inserting some elements and double click on some, we obtain:

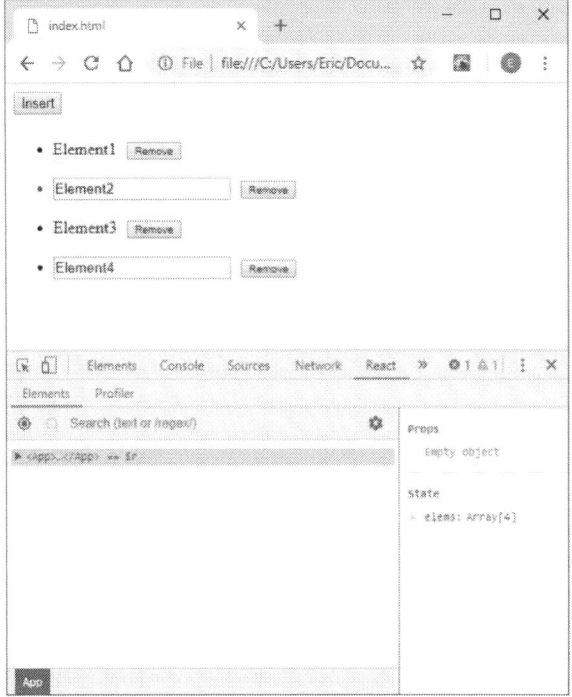

The double-clicked list items are transformed into input fields, initialized with the content of the item (here this.props.txt).

However, the entry in each field is not taken into account ... This is the next step!

Entering in the field

At this stage of our development, the input fields are displayed with a double click, but can not be modified. Why ? In fact, each input field is now managed by React, and an input field managed by React does not have the same behavior as a traditional HTML input field! Among other things, it is not modifiable by default, and to be able to modify it, it would be necessary to carry out a new render(), which can not be done ... only by modifying the state!

You will notice that React gives us some possible solutions, thanks to the error message displayed in the console: it advises us to implement the onChange event so that the input field is no longer read-only. The method associated with the onChange event will be called each time a key is pressed, while the text entered in the field can be retrieved using event.target.value (event being the event parameter passed in the handlerChange(event) method associated with the onChange event).

Let's make these changes in the Element component by displaying for the moment the text typed in the console (using console.log(event.target.value)):

Implement the onChange event to manage the input field

```
class Element extends React.Component {
 constructor(props) {
  super(props);
  this.ukey = props.ukey;
  this.state = { style : {}, removed : false, modifyOn : false };
 }
 mouseOver() {
  var style = { color : "red", fontStyle : "italic" };
  this.setState({style : style });
 }
 mouseOut() {
  var style = { color : "", fontStyle : "" };
  this.setState({style : style });
 }
 handlerRemoveElem() {
  this.props.app.removeElem(this);
 }
 modifyElem() {
  this.setState({ modifyOn : true });
 }
 handlerChange(event) {
  console.log(event.target.value);  // display the entered text
 }
 render() {
  return (
   this.state.removed ? null :
     <li style={this.state.style}
        onMouseOver={this.mouseOver.bind(this)}
        onMouseOut={this.mouseOut.bind(this)}
      onDoubleClick={this.modifyElem.bind(this)} >
       { this.state.modifyOn ?
      <input type="text" value={this.props.txt}
         onChange={this.handlerChange.bind(this)}/> :
        <span>{this.props.txt}</span>
    }
     <button style={{margin:"10px", fontSize:"10px"}}
       onClick={this.handlerRemoveElem.bind(this)}
```

```
      >
        Remove
      </button>
    </li>
  )
  }
}
```

The only change made is the implementation of the onChange event when typing.

After trying to modify the contents of "Element1" by typing "a", then "b", then "c" in the field:

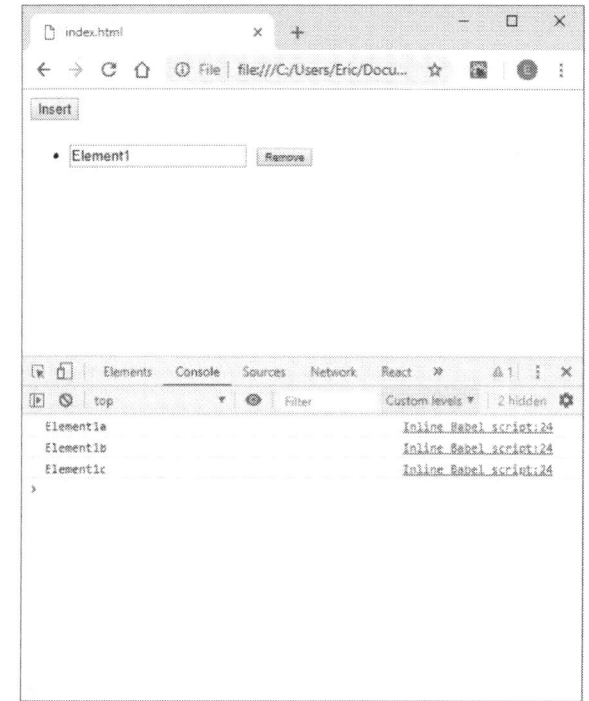

The content of the field is not modified despite the entry, and only the last entered character is retrieved in event.target.value at each character entry. Although strange, this is normal considering the internal functioning of React, which can change the display only during a change of state, which has not been done yet!

The value of the element must therefore be added to the state in the input field, so that each time the field is changed, this new value is reflected in the value attribute of the <input> element. For that, it is necessary moreover that the displayed value does not come from this.props.txt (which is the initial value of the field) but from this.state.txt (which is the real value of the field at every moment, provided that the state be updated every time you hit the keyboard). To do this, we introduce a new txt property in the state of the Element class, which will permanently contain the value entered in the field.

Manage the value entered in the field by the state

```
class Element extends React.Component {
 constructor(props) {
  super(props);
  this.ukey = props.ukey;
   this.state = {
      style : {},
      removed : false,
   modifyOn : false,
   txt : props.txt
  };
 }
 mouseOver() {
  var style = { color : "red", fontStyle : "italic" };
  this.setState({style : style });
 }
 mouseOut() {
  var style = { color : "", fontStyle : "" };
  this.setState({style : style });
 }
 handlerRemoveElem() {
  this.props.app.removeElem(this);
 }
 modifyElem() {
  this.setState({ modifyOn : true });
 }
 handlerChange(event) {
  console.log(event.target.value);
  this.setState({ txt : event.target.value }); // display the entered text
 }
 render() {
  return (
   this.state.removed ? null :
     <li style={this.state.style}
        onMouseOver={this.mouseOver.bind(this)}
        onMouseOut={this.mouseOut.bind(this)}
      onDoubleClick={this.modifyElem.bind(this)} >
       { this.state.modifyOn ?
      <input type="text" value={this.state.txt}
```

```
            onChange={this.handlerChange.bind(this)}/> :
        <span>{this.state.txt}</span>
      }
      <button style={{margin:"10px", fontSize:"10px"}}
          onClick={this.handlerRemoveElem.bind(this)}
      >
        Remove
      </button>
    </li>
  )
 }
}
```

We introduce the txt property into the state, initialized from this.props.txt. And for this value to be displayed in the field, it is indicated in the value attribute of the <input> element and in the associated <span> content.

This value is updated by this.setState() when processing the onChange event.

As before, type the characters "abcde" in the input field:

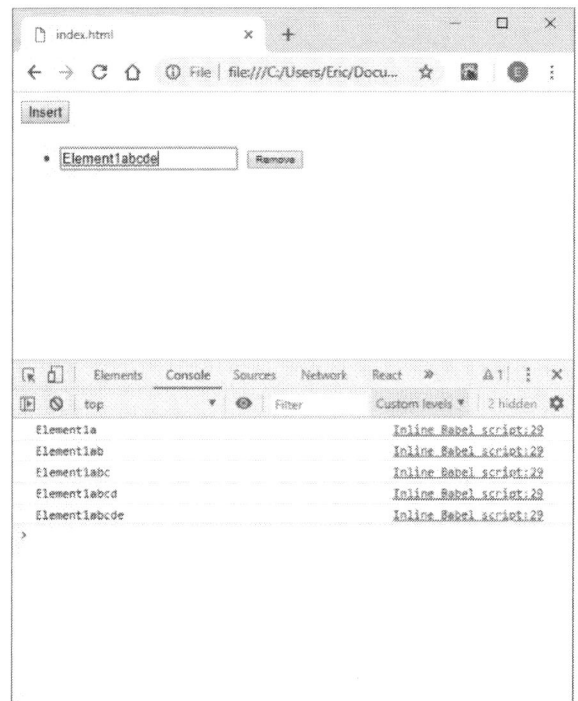

The characters typed in the field are now visible, while the Console shows the evolution of the text as you type. It now remains to manage the support on Enter which allows to validate the entered text.

Confirmation of the change by pressing Enter

It is now necessary to detect pressing the `Enter` key. Looking at React's documentation on events (see https://reactjs.org/docs/events.html) we see that we can use `event.charCode` which contains the code of the key pressed. But for that, the documentation indicates that it is necessary to use one of the following three events:

- `onKeyDown`: occurs when the key is pressed,
- `onKeyUp`: occurs when the key is up (after being pressed),
- `onKeyPress`: indicates that the key has been pressed.

The final event `onKeyPress` can be used in our case (but the other two could have been). Let's implement this event on the `<input>` element of the input field.

> Note that `event.charCode` is not initialized if you use it in the `onChange` event, hence the obligation to use one of the three previous events (which initialize it).

The processing will consist in modifying the state of the element in order to transform the input field in static field (setting of `this.state.modifyOn` to `false`), then to update the `state.elems` of the component `<App>` in order to tell it the new text entered. For that we create a `modifyElem(objElem, newValue)` method defined in the `<App>` component that will update `this.state.elems` with the new text of the element. The `modifyElem()` method is called from the `Element` class with the `app` property stored in the `Element` class (called via `this.props.app.modifyElem()`).

Processing the Enter key in the input field

```
class Element extends React.Component {
  constructor(props) {
    super(props);
    this.ukey = props.ukey;
      this.state = {
        style : {},
        removed : false,
      modifyOn : false,
      txt : props.txt
    };
  }
  mouseOver() {
    var style = { color : "red", fontStyle : "italic" };
    this.setState({style : style });
  }
  mouseOut() {
```

```
    var style = { color : "", fontStyle : "" };
    this.setState({style : style });
  }
  handlerRemoveElem() {
    this.props.app.removeElem(this);
  }
  modifyElem() {
    this.setState({ modifyOn : true });
  }
  handlerChange(event) {
    console.log(event.target.value);
    this.setState({ txt : event.target.value });
  }
  handlerKeyPress(event) {
    if (event.charCode == 13) {  // Enter key
      this.setState({ modifyOn : false });
      this.props.app.modifyElem(this, event.target.value);
    }
  }
  render() {
    return (
      this.state.removed ? null :
        <li style={this.state.style}
            onMouseOver={this.mouseOver.bind(this)}
            onMouseOut={this.mouseOut.bind(this)}
          onDoubleClick={this.modifyElem.bind(this)} >
            { this.state.modifyOn ?
          <input type="text" value={this.state.txt}
              onChange={this.handlerChange.bind(this)}
              onKeyPress={this.handlerKeyPress.bind(this)}/> :
              <span>{this.state.txt}</span>
        }
        <button style={{margin:"10px", fontSize:"10px"}}
            onClick={this.handlerRemoveElem.bind(this)}
        >
          Remove
        </button>
      </li>
    )
  }
}
class ElementsList extends React.Component {
  constructor(props) {
```

```
    super(props);
  }
  render() {
   return (
    <ul>
     {
     this.props.elems.map((elem, index) => {
       var { ukey, txt } = elem;
       return <Element key={ukey} ukey={ukey} txt={txt} app={this.props.app} />
     })
     }
    </ul>
   )
  }
}
class App extends React.Component {
 constructor(props) {
  super(props);
  this.state = { elems : [] };
 }
 getUniqueKey() {
  var key = Math.random() + "";
  return key;
 }
 insertElem() {
  var elems = this.state.elems;
  var txt = "Element" + (elems.length + 1);
  var ukey = this.getUniqueKey();
  var elem = { txt : txt, ukey : ukey };
  elems.push(elem);
  this.setState({ elems : elems });
 }
 removeElem(objElem) {    // Element class object
  var elems = this.state.elems;
  elems = elems.filter(function(elem) {
   if (objElem.ukey != elem.ukey) return true;
  });
  this.setState({ elems : elems });
 }
 modifyElem(objElem, newValue) {   // Element class object
  var elems = this.state.elems;
  elems = elems.map(function(elem) {
```

```
    var { txt, ukey } = elem;
    if (objElem.ukey == ukey) elem.txt = newValue;   // modify element
    return elem;
   });
   this.setState({ elems : elems });
  }
  render() {
   return (
    <div>
     <button onClick={this.insertElem.bind(this)}>Insert</button>
     <ElementsList elems={this.state.elems} app={this} />
    </div>
   )
  }
 }
 ReactDOM.render(<App />, document.getElementById("root"));
```

Detection of the Enter key is performed in the handlerKeyPress() method called whenever a keyboard key is pressed. This method calls the modifyElem() method defined in the App class in the same way that the removeElem() method was called during a deletion.

After insertion and modification of some elements (including a deletion):

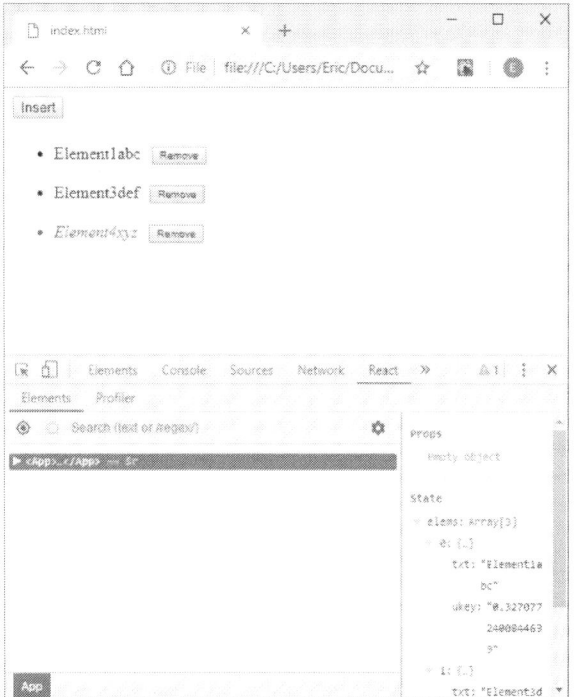

The React tab makes it possible to check that the states are updated by React (although it can also be seen thanks to the display on the page, because it reflects the content of the state).

Enlargement of the window

The goal will be to manage the enlargement of the browser window, to change the size of the font with larger characters (or smaller if the window shrinks).

The interest here is to show how to implement an event that React does not support, in this case the resize event managed on the browser's window object. This event is supported in HTML, but React does not provide the onResize property to handle it. We must implement it ourselves...

To implement a new event that is not managed by React, the addEventListener() and removeEventListener() JavaScript methods are used directly. These methods will be used here to manage the resize event received by the window object:

- The window.addEventListener() method will be implemented in the componentDidMount() method defined in the <App> component. The window.addEventListener("resize", callback) method is used to attach a callback function when the resize event is received by the window object. The addEventListener() method is implemented in the componentDidMount() method of the App class and is called when creating the <App> component.

• The window.removeEventListener() method will be implemented in the componentWillUnmount() method defined in the <App> component. The window.removeEventListener("resize", callback) method allows you to ignore the associated callback function during the resize event. The removeEventListener() method is implemented in the componentWillUnmount() method of the App class and is therefore called when the <App> component is destroyed.

> Note that to avoid memory management issues, every call to an addEventListener() method must be associated with a call to the corresponding removeEventListener() method.

The processing to be performed in the callback function (called during the resize event) will consist in modifying the size of the font used to write the elements of the list. For now, we did not manage this font size because we used the default size set in the browser. How to take into account a new size of the font to display the list? Simply by modifying the state used in the App class (knowing that the list of displayed elements is already in the state of the App class (this.state.elems)).

The style of the list (positioned in this.state.style of the App class) will be passed in the props object to the different used components, ie <ElementsList> then <Element>. The <Element> component is the one that will eventually use the style of the list to display each element.

Manage the resize event on the window

```
class Element extends React.Component {
 constructor(props) {
  super(props);
  this.ukey = props.ukey;
   this.state = {
   style : { ...this.props.style },
      removed : false,
   modifyOn : false,
   txt : props.txt
  };
 }
 mouseOver() {
  var style = { ...this.state.style, color : "red", fontStyle : "italic" };
  this.setState({style : style });
 }
```

```jsx
  mouseOut() {
    var style = { ...this.state.style, color : "", fontStyle : "" };
    this.setState({style : style });
  }
  handlerRemoveElem() {
    this.props.app.removeElem(this);
  }
  modifyElem() {
    this.setState({ modifyOn : true });
  }
  handlerChange(event) {
    console.log(event.target.value);
    this.setState({ txt : event.target.value });
  }
  handlerKeyPress(event) {
    if (event.charCode == 13) {
      this.setState({ modifyOn : false });
      this.props.app.modifyElem(this, event.target.value);
    }
  }
  render() {
    return (
      this.state.removed ? null :
      <li style={this.state.style}
          onMouseOver={this.mouseOver.bind(this)}
          onMouseOut={this.mouseOut.bind(this)}
        onDoubleClick={this.modifyElem.bind(this)} >
          { this.state.modifyOn ?
        <input type="text" value={this.state.txt}
            onChange={this.handlerChange.bind(this)}
            onKeyPress={this.handlerKeyPress.bind(this)}/> :
            <span>{this.state.txt}</span>
      }
       <button style={{margin:"10px", fontSize:"10px"}}
          onClick={this.handlerRemoveElem.bind(this)}
       >
        Remove
       </button>
      </li>
    )
  }
}
class ElementsList extends React.Component {
```

```
  constructor(props) {
    super(props);
  }
  render() {
    return (
      <ul>
        {
         this.props.elems.map((elem, index) => {
           var { ukey, txt } = elem;
              return <Element key={ukey} ukey={ukey} txt={txt}
                   app={this.props.app} style={this.props.style} />
         })
        }
      </ul>
    )
  }
}
class App extends React.Component {
  constructor(props) {
    super(props);
    this.state = {
      elems : [],
      style : { fontSize : this.getFontSize() }
    };
  }
  getUniqueKey() {
    var key = Math.random() + "";
    return key;
  }
  insertElem() {
    var elems = this.state.elems;
    var txt = "Element" + (elems.length + 1);
    var ukey = this.getUniqueKey();
    var elem = { txt : txt, ukey : ukey };
    elems.push(elem);
    this.setState({ elems : elems });
  }
  removeElem(objElem) {    // objet de classe Element
    var elems = this.state.elems;
    elems = elems.filter(function(elem) {
      if (objElem.ukey != elem.ukey) return true;
    });
    this.setState({ elems : elems });
```

```
}
modifyElem(objElem, newValue) {
 var elems = this.state.elems;
 elems = elems.map(function(elem) {
  var { txt, ukey } = elem;
  if (objElem.ukey == ukey) elem.txt = newValue;
  return elem;
 });
 this.setState({ elems : elems });
}
getFontSize() { // returns fontSize according to the height of the window
 var fontSize;
 if (window.innerHeight < 150) fontSize = 12;
 else if (window.innerHeight < 200) fontSize = 13;
 else if (window.innerHeight < 250) fontSize = 15;
 else if (window.innerHeight < 300) fontSize = 16;
 else if (window.innerHeight < 350) fontSize = 18;
 else if (window.innerHeight < 400) fontSize = 20;
 else if (window.innerHeight < 450) fontSize = 22;
 else if (window.innerHeight < 500) fontSize = 24;
 else if (window.innerHeight < 550) fontSize = 30;
 else fontSize = 40;
 return fontSize + "px";
}
handlerResize(event) {
 var fontSize = this.getFontSize();
 this.setState({ style : { fontSize : fontSize }});
}
componentDidMount() {
 window.addEventListener("resize", this.handlerResize.bind(this));
}
componentWillUnmount() {
 window.removeEventListener("resize", this.handlerResize);
}
render() {
 return (
  <div>
   <button onClick={this.insertElem.bind(this)}>Insert</button>
   <ElementsList elems={this.state.elems} app={this}
         style={this.state.style} />
  </div>
 )
```

```
    }
}
ReactDOM.render(<App />, document.getElementById("root"));
```

The getFontSize() method defined in the App class retrieves a font size based on the height of the window. This size will be reflected in the style property of the state associated with the App class.

This style is passed as a property (props.style) when creating the <ElementsList> component, and then transferred in the same way when creating <Element> components.

> Note the use of the ... operator to destructure an object, and group its properties within a new object. Indeed, the Element class already supports a style property in its state, and the new styles passed must be concatenated with existing ones, and not replace them. The operator ... allows you to perform this operation in a very simple way.

Let's run this program, and enlarge the browser window (beyond 200 pixels high, which should produce a character height of at least 15 pixels):

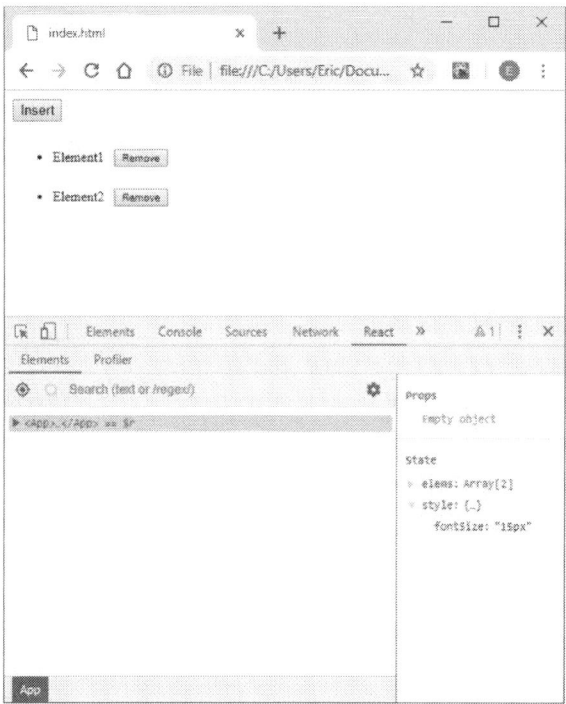

We see that the initial size of the list items is quite different from the default one (smaller characters), and we also see that the fontSize property defined in the state of the App class varies depending on the height of the window and here indicates

"15px".

However, the size of the characters on the screen does not vary ...

Let's look at the value of the props object associated with an Element class object using the React tab. Just open each component displayed on the left side of the React tab and select an <Element> component (here the first one in the list):

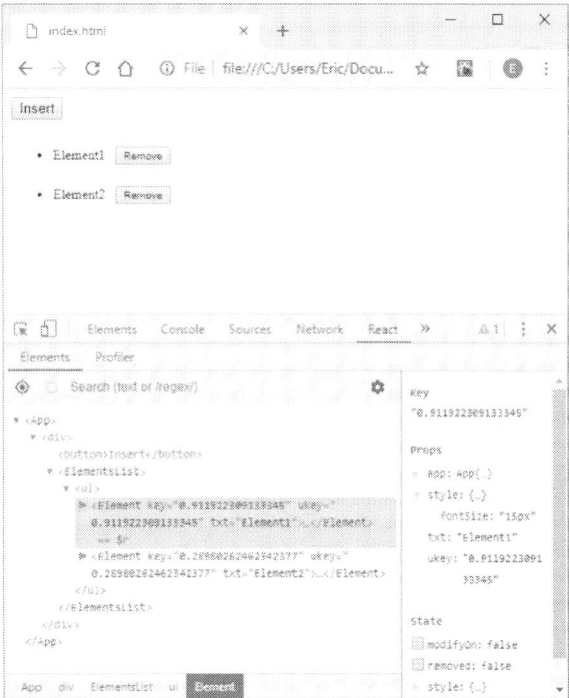

The fontSize property in the style associated with the props object indicates "15px" (which is the correct value found in the App component's state), but obviously this fontSize property is not reflected in the screen. Why ?

In fact, the value of the props object is not reflected on the screen because the <Element> component is already created. React defines the method componentDidUpdate(prevProps, prevState) in order to handle the case where a component already created receives new props, which is the case here.

Let's implement this method in the <Element> component and make a call to setState() indicating the new style (included in the this.props object of the component).

Use componentDidUpdate() to update the state
```
class Element extends React.Component {
```

```
constructor(props) {
 super(props);
 this.ukey = props.ukey;
   this.state = {
     style : { ...this.props.style },
     removed : false,
   modifyOn : false,
   txt : props.txt
 };
}
mouseOver() {
 var style = { ...this.state.style, color : "red", fontStyle : "italic" };
 this.setState({style : style });
}
mouseOut() {
 var style = { ...this.state.style, color : "", fontStyle : "" };
 this.setState({style : style });
}
handlerRemoveElem() {
 this.props.app.removeElem(this);
}
modifyElem() {
 this.setState({ modifyOn : true });
}
handlerChange(event) {
 console.log(event.target.value);
 this.setState({ txt : event.target.value });
}
handlerKeyPress(event) {
 if (event.charCode == 13) {
   this.setState({ modifyOn : false });
   this.props.app.modifyElem(this, event.target.value);
 }
}
componentDidUpdate(prevProps, prevState) {
 if (prevProps.style != this.props.style) {
   // the style property has been modified: update the state
   this.setState({ style : this.props.style });
 }
}
render() {
 return (
   this.state.removed ? null :
```

```
      <li style={this.state.style}
          onMouseOver={this.mouseOver.bind(this)}
          onMouseOut={this.mouseOut.bind(this)}
        onDoubleClick={this.modifyElem.bind(this)} >
          { this.state.modifyOn ?
        <input type="text" value={this.state.txt}
            onChange={this.handlerChange.bind(this)}
            onKeyPress={this.handlerKeyPress.bind(this)}/> :
            <span>{this.state.txt}</span>
        }
        <button style={{margin:"10px", fontSize:"10px"}}
            onClick={this.handlerRemoveElem.bind(this)}
        >
          Remove
        </button>
      </li>
    )
  }
}
class ElementsList extends React.Component {
  constructor(props) {
    super(props);
  }
  render() {
    return (
      <ul>
        {
        this.props.elems.map((elem, index) => {
          var { ukey, txt } = elem;
            return <Element key={ukey} ukey={ukey} txt={txt}
                app={this.props.app} style={this.props.style} />
        })
        }
      </ul>
    )
  }
}
class App extends React.Component {
  constructor(props) {
    super(props);
      this.state = {
      elems : [],
      style : { fontSize : this.getFontSize() }
    };
```

```
}
getUniqueKey() {
  var key = Math.random() + "";
  return key;
}
insertElem() {
  var elems = this.state.elems;
  var txt = "Element" + (elems.length + 1);
  var ukey = this.getUniqueKey();
  var elem = { txt : txt, ukey : ukey };
  elems.push(elem);
  this.setState({ elems : elems });
}
removeElem(objElem) {
  var elems = this.state.elems;
  elems = elems.filter(function(elem) {
    if (objElem.ukey != elem.ukey) return true;
  });
  this.setState({ elems : elems });
}
modifyElem(objElem, newValue) {
  var elems = this.state.elems;
  elems = elems.map(function(elem) {
    var { txt, ukey } = elem;
    if (objElem.ukey == ukey) elem.txt = newValue;
    return elem;
  });
  this.setState({ elems : elems });
}
getFontSize() {
  var fontSize;
  if (window.innerHeight < 150) fontSize = 12;
  else if (window.innerHeight < 200) fontSize = 13;
  else if (window.innerHeight < 250) fontSize = 15;
  else if (window.innerHeight < 300) fontSize = 16;
  else if (window.innerHeight < 350) fontSize = 18;
  else if (window.innerHeight < 400) fontSize = 20;
  else if (window.innerHeight < 450) fontSize = 22;
  else if (window.innerHeight < 500) fontSize = 24;
  else if (window.innerHeight < 550) fontSize = 30;
  else fontSize = 40;
  return fontSize + "px";
```

```
}
handlerResize(event) {
  var fontSize = this.getFontSize();
  this.setState({ style : { fontSize : fontSize }});
}
componentDidMount() {
  window.addEventListener("resize", this.handlerResize.bind(this));
}
componentWillUnmount() {
  window.removeEventListener("resize", this.handlerResize);
}
render() {
  return (
    <div>
      <button onClick={this.insertElem.bind(this)}>Insert</button>
      <ElementsList elems={this.state.elems} app={this}
            style={this.state.style} />
    </div>
  )
}
}
ReactDOM.render(<App />, document.getElementById("root"));
```

The only change is the addition of the `componentDidUpdate()` method in the `Element` class. It updates the state of the element.

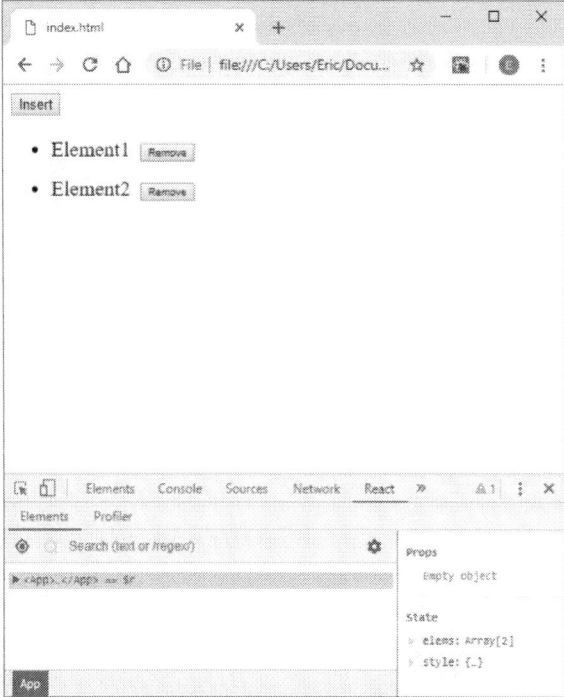

The size of the elements now varies according to the height of the window.

7 – MANAGE FORMS WITH REACT

In previous chapters we have used two types of HTML elements that we have learned to deal with using React. These are the buttons and input fields. However, there are several types of HTML elements that can interact in our HTML pages:
- Input fields of a single line (`<input>` elements of `text` type). They have already been studied previously.
- The classic buttons (`<button>` or `<input>` elements of `button` type). They have also been studied previously.
- Multiline input fields (`<textarea>` elements).
- Selection lists (`<select>` elements including `<option>` elements).
- The radio buttons (`<input>` elements of `radio` type).
- The checkboxes (`<input>` elements of `checkbox` type).

Let's take a look at the new elements in this chapter.

Manage multiline input fields

A multiline input field is defined by the `<textarea>` element. Let's create a `<TextArea>` component that "enhances" the traditional `<textarea>` element.

Basic <TextArea> component

Let's start with a basic component to create a basic `<textarea>`. It will be used in the following form:

Using a basic <TextArea> component
```
<TextArea cols={40} rows={10} value="Type your text here" />
```

The `cols`, `rows` and `value` attributes are respectively indicated:
- The number of columns of the `<textarea>` (`cols` attribute),

- The number of lines of the `<textarea>` (`rows` attribute),
- The default value displayed in the field (`value` attribute).

As we saw previously for the input fields, it is necessary to implement the `onChange` event so that the input is taken into account in the field. In addition, the state must include the value entered in the field, so that this value is automatically refreshed when entering.

The `value` property defined in the component should therefore be used to initialize the `value` property of the state.

Implementing the basic <TextArea> component

```
<html>
<head>
<script crossorigin
  src="https://unpkg.com/react@16/umd/react.development.js"></script>
<script crossorigin
  src="https://unpkg.com/react-dom@16/umd/react-dom.development.js"></script>
<script src="https://unpkg.com/babel-standalone@6/babel.min.js"></script>
</head>
<body>
 <div id="root"></div>
</body>
<script type="text/babel">
class TextArea extends React.Component {
 constructor(props) {
  super(props);
  this.state = { value : props.value };
 }
 handlerChange(event) {
  this.setState({value : event.target.value});
 }
 render() {
  return (
   <textarea cols={this.props.cols}
        rows={this.props.rows}
        value={this.state.value}
        onChange={this.handlerChange.bind(this)}
   />
```

```
    )
  }
}
ReactDOM.render(
 <TextArea cols={40} rows={10} value="Type your text here" />,
 document.getElementById("root")
);
</script>
</html>
```

The operation of a multiline input field (`<textarea>`) is similar to that of an `<input>` field of a single line.

After displaying the component, and typing a few characters in the input field:

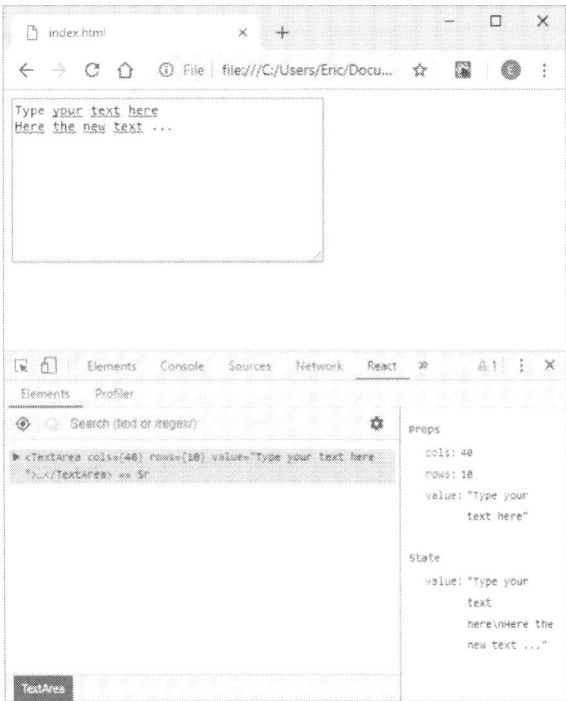

The entered text appears in the field, only because the onChange event was implemented in the class and the state handles the value entered in the field...

`<TextArea>` component with automatic focus

React provides the boolean autoFocus property to give focus to a field (value {true} or {false}).

To give focus to a <textarea> field automatically (when loading the associated component), just write the following JSX code:

Give focus to the <textarea> element as soon as it is displayed
```
<textarea autoFocus={true} />
```

Let's implement the focus property ({true} or {false}) in the <TextArea> component to give focus to the input field (or no focus if the value is {false} or the property is not specified).

<TextArea> component implementing the focus property
```
class TextArea extends React.Component {
  constructor(props) {
    super(props);
    this.state = { value : props.value };
  }
  handlerChange(event) {
    this.setState({value : event.target.value});
  }
  render() {
    return (
        <textarea cols={this.props.cols}
                  rows={this.props.rows}
                  value={this.state.value}
                  onChange={this.handlerChange.bind(this)}
            autoFocus={this.props.focus}
        />
    )
  }
}
ReactDOM.render(
  <TextArea cols={40} rows={10} value="Type your text here" focus={true} />,
  document.getElementById("root")
);
```

The focus property is transferred into the autoFocus property of the <textarea> element.

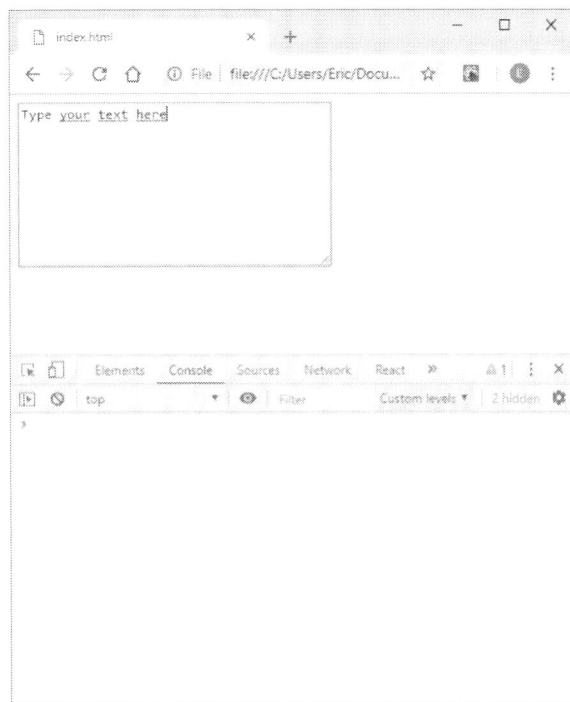

As soon as the program is launched, the input field has the focus.

The `autoFocus` property is accessible for all React elements that can have focus (not just `<textarea>` elements).

<TextArea> component with field deletion when taking focus

We now want to clear the contents of the field when it gets the focus. This allows you to be ready to type in the field without having to delete it ourselves (for example when it contains an error).

For that, we will use the `onFocus` event indicating that `this.state.value` is empty (`""`). Updating the state causes (as we have already seen many times) a refresh of the component.

Clear the field when it gets the focus

```
class TextArea extends React.Component {
 constructor(props) {
  super(props);
  this.state = { value : props.value };
 }
 handlerChange(event) {
```

```
    this.setState({value : event.target.value});
  }
  handlerFocus(event) {
    this.setState({value : ""});
  }
  render() {
    return (
        <textarea cols={this.props.cols}
              rows={this.props.rows}
              value={this.state.value}
              onChange={this.handlerChange.bind(this)}
          onFocus={this.handlerFocus.bind(this)}
        autoFocus={this.props.focus}
    />
    )
  }
}
ReactDOM.render(
  <TextArea cols={40} rows={10} value="Type your text here" focus={false} />,
  document.getElementById("root")
);
```

The `onFocus` event is implemented using the `handlerFocus()` intermediate method, in which the `value` property of the state is updated.

To see how clear the field is when it gets focus, we set the `focus` property to `false` when creating the `<TextArea>` component.

Let's show the component before it gets focus:

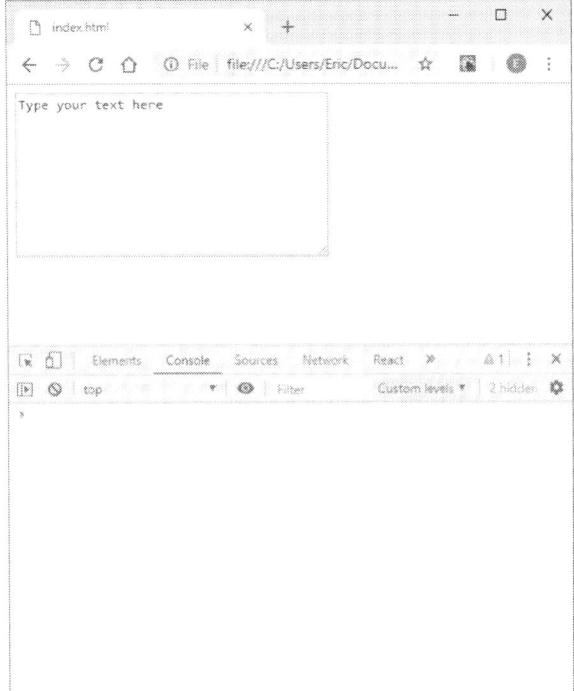

The default value of the field is still displayed ...

Then click in the input field:

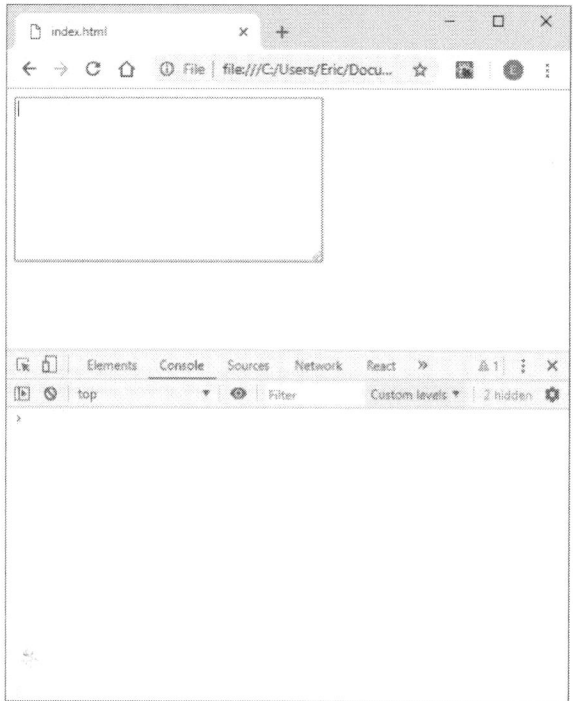

The content of the input field is cleared as soon as you click inside ...

<TextArea> component with processing function

A very practical feature of React is to allow you to set up a processing function in the properties of a component. This allows you to create a component by specifying a different processing function depending on where this component is used.

For example, we want to activate a function validTextArea(text) when we want to validate the contents of <textarea>. The <TextArea> component would then have a new property called here onValid whose value would be {validTextArea}:

<TextArea> component with the defined onValid property

```
<TextArea cols={40} rows={10} value="Type your text here"
    onValid={validTextArea} />
```

The validTextArea(text) function is defined in the JavaScript code. It uses the text parameter indicating the text that has been entered in the <textarea> field. For example, here is his definition:

Defining the validTextArea(text) function

```
function validTextArea(text) { // validation function
```

```
console.log(text);  // display of typed text in the console
}
```

For now, the validation function simply displays the text indicated in the parameter in the console.

It remains to define when the validation function must be activated. It could be :
- When exiting the input field (onBlur event),
- When pressing a key combination when typing (eg Shift + Enter),
- When clicking a button outside the input field (click on a Validate button).

Let's look at these different possibilities below.

Validation of the field when leaving the field

The output of the input field is detected with the onBlur event on the field.

Validation thanks to onBlur event on the field

```
class TextArea extends React.Component {
 constructor(props) {
  super(props);
  this.state = { value : props.value };
 }
 handlerChange(event) {
  this.setState({value : event.target.value});
 }
 handlerFocus(event) {
  this.setState({value : ""});
 }
 handlerBlur(event) {
  var value = event.target.value;
  this.props.onValid(value);  // calling the validTextArea(value) method
 }
 render() {
  return (
     <textarea cols={this.props.cols}
               rows={this.props.rows}
               value={this.state.value}
               onChange={this.handlerChange.bind(this)}
               onFocus={this.handlerFocus.bind(this)}
         onBlur={this.handlerBlur.bind(this)}
         autoFocus={this.props.focus}
   />
  )
 }
}
```

```
function validTextArea(text) { // validation function
  console.log(text);  // display of typed text in the console
}
ReactDOM.render(
  <TextArea cols={40} rows={10} value="Type your text here"
      onValid={validTextArea} />,
  document.getElementById("root")
);
```

The onBlur event is associated with the handlerBlur() intermediate method, which makes the call to the processing function passed in the component properties (onValid property).

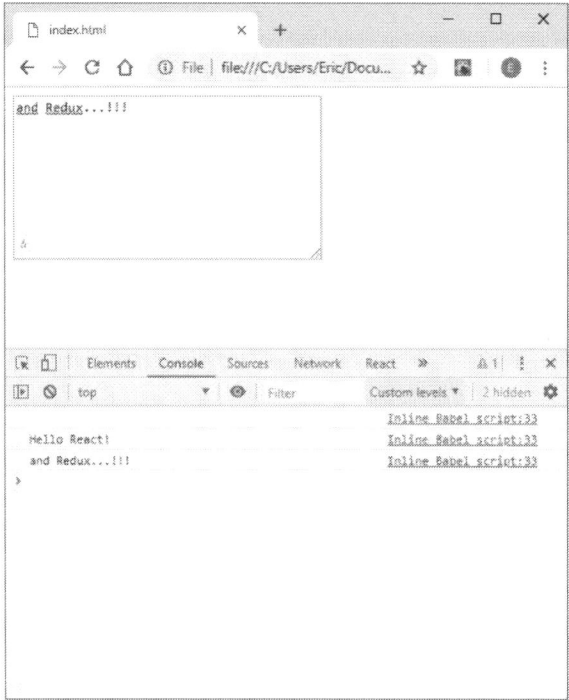

At each exit of the field, the text entered is displayed in the console.

Validating the field with a combination of keys

Another form of validation would be to use a combination of keys when typing, for example pressing the Shift + Enter keys simultaneously.

To do this, use the onKeyPress event, which allows you to detect pressing any key on the keyboard.

Validating the field with a combination of keys

```
class TextArea extends React.Component {
 constructor(props) {
  super(props);
  this.state = { value : props.value };
 }
 handlerChange(event) {
  this.setState({value : event.target.value});
 }
 handlerFocus(event) {
  this.setState({value : ""});
 }
 handlerKeyPress(event) {
  if (event.shiftKey && event.charCode == 13) { // Shift + Enter
   var value = event.target.value;
   this.props.onValid(value); // calling the validTextArea(value) method
  }
 }
 render() {
  return (
      <textarea cols={this.props.cols}
             rows={this.props.rows}
             value={this.state.value}
             onChange={this.handlerChange.bind(this)}
             onFocus={this.handlerFocus.bind(this)}
         onKeyPress={this.handlerKeyPress.bind(this)}
        autoFocus={this.props.focus}
   />
  )
 }
}
function validTextArea(text) {
 console.log(text);
}
ReactDOM.render(
 <TextArea cols={40} rows={10} value="Type your text here"
      onValid={validTextArea} />,
 document.getElementById("root")
);
```

The principle is the same as before. The `onKeyPress` event is associated with the `handlerKeyPress()` method that detects simultaneous pressing on the `Shift + Enter` keys. Following this key detection, the `validTextArea()` method is called via the call to `this.props.onValid()`.

Validation of the field thanks to a click on a validation button

We propose to use a button to validate the input field. When the button is clicked, the method indicated in the onValid attribute is called (by sending the text entered as a parameter).

Two React components will be used here:

- The first component, named <TextArea>, is the component that was previously used to authorize input in the <textarea> input field.
- The second component, named <TextAreaWithButton>, includes the first <TextArea> component and a <button> validation button for validation. It is therefore an aggregation of components, responsible for cooperating together.

The new <TextAreaWithButton> component is used as follows:

Using the <TextAreaWithButton> component
```
<TextAreaWithButton cols={40} rows={10} value="Type your text here"
        onValid={validTextArea} />
```

The user interface of the <TextAreaWithButton> component is similar to the previous component used <TextArea>.

Let us write the <TextArea> and <TextAreaWithButton> components, displaying for the moment only the text "Validation" with each click on the validation button.

Validation by a validation button
```
class TextArea extends React.Component {
 constructor(props) {
  super(props);
  this.state = { value : this.props.value };
 }
 handlerChange(event) {
  this.setState({value : event.target.value});
 }
 handlerFocus(event) {
  this.setState({value : ""});
 }
 render() {
  return (
     <textarea cols={this.props.cols}
               rows={this.props.rows}
               value={this.state.value}
               onChange={this.handlerChange.bind(this)}
               onFocus={this.handlerFocus.bind(this)}
   />
```

```
    )
  }
}
class TextAreaWithButton extends React.Component {
  constructor(props) {
    super(props);
  }
  handlerValid() {
    console.log("Validation");   // display "Validation" with each click
  }
  render() {
    return (
      <div>
        <TextArea cols={this.props.cols} rows={this.props.rows}
             value={this.props.value} />
        <br/><br/>
        <button onClick={this.handlerValid.bind(this)}>Validate</button>
      </div>
    )
  }
}
function validTextArea(text) {
  console.log(text);
}
ReactDOM.render(
  <TextAreaWithButton cols={40} rows={10} value="Type your text here"
             onValid={validTextArea} />,
  document.getElementById("root")
);
```

The properties specified for creating the `<TextAreaWithButton>` component are passed to the `<TextArea>` component.

The `handlerValid()` validation function is now integrated into the `<TextAreaWithButton>` main component, and is activated when clicking on the validation button.

Let's check that the combination of the two components is working correctly for now:

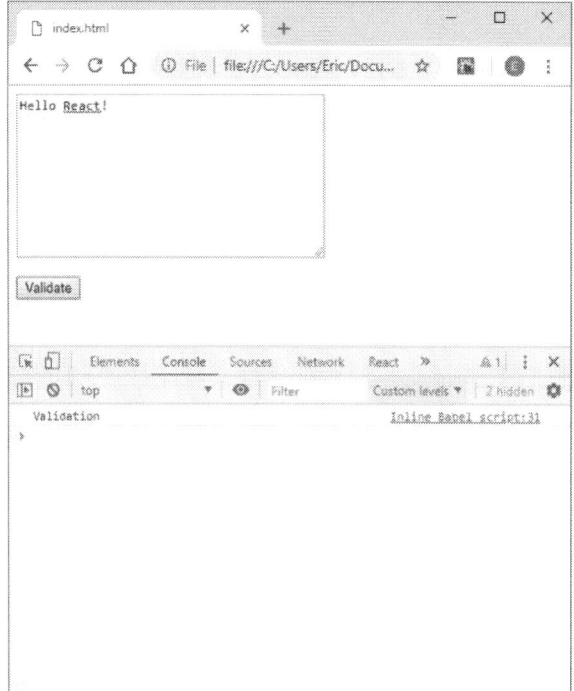

The input works (the input field is updated each time you type on the keyboard), and the text "Validation" appears in the console when the Validate button is clicked.

It now remains to recover the text entered in the input field to display it in the console during validation. The handlerValid() method of the TextAreaWithButton class should be able to write an instruction of the following form:

handlerValid method ()
```
handlerValid() {
  // console.log("Validation");
  this.props.onValid(input text);  // validate input text
}
```

The validation method is passed into the props object of the <TextAreaWithButton> component, and is called through this.props.onValid().

However, it remains to recover the text entered (accessible in the <TextArea> component), but not yet accessible in the <TextAreaWithButton> parent component ...

How to retrieve the text entered in a child component? For this, the easiest way is to integrate it into the state of the parent component. Whenever the child component notices a change in the entered text, it updates the state of the parent component (which includes the text entered in its state). For a child component to update the parent's state, the child component must have access to the parent component. How to allow this access? Simply by passing the instance of the parent component to the child in its props object (we had already used this possibility in the previous chapter).

Update the parent's state from the child component

```
class TextArea extends React.Component {
 constructor(props) {
  super(props);
  this.state = { value : this.props.value }; // child's state
 }
 handlerChange(event) {
  this.setState({value : event.target.value});      // child's state
  this.props.app.setState({value : event.target.value}); // parent's state
 }
 handlerFocus(event) {
  this.setState({value : ""});
 }
 render() {
  return (
     <textarea cols={this.props.cols}
               rows={this.props.rows}
               value={this.state.value}
               onChange={this.handlerChange.bind(this)}
               onFocus={this.handlerFocus.bind(this)}
     />
  )
 }
}
class TextAreaWithButton extends React.Component {
 constructor(props) {
  super(props);
  this.state = { value : this.props.value }; // parent's state
 }
 handlerValid() {
  // console.log("Validation");
  this.props.onValid(this.state.value);
 }
 render() {
  return (
   <div>
    <TextArea cols={this.props.cols} rows={this.props.rows}
```

```
        value={this.props.value} app={this} />
    <br/><br/>
    <button onClick={this.handlerValid.bind(this)}>Validate</button>
    </div>
  )
 }
}
function validTextArea(text) {
 console.log(text);
}
ReactDOM.render(
 <TextAreaWithButton cols={40} rows={10} value="Type your text here"
         onValid={validTextArea} />,
 document.getElementById("root")
);
```

The instance of the parent component is passed into the app property when the <TextArea> child component is created.

Each time the value entered is changed, the state of the child component is updated, as well as the state of the parent component. The parent component can then use its state when validating the button.

The entered text is displayed in the console each time you click on the validation button.

Manage selection lists

The selection lists correspond to the `<select>` elements integrating the `<option>` elements describing the items in the list. Here is for example a list written in HTML integrating five elements of list:

Selection list in HTML
```
<select>
 <option value="1">Element1</option>
 <option value="2">Element2</option>
 <option value="3">Element3</option>
 <option value="4">Element4</option>
 <option value="5">Element5</option>
</select>
```

The `value` attribute specified for each list item is used to assign a value that will be retrieved when the associated item is selected.

This list is displayed as follows:

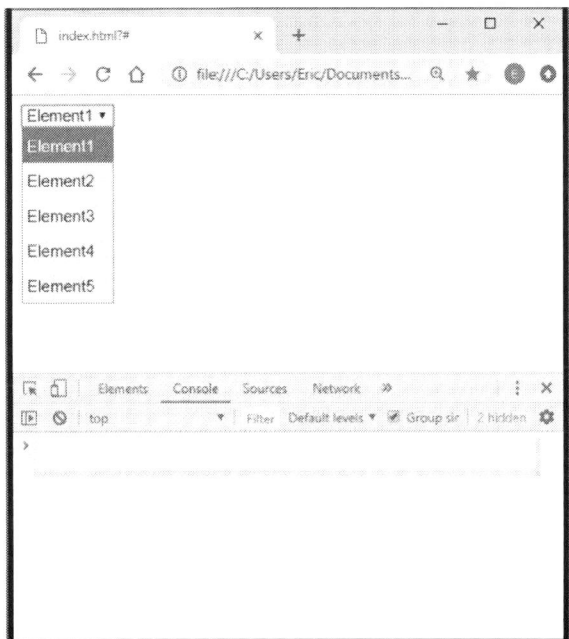

The selection list was opened after clicking on it.

Create the selection list with React

Use React to create the same list as previously displayed. We use a <Select> component in which we pass an options property which is an array indicating the list of elements to be displayed (in the form of strings). React elements are created with JSX.

Create the selection list using JSX and React

```
class Select extends React.Component {
 constructor(props) {
  super(props);
 }
 render() {
  return (
   <select>
   {
    this.props.options.map(function(option, index) {
     return <option key={index+1} value={index+1}>{option}</option>
    })
   }
   </select>
  )
 }
}
ReactDOM.render(
 <Select
  options={["Element1", "Element2", "Element3", "Element4", "Element5"]} />,
 document.getElementById("root")
);
```

The key attribute set when creating the <option> element is needed because React uses it to uniquely identify each item in the list. We use index + 1 (instead of just index) to start the numbering at 1 and not 0 (to be similar to the previous HTML list).

By displaying the list and selecting the React tab of the window:

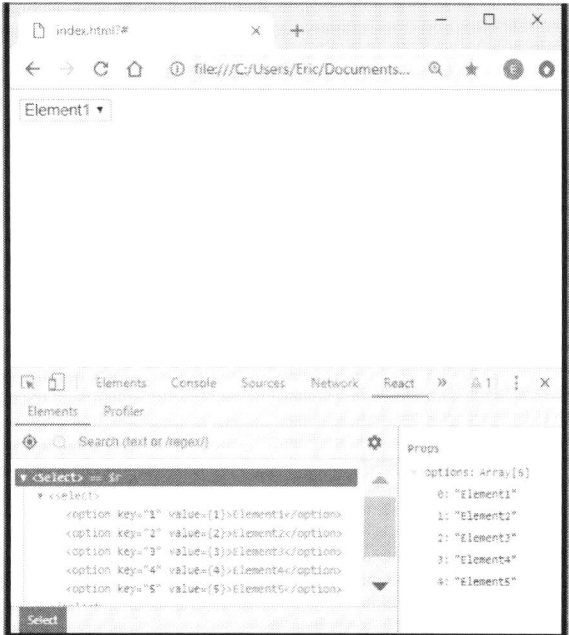

Retrieve the value selected in the selection list

The new goal is now to be able to retrieve the selected value from a list in a process function. This consists in displaying in the console the value attribute of the element selected in the list.

The onChange attribute is used on the <select> element to perform processing when selecting a new item in the list.

Display the value attribute of the selected item

```
class Select extends React.Component {
 constructor(props) {
  super(props);
 }
 handlerChange(event) {
  console.log(event.target.value);
 }
 render() {
  return (
   <select onChange={this.handlerChange.bind(this)}>
   {
    this.props.options.map(function(option, index) {
     return <option key={index+1} value={index+1}>{option}</option>
```

```
    })
   }
   </select>
  )
 }
}
ReactDOM.render(
  <Select
  options={["Element1", "Element2", "Element3", "Element4", "Element5"]} />,
  document.getElementById("root")
);
```

The value of the selected item is retrieved using event.target.value.

After selecting multiple items from the list:

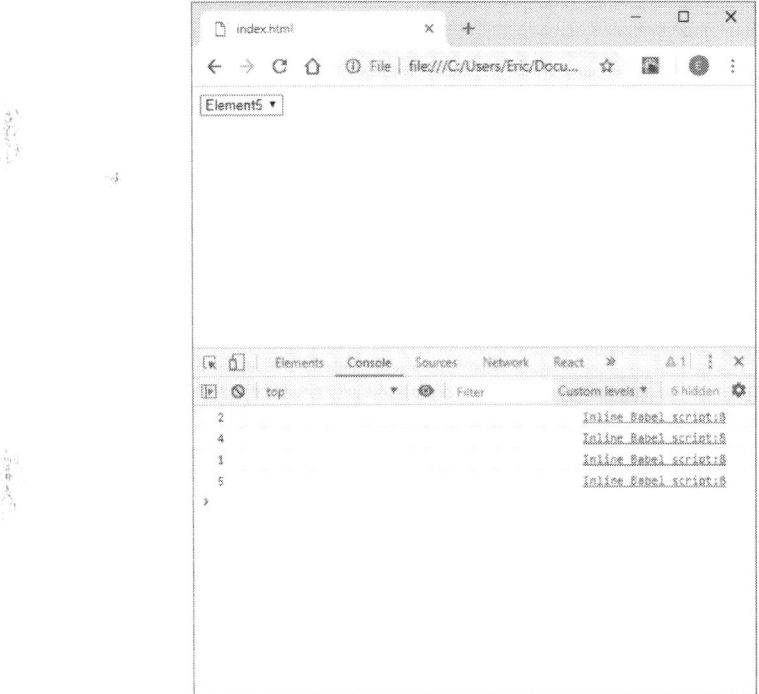

The values associated with the selected elements are displayed in the console.

Implement a processing function as an attribute

You can also specify a processing function in the attributes of the <Select> element, for example by using the onSelect attribute and assigning it the name of a processing function. This makes it possible to indicate different processing functions according to the `<Select>` components used.

Use the onSelect attribute to assign a processing function

```
class Select extends React.Component {
 constructor(props) {
  super(props);
 }
 handlerChange(event) {
  this.props.onSelect(event.target.value); // call of onSelectElement ()
 }
 render() {
  return (
   <select onChange={this.handlerChange.bind(this)}>
   {
    this.props.options.map(function(option, index) {
     return <option key={index+1} value={index+1}>{option}</option>
    })
   }
   </select>
  )
 }
}
function onSelectElement(value) {
 console.log(value);
}
ReactDOM.render(
  <Select options={["Element1", "Element2", "Element3", "Element4", "Element5"]}
     onSelect={onSelectElement} />,
  document.getElementById("root")
);
```

The `onSelectElement()` processing function is specified in the `onSelect` attribute of the `<Select>` component.

It is called when processing the `onChange` event on the `<select>` element.

Select a default item in the selection list

The first item in the list is the one that is selected by default. To select another, you must specify its value in the `defaultValue` attribute of the `<select>` element. For example, to select the list item whose value attribute is 4, write in JSX:

Select the list item with value equal to 4

```
<select defaultValue={4} >
```

> Be careful because this works in JSX but not in HTML! (The defaultValue attribute is unknown on the <select> HTML element). But we do not write HTML in React programs, so everything is fine ...

In the following example, the selected element with the default attribute in the <Select> component is indicated. The value of the attribute must correspond to the value attribute of an element inserted in the list (if it is not the case, the first element of the list is selected by default, as if nothing was indicated).

Use the default attribute to preselect an item from the list

```
class Select extends React.Component {
 constructor(props) {
  super(props);
 }
 render() {
  return (
   <select defaultValue={this.props.default}>
   {
    this.props.options.map(function(option, index) {
     return <option key={index+1} value={index+1}>{option}</option>
    })
   }
   </select>
  )
 }
}
ReactDOM.render(
  <Select options={["Element1", "Element2", "Element3", "Element4", "Element5"]}
    default="5" />,
  document.getElementById("root")
);
```

The default attribute (or other name as needed) is used in the <Select> component, but the defaultValue attribute must be used in the React <select> element.

Let's check that the element whose value is 5 is selected by default:

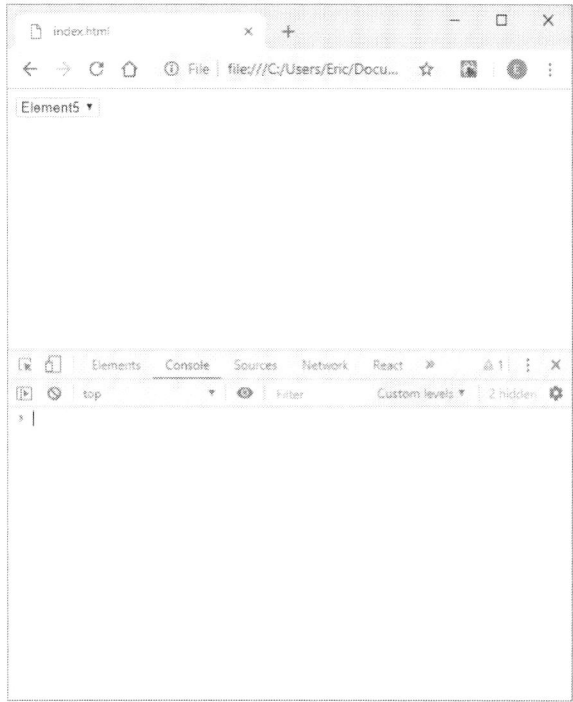

Element5 is the one selected by default when displaying the list.

Manage radio buttons

Let's use the radio buttons to perform the most usual operations on these elements:
- Display a group of radio buttons (with a single component or with two React components).
- Preselect a radio button in the group.
- Trigger an action when selecting a radio button or using an external button.

View a group of radio buttons using a single React component

We use here a single React component named <RadioGroup> which is responsible for managing the radio buttons that are transmitted to it. The component is used as follows:

Using the RadioGroup component (grouping radio buttons)
```
var radios = [
 { value : 1, text : "radio1" },
```

```
  { value : 2, text : "radio2" },
  { value : 3, text : "radio3" },
  { value : 4, text : "radio4" }
];
ReactDOM.render(
  <RadioGroup radios={radios} name="group1" />,
  document.getElementById("root")
);
```

The radio buttons are put here in an array of {value, text} objects in which the value property matches the value of the button when selected, while the text property represents the text that will be displayed for that button.

The name property specifies a name for the group of these buttons, which allows the mutual exclusion of these buttons from each other (a button selected in a group deselects other buttons in the same group). If the name property is not specified in a radio button, this radio button will not participate in excluding other radio buttons even if they are visually in the same group.

Let's write the <RadioGroup> component to display these radio buttons. Each radio button will consist of a <label> element containing the button text (<span> element) and the radio button (<input type="radio"> element).

RadioGroup component to display the radio buttons of the same group

```
class RadioGroup extends React.Component {
 constructor(props) {
  super(props);
 }
 render() {
  return (
   <div>
   {
    this.props.radios.map((radio, index) => {
     return (
      <label key={index}>
       <span>{radio.text}</span>
       <input type="radio" value={radio.value} name={this.props.name} />
       <br/>
      </label>
     )
    })
   }
   </div>
```

```
    )
  }
}
var radios = [
  { value : 1, text : "radio1" },
  { value : 2, text : "radio2" },
  { value : 3, text : "radio3" },
  { value : 4, text : "radio4" }
];
ReactDOM.render(
  <RadioGroup radios={radios} name="group1" />,
  document.getElementById("root")
);
```

Notice the use of the ES6 notation for writing the callback function in the `map()` method. Indeed, this callback function uses the `this.props.name` statement containing the name of the radio button group. Thanks to the ES6 notation with `=>` to indicate the function of treatment, the value of `this` is not lost in the callback function (it is then the same as that of the higher level). Without the ES6 notation, the value of `this` would be lost in the callback function and a JavaScript error would occur.

In addition, React specifies to use the `key` property when writing an iteration function so that each element is differentiated from other elements, hence the use of this property.

Let's check that the radio button group is displayed and that the radio buttons are mutually exclusive:

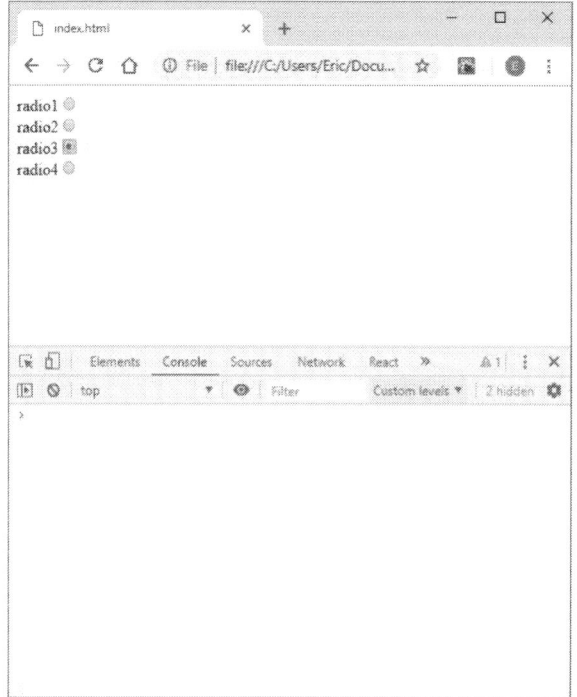

Each selected button deselects the previously selected button.

View a group of radio buttons using two React components

The `<RadioGroup>` component can be broken down into two React components:
- A `<Radio>` component to display a single radio button,
- A `<RadioGroup>` component to display multiple `<Radio>` components.

Let's write these two components. The final result will be similar to the previous program, but corresponds more to the architecture of React which advises decomposing as much as possible into components to assemble them later.

Radio buttons using two React components

```
class Radio extends React.Component {
 constructor(props) {
  super(props);
 }
 render() {
  return (
   <label>
    <span>{this.props.text}</span>
```

```
    <input type="radio" value={this.props.value} name={this.props.name} />
    <br/>
   </label>
  )
 }
}
class RadioGroup extends React.Component {
 constructor(props) {
  super(props);
 }
 render() {
  return (
   <div>
   {
    this.props.radios.map((radio, index) => {
     return (
      <Radio key={index} text={radio.text} value={radio.value}
         name={this.props.name} />
     )
    })
   }
   </div>
  )
 }
}
var radios = [
 { value : 1, text : "radio1" },
 { value : 2, text : "radio2" },
 { value : 3, text : "radio3" },
 { value : 4, text : "radio4" }
];
ReactDOM.render(
 <RadioGroup radios={radios} name="group1" />,
 document.getElementById("root")
);
```

The `<Radio>` component describes a radio button, while the `<RadioGroup>` component assembles several `<Radio>` components.

The mandatory `key` attribute for React is now set when building each `<Radio>` element.

Preselect a radio button

By default, no radio button is preselected when buttons are displayed in the group. To preselect a radio button in the group, it is necessary, as in HTML, to indicate the checked attribute set to true. Setting this attribute to false deselects the radio button.

Preset radio button "radio3" in JSX
```
<input type="radio" value={this.props.value} name={this.props.name}
    checked={true} />
```

The checked attribute set to true pre-selects the specified radio button.

In the description of the list of radio buttons, insert a new field, here named checked, describing the radio buttons selected (checked set to true) or not (checked set to false or unspecified).

For example to indicate that the radio button "radio3" is preselected, we write:

Preselect the radio button "radio3"
```
var radios = [
  { value : 1, text : "radio1" },
  { value : 2, text : "radio2" },
  { value : 3, text : "radio3", checked : true },  // preselected by default
  { value : 4, text : "radio4" }
];
```

> Only one radio button in the same group must have the checked attribute set to true. Other radio buttons in the group may have the checked property set to false, or not specified as here.

Take into account the checked attribute for radio buttons
```
class Radio extends React.Component {
 constructor(props) {
  super(props);
 }
 render() {
  return (
   <label>
    <span>{this.props.text}</span>
       <input type="radio" value={this.props.value}
              name={this.props.name}
       checked={this.props.checked}
    />
    <br/>
   </label>
  )
```

```
    }
}
class RadioGroup extends React.Component {
 constructor(props) {
  super(props);
 }
 render() {
  return (
    <div>
    {
     this.props.radios.map((radio, index) => {
      return (
           <Radio key={index} text={radio.text} value={radio.value}
          name={this.props.name} checked={radio.checked}
       />
      )
     })
    }
    </div>
  )
 }
}
var radios = [
 { value : 1, text : "radio1" },
 { value : 2, text : "radio2" },
 { value : 3, text : "radio3", checked : true },
 { value : 4, text : "radio4" }
];
ReactDOM.render(
 <RadioGroup radios={radios} name="group1" />,
 document.getElementById("root")
);
```

The `checked` attribute is passed in the `props` of each component.

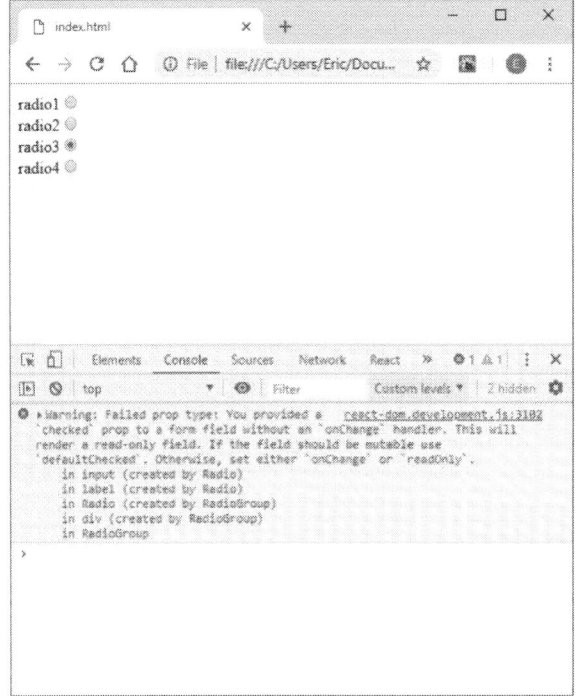

The "radio3" radio button is actually selected, but an error message is displayed by React in the console, indicating that the onChange event must be implemented on the radio button.

Moreover the clicks on the radio buttons do not work ... Only the preselected button "radio3" can be selected, the other buttons are inactive.

Let's implement the onChange event in the Radio class. For now, just display the value of the selected item.

Implement the onChange event on radio buttons

```
class Radio extends React.Component {
 constructor(props) {
  super(props);
 }
 handlerChange(event) {
  console.log(event.target.value);
 }
 render() {
  return (
   <label>
    <span>{this.props.text}</span>
```

```
            <input type="radio" value={this.props.value}
                name={this.props.name}
            checked={this.props.checked}
            onChange={this.handlerChange.bind(this)}
        />
        <br/>
      </label>
    )
  }
}
class RadioGroup extends React.Component {
  constructor(props) {
    super(props);
  }
  render() {
    return (
      <div>
      {
        this.props.radios.map((radio, index) => {
          return (
              <Radio key={index} text={radio.text} value={radio.value}
                  name={this.props.name} checked={radio.checked}
            />
          )
        })
      }
      </div>
    )
  }
}
var radios = [
  { value : 1, text : "radio1" },
  { value : 2, text : "radio2" },
  { value : 3, text : "radio3", checked : true },
  { value : 4, text : "radio4" }
];
ReactDOM.render(
  <RadioGroup radios={radios} name="group1" />,
  document.getElementById("root")
);
```

The `onChange` event has been implemented on the `<input>` element defining the radio button (in the `Radio` class). The value of the clicked button is displayed in the console.

Let's check if it works better now:

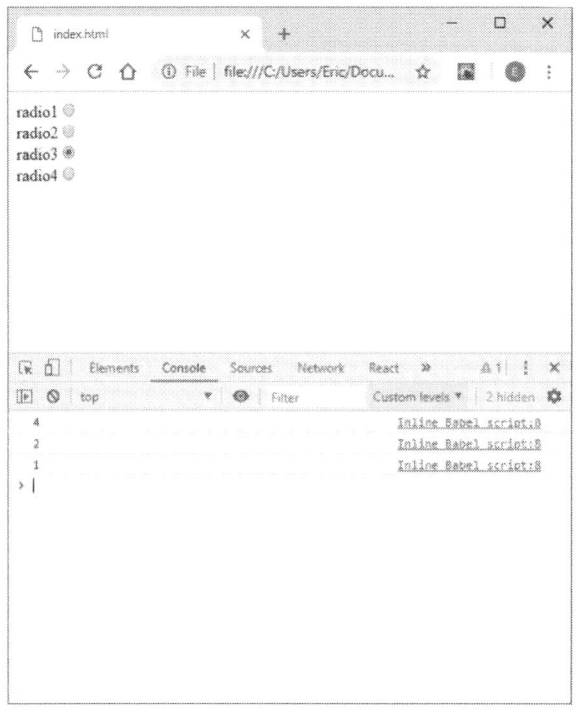

The error message displayed by React disappeared (since we implemented the onChange event as it required). However, clicks on the other radio buttons display the value associated with the button in the console, but the radio button is not selected on the screen... Why ???...

Why are radio buttons not selected on the screen when selected with the mouse? Let's not forget that what is displayed on the screen is the result of the automatic call of render() by React when creating components. So that what is displayed on the screen is modified (for example following a click on another radio button), the render() method should be called again, which can only be done if one modify the state. Now, we have not mentioned the state in any of the two classes Radio and RadioGroup.

We will indicate in the state of the Radio class, the checked state (true or false) of the radio button associated with this component (this.state.checked). Clicking a radio button will have to set the checked state of this radio button to true, but will have to set the checked states of the other radio buttons to false (only one radio button can be selected in the group). To do this, we introduce in the state associated with the <RadioGroup> component the radios property (this.state.radios) which contains the values of the radios variable indicating the initial state of the radio buttons.

When clicking on a radio button, this.state.radios state of the <RadioGroup> component will need to be updated, which will cause a refresh of all <RadioGroup> radio buttons.

In order for the click on a radio button (<Radio> component) to update the state in the <RadioGroup> parent component, the parent component must pass its instance to the child component. This instance transfer takes place in the props object (as we did previously), and we name app the transmitted property for example.

The program taking these developments into account is as follows:

Taking into account states in <Radio> and <RadioGroup> components

```
class Radio extends React.Component {
 constructor(props) {
  super(props);
  this.state = { checked : props.checked || false };
 }
 handlerChange(event) {
  console.log(event.target.value);
  var radios = this.props.app.state.radios;
  radios = radios.map((radio, index) => {
   if (radio.value == event.target.value) radio.checked = true;
   else radio.checked = false;
   return radio;
  });
  this.props.app.setState({radios : radios}); // refresh of the group
 }
 render() {
  return (
   <label>
    <span>{this.props.text}</span>
     <input type="radio" value={this.props.value}
         name={this.props.name}
      checked={this.state.checked}
      onChange={this.handlerChange.bind(this)}
    />
    <br/>
   </label>
  )
 }
```

```
}
class RadioGroup extends React.Component {
 constructor(props) {
  super(props);
  this.state = { radios : props.radios };
 }
 render() {
  return (
   <div>
   {
     this.state.radios.map((radio, index) => {
      return (
         <Radio key={index} text={radio.text} value={radio.value}
         name={this.props.name} checked={radio.checked} app={this}
       />
      )
     })
   }
   </div>
  )
 }
}
var radios = [
 { value : 1, text : "radio1" },
 { value : 2, text : "radio2" },
 { value : 3, text : "radio3", checked : true },
 { value : 4, text : "radio4" }
];
ReactDOM.render(
 <RadioGroup radios={radios} name="group1" />,
 document.getElementById("root")
);
```

Updating the state associated with this.state.radios (when clicking a radio button) causes a new render() of the radio buttons (render() method of the <RadioGroup> component), which causes the render() of each radio button (render() method of the <Radio> component).

Note that this.state.checked must be initialized in all cases (hence false if props.checked does not exist), otherwise React produces an error (when selecting another radio button) indicating that the component goes from an "uncontrolled" state to a "controlled" state: in fact this means that sometimes the component is managed with the state, sometimes no. To remedy this, we initialize the state in all cases.

However, the click on the radio buttons is still not taken into account on the screen, even if the processing function is activated as can be seen in the console:

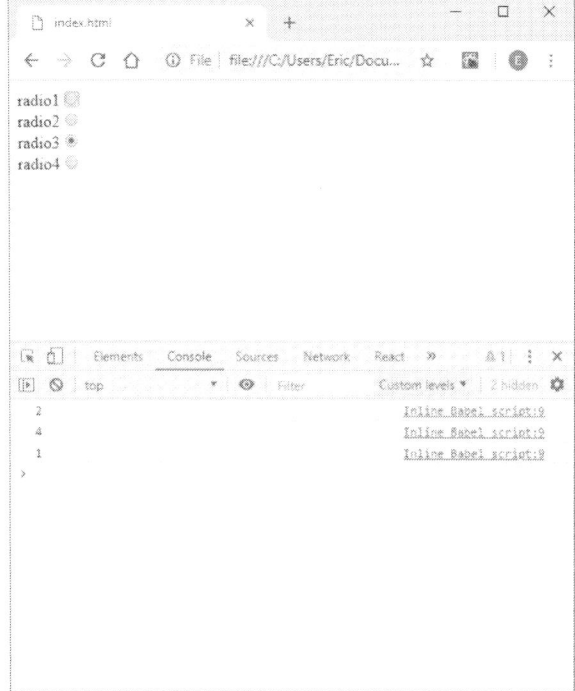

The clicks on the buttons are well taken into account, but the display does not change ...

The non-update on the screen of the selected radio buttons is easily explained. Just display the React tab and display the last `<Radio>` component that was clicked in the list (here "radio1").

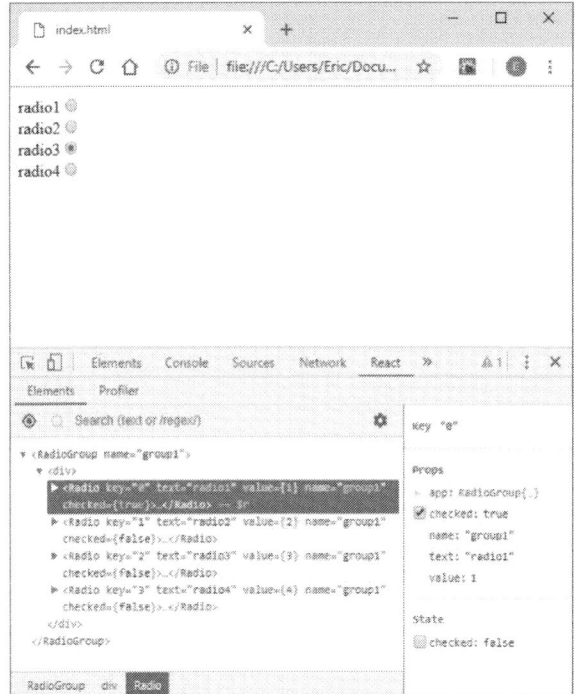

We see that the props object has the checked property of this element at true (the others are at false), but the problem is that the this.state.checked property of this element remains at false, in contradiction with its this.props.checked property. The checked property is updated for this element, but not its state …

In fact, this behavior is normal. We have already seen that the update of new properties for an already displayed element does not cause the refreshing of this element (no new call to the render() method), because only the updating of the state allows it. Therefore, you must use the componentDidUpdate(prevProps, prevState) method to be notified that new properties have been passed to a component, and update the component's state to refresh it on the screen.

So we add the componentDidUpdate(prevProps, prevState) method in the <Radio> component.

Adding the componentDidUpdate(prevProps, prevState) method to the Radio class

```
class Radio extends React.Component {
 constructor(props) {
  super(props);
  this.state = { checked : props.checked || false };
 }
```

```
handlerChange(event) {
 console.log(event.target.value);
 var radios = this.props.app.state.radios;
 radios = radios.map((radio, index) => {
  if (radio.value == event.target.value) radio.checked = true;
  else radio.checked = false;
  return radio;
 });
 this.props.app.setState({radios : radios});
}
componentDidUpdate(prevProps, prevState) {
   if (prevProps.checked != this.props.checked)
   this.setState({ checked : this.props.checked });
}
render() {
 return (
  <label>
   <span>{this.props.text}</span>
      <input type="radio" value={this.props.value}
            name={this.props.name}
        checked={this.state.checked}
        onChange={this.handlerChange.bind(this)}
   />
   <br/>
  </label>
 )
}
}
class RadioGroup extends React.Component {
 constructor(props) {
  super(props);
  this.state = { radios : props.radios };
 }
 render() {
  return (
   <div>
    {
     this.state.radios.map((radio, index) => {
      return (
          <Radio key={index} text={radio.text} value={radio.value}
              name={this.props.name} checked={radio.checked} app={this}
       />
      )
```

```
      })
    }
   </div>
  )
 }
}
var radios = [
 { value : 1, text : "radio1" },
 { value : 2, text : "radio2" },
 { value : 3, text : "radio3", checked : true },
 { value : 4, text : "radio4" }
];
ReactDOM.render(
 <RadioGroup radios={radios} name="group1" />,
 document.getElementById("root")
);
```

The componentDidUpdate() method will be called by React for each <Radio> component to refresh. Updating the state performed in the method causes the component to refresh on the screen.

Let's display the window and click on the first radio button (which deselects the third one that was selected by default):

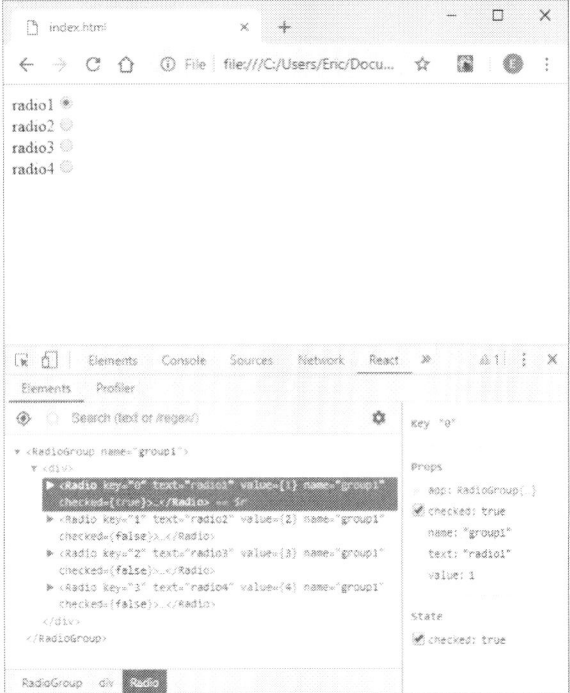

The update of the checked property is now passed to the state, which allows the update on the screen.

Validate the selection of a radio button

You want to perform a treatment when a radio button is selected. The treatment can be performed:
- As soon as the radio button is selected,
- As soon as an external validation button is clicked.

Let's look at these two cases below.

Validate as soon as a radio button is selected

A new onSelect attribute is specified in the <RadioGroup> component. It allows to define a processing function that will be activated when selecting a radio button in the group.

For example, we define the selectRadio(value) processing function that will be specified in the onSelect attribute of the <RadioGroup> component.

<u>Use the onSelect attribute to enable the selectRadio() function when selecting a radio button</u>

```
function selectRadio(value) {
```

```
  console.log(value);  // value of the selected radio button
}
ReactDOM.render(
 <RadioGroup radios={radios} name="group1" onSelect={selectRadio} />,
 document.getElementById("root")
);
```

The selectRadio() function is specified in the onSelect attribute of the <RadioGroup> component.

Taking this new attribute into account causes changes in the <Radio> and <RadioGroup> components.

Taking into account the onSelect attribute in the radio buttons

```
class Radio extends React.Component {
 constructor(props) {
  super(props);
  this.state = { checked : props.checked || false };
 }
 handlerChange(event) {
  var radios = this.props.app.state.radios;
  radios = radios.map((radio, index) => {
   if (radio.value == event.target.value) radio.checked = true;
   else radio.checked = false;
   return radio;
  });
  this.props.app.setState({radios : radios});
  this.props.onSelect(event.target.value);  // selectRadio() call
 }
 componentDidUpdate(prevProps, prevState) {
   if (prevProps.checked != this.props.checked)
   this.setState({ checked : this.props.checked });
 }
 render() {
  return (
   <label>
    <span>{this.props.text}</span>
      <input type="radio" value={this.props.value}
          name={this.props.name}
      checked={this.state.checked}
      onChange={this.handlerChange.bind(this)}
   />
   <br/>
   </label>
```

```
    )
  }
}
class RadioGroup extends React.Component {
  constructor(props) {
    super(props);
    this.state = { radios : props.radios };
  }
  render() {
    return (
      <div>
      {
        this.state.radios.map((radio, index) => {
          return (
            <Radio key={index} text={radio.text} value={radio.value}
                name={this.props.name} checked={radio.checked} app={this}
              onSelect={this.props.onSelect}
            />
          )
        })
      }
      </div>
    )
  }
}
var radios = [
  { value : 1, text : "radio1" },
  { value : 2, text : "radio2" },
  { value : 3, text : "radio3", checked : true },
  { value : 4, text : "radio4" }
];
function selectRadio(value) {
  console.log(value);  // value of the selected radio button
}
ReactDOM.render(
  <RadioGroup radios={radios} name="group1" onSelect={selectRadio} />,
  document.getElementById("root")
);
```

The call to the function transmitted in the `onSelect` attribute is performed each time a radio button is clicked, so in the `handlerChange()` method.

Let's click on different radio buttons in the window:

ERIC SARRION

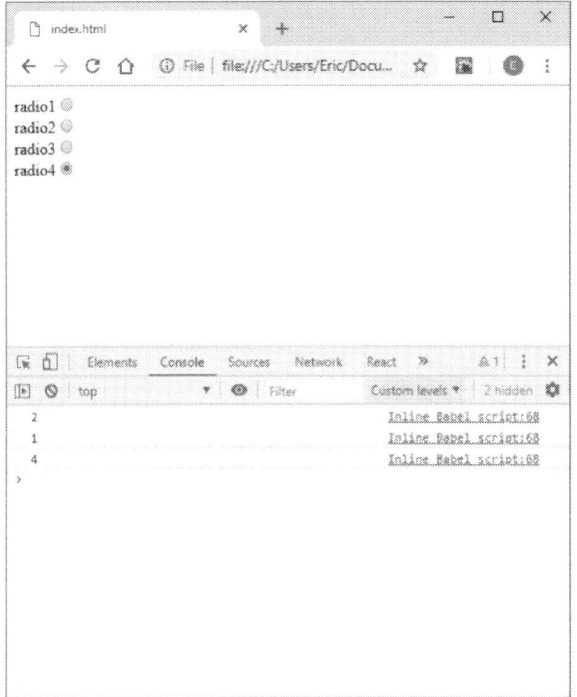

Clicking on each radio button causes the processing function to be called, which displays the value of the radio button in the console.

Validate using an external validation button

Rather than validate as soon as the radio button is selected, you can choose to validate by pressing an external Validate button. To achieve this, we create a new React component that integrates the validation button with the previous radio buttons. Let's call this new component <RadioGroupWithButton>. It is used as follows:

<u>Using the <RadioGroupWithButton> Component</u>

```
function validRadio(value) {
  console.log(value);
}
ReactDOM.render(
  <RadioGroupWithButton radios={radios} name="group1" onValid={validRadio} />,
  document.getElementById("root")
);
```

The onValid attribute specifies a processing function that has the value of the selected radio button as a parameter. This processing function is activated when

212

clicking on the Validate validation button displayed by the <RadioGroupWithButton> component.

The onSelect attribute used previously is here deleted, but could have been retained in the case where it is also desired to perform a processing during the immediate selection of a radio button.

Let's implement this new RadioGroupWithButton class, in addition to the Radio and RadioGroup classes already written.

RadioGroupWithButton component

```
class Radio extends React.Component {
 constructor(props) {
  super(props);
  this.state = { checked : props.checked || false };
 }
 handlerChange(event) {
  var radios = this.props.app.state.radios;
  radios = radios.map((radio, index) => {
   if (radio.value == event.target.value) radio.checked = true;
   else radio.checked = false;
   return radio;
  });
  this.props.app.setState({radios : radios});
 }
 componentDidUpdate(prevProps, prevState) {
    if (prevProps.checked != this.props.checked)
    this.setState({ checked : this.props.checked });
 }
 render() {
  return (
   <label>
    <span>{this.props.text}</span>
       <input type="radio" value={this.props.value}
            name={this.props.name}
       checked={this.state.checked}
       onChange={this.handlerChange.bind(this)}
    />
    <br/>
   </label>
  )
 }
}
class RadioGroup extends React.Component {
```

```
  constructor(props) {
   super(props);
   this.state = { radios : props.radios };
  }
  render() {
   return (
    <div>
    {
     this.state.radios.map((radio, index) => {
      return (
          <Radio key={index} text={radio.text} value={radio.value}
              name={this.props.name} checked={radio.checked} app={this}
       />
      )
     })
    }
    </div>
   )
  }
 }
 class RadioGroupWithButton extends React.Component {
  constructor(props) {
   super(props);
  }
  handlerValid(event) {
   var value; // value of the selected radio button
   this.props.radios.forEach(function(radio, index) {
    if (radio.checked) value = radio.value; // selected radio button
   });
   this.props.onValid(value); // validRadio(value) call
  }
  render() {
   return (
    <div>
     <RadioGroup radios={this.props.radios} name={this.props.name} />
     <br/>
     <button onClick={this.handlerValid.bind(this)}>Validate</button>
    </div>
   )
  }
 }
 var radios = [
```

```
  { value : 1, text : "radio1" },
  { value : 2, text : "radio2" },
  { value : 3, text : "radio3", checked : true },
  { value : 4, text : "radio4" }
];
function validRadio(value) {
  console.log(value);  // value of the selected radio button
}
ReactDOM.render(
  <RadioGroupWithButton radios={radios} name="group1" onValid={validRadio} />,
  document.getElementById("root")
);
```

The handlerValid() method is activated when the validation button is clicked. It detects the possibly selected radio button, and calls the method specified in the onValid property of the component.

The forEach() method used on the radios array associated with the radio buttons allows you to perform a treatment for each element of the radios array. It is used here to detect the radio button that may be selected and to retrieve the associated value (undefined if none).

After selecting different radio buttons and clicking the Validate button:

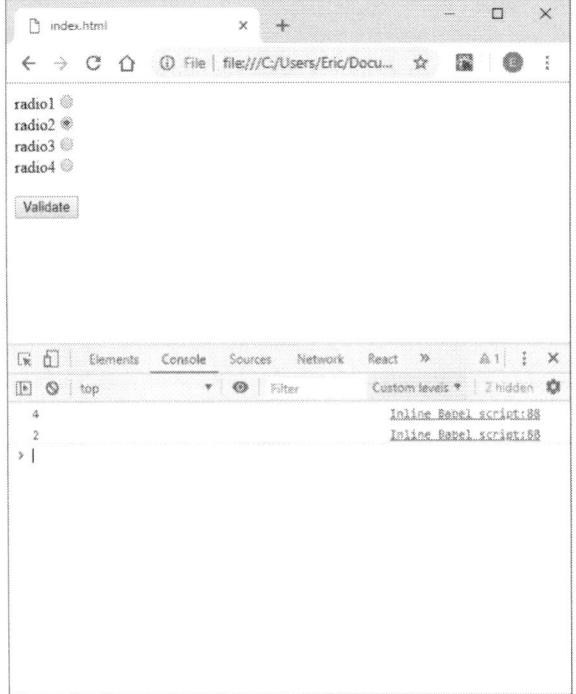

The values of the selected radio buttons are displayed in the console each time you click the Validate button.

Manage checkboxes

The management of the checkboxes is similar to that of the radio buttons. However, several checkboxes can be selected at the same time, unlike the radio buttons of the same group.

As we did for the radio buttons, let's look at the most common actions that can be done with the checkboxes:
- Display checkboxes and manage their preselection,
- Validate the selection or deselection of a checkbox.

Each of these actions is similar to those we had done during the study of radio buttons.

However, each check box being independent of the others (unlike the radio buttons), global state management is not necessary in this case (as when using this.state.radios). So we will use only one state for each checkbox, which will memorize the checked property of it (with this.state.checked).

REACT STEP BY STEP

We will use two React components:
- The `<CheckBox>` component will manage a check box (via this.state.checked),
- The `<CheckBoxGroup>` component will manage all the checkboxes to display.

Show checkboxes and manage their eventual preselection

We use the checkboxes array that contains the checkboxes to display, indicating in the checked property whether the checkbox is preselected (true) or not (false).

`<CheckBox>` and `<CheckBoxGroup>` Components

```
class CheckBox extends React.Component {
 constructor(props) {
  super(props);
  this.state = { checked : props.checked || false };
 }
 handlerChange(event) {
  this.setState({checked : event.target.checked});
 }
 render() {
  return (
   <label>
    <span>{this.props.text}</span>
       <input type="checkbox" value={this.props.value}
       checked={this.state.checked}
       onChange={this.handlerChange.bind(this)}
    />
    <br/>
   </label>
  )
 }
}
class CheckBoxGroup extends React.Component {
 constructor(props) {
  super(props);
 }
 render() {
  return (
   <div>
    {
     this.props.checkboxes.map((checkbox, index) => {
      return (
          <CheckBox key={index} text={checkbox.text} value={checkbox.value}
```

217

```
                    checked={checkbox.checked}
            />
        )
    })
    }
    </div>
  )
 }
}
var checkboxes = [
 { value : 1, text : "check1" },
 { value : 2, text : "check2", checked : true },
 { value : 3, text : "check3", checked : true },
 { value : 4, text : "check4" }
];
ReactDOM.render(
 <CheckBoxGroup checkboxes={checkboxes} />,
 document.getElementById("root")
);
```

The principle is similar to that of radio buttons, but simpler because you no longer need to manage the state in the `CheckBoxGroup` class.

For this, the state of each checkbox is managed directly when clicking on it (via `this.state.checked`).

After selecting and deselecting the checkboxes:

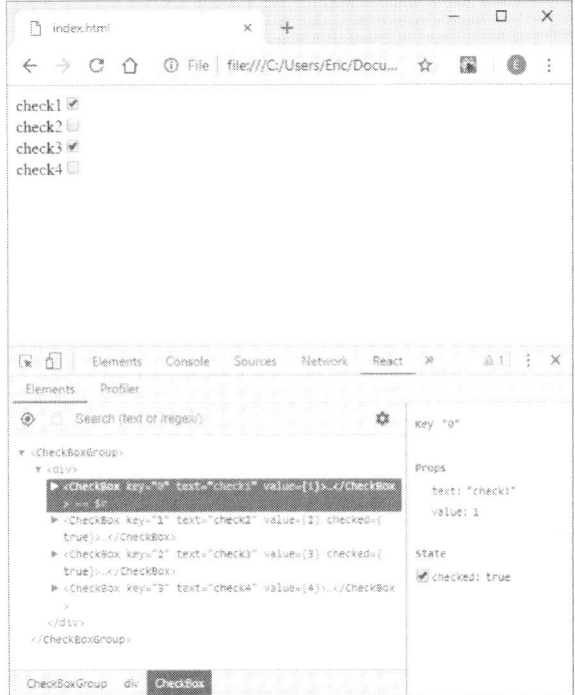

The state of each check box, visible in the React tab, corresponds to what is visible on the screen.

Perform a treatment when selecting or deselecting a check box

We want to call a processing function when selecting a checkbox, and call another when deselecting. Both the onSelect and onUnselect attributes are used to indicate which processing functions to call.

Here is an example of using these attributes used in the <CheckBoxGroup> component:

Using the onSelect and onUnselect attributes for the checkboxes

```
function selectCheckbox(checkbox) {
  console.log(checkbox + " selected");
}
function unselectCheckbox(checkbox) {
  console.log(checkbox + " unselected");
}
ReactDOM.render(
  <CheckBoxGroup checkboxes={checkboxes}
        onSelect={selectCheckbox} onUnselect={unselectCheckbox} />,
```

```
  document.getElementById("root")
);
```

- The onSelect attribute indicates to call the selectCheckbox(value) function,
- The onUnselect attribute indicates to call the function unselectCheckbox(value).

The value parameter in both cases corresponds to the value attribute specified in the checkboxes object.

The React program implementing these two new attributes is as follows:

Implement the onSelect and onUnselect attributes in the CheckBoxGroup component

```
class CheckBox extends React.Component {
 constructor(props) {
  super(props);
  this.state = { checked : props.checked || false };
 }
 handlerChange(event) {
  this.setState({checked : event.target.checked});
  if (event.target.checked) this.props.app.props.onSelect(event.target.value);
  else this.props.app.props.onUnselect(event.target.value);
 }
 render() {
  return (
   <label>
    <span>{this.props.text}</span>
       <input type="checkbox" value={this.props.value}
       checked={this.state.checked}
       onChange={this.handlerChange.bind(this)}
    />
    <br/>
   </label>
  )
 }
}
class CheckBoxGroup extends React.Component {
 constructor(props) {
  super(props);
 }
 render() {
  return (
   <div>
    {
```

```
      this.props.checkboxes.map((checkbox, index) => {
        return (
            <CheckBox key={index} text={checkbox.text} value={checkbox.value}
                checked={checkbox.checked} app={this}
        />
        )
      })
    }
    </div>
  )
 }
}
var checkboxes = [
 { value : 1, text : "check1" },
 { value : 2, text : "check2", checked : true },
 { value : 3, text : "check3", checked : true },
 { value : 4, text : "check4" }
];
function selectCheckbox(checkbox) {
 console.log(checkbox + " selected");
}
function unselectCheckbox(checkbox) {
 console.log(checkbox + " unselected");
}
ReactDOM.render(
  <CheckBoxGroup checkboxes={checkboxes}
         onSelect={selectCheckbox} onUnselect={unselectCheckbox} />,
 document.getElementById("root")
);
```

Because the onSelect and onUnselect properties are not passed into the props object when creating <CheckBox> components, the app property is used so that each <CheckBox> component can access these <CheckBoxGroup> component properties.

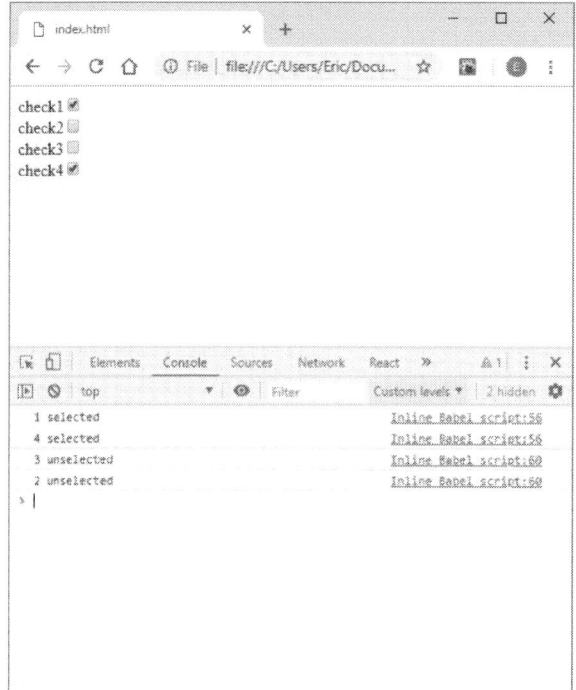

With each selection or deselection of check box, the corresponding processing function is called.

Perform a treatment by validating an external button

A variant of the previous program consists in calling the processing function by clicking on an external Validate button. Here we want the click on this button to display the value and status of all the checkboxes displayed.

To do this, we proceed as usual by creating a new `<CheckBoxGroupWithButton>` component that includes the checkboxes and the validation button.

Clicking on the Validate button to display the status of all the checkboxes, it will be necessary to store in the state object the different status in progress. We will use the checkboxes property that will be integrated into the state defined in the CheckBoxGroupWithButton class. The this.state.checkboxes value will be updated with each click on a checkbox (so from the handlerChange() method of the CheckBox class). For this we use the app property to access the state of a parent component.

Validate the checkboxes with an external Validate button

```
class CheckBox extends React.Component {
```

```
  constructor(props) {
   super(props);
   this.state = { checked : props.checked || false };
  }
  handlerChange(event) {
   this.setState({checked : event.target.checked});
   var checkboxes =
    this.props.app.state.checkboxes.map(function(checkbox, index) {
       if (checkbox.value == event.target.value)
      checkbox.checked = event.target.checked; // new value
     return checkbox;
    });
   this.props.app.setState({checkboxes : checkboxes});
  }
  render() {
   return (
    <label>
     <span>{this.props.text}</span>
       <input type="checkbox" value={this.props.value}
        checked={this.state.checked}
        onChange={this.handlerChange.bind(this)}
     />
     <br/>
    </label>
   )
  }
 }
 class CheckBoxGroup extends React.Component {
  constructor(props) {
   super(props);
  }
  render() {
   return (
    <div>
    {
     this.props.checkboxes.map((checkbox, index) => {
      return (
          <CheckBox key={index} text={checkbox.text} value={checkbox.value}
           checked={checkbox.checked} app={this.props.app}
       />
      )
     })
    }
```

```
      </div>
    )
  }
}
class CheckBoxGroupWithButton extends React.Component {
  constructor(props) {
    super(props);
    this.state = { checkboxes : props.checkboxes };
  }
  handlerValid(event) {
    this.props.onValid(this.state.checkboxes); // validCheckBox(checkboxes)
  }
  render() {
    return (
      <div>
        <CheckBoxGroup checkboxes={this.props.checkboxes} app={this} />
        <br/>
        <button onClick={this.handlerValid.bind(this)}>Validate</button>
      </div>
    )
  }
}
var checkboxes = [
  { value : 1, text : "check1" },
  { value : 2, text : "check2", checked : true },
  { value : 3, text : "check3", checked : true },
  { value : 4, text : "check4" }
];
function validCheckboxes(checkboxes) {
  console.log(checkboxes);
}
ReactDOM.render(
  <CheckBoxGroupWithButton checkboxes={checkboxes} onValid={validCheckboxes} />,
  document.getElementById("root")
);
```

The main part of the process is performed to update this.state.checkboxes in the handlerChange() method. The goal is to update the checked property (true or false) of the checkbox in the state (in this.state.checkboxes of the CheckBoxGroupWithButton class), so that this.state.checkboxes can be used during validation of the button.

Select and deselect checkboxes and validate:

The `this.state.checkboxes` value displayed in the console reflects the status of the checkboxes on the screen.

Use DOM features with React

If you have already used JavaScript or libraries such as jQuery to manipulate the DOM, you must notice that React's approach is completely different. Even though rendering the React code is HTML, we do not manipulate any DOM element, but rather React elements that can be considered as a virtual DOM. It is React that makes the correspondence between its virtual DOM and the real DOM, which is mandatory otherwise nothing could be displayed on the screen.

However, it may sometimes be useful to access the actual DOM, although this is not a preferred situation when developing with React. Indeed the direct manipulation of the real DOM makes that the virtual DOM is not any more in correspondence (since React does the correspondence itself, but in the opposite direction!). In particular, if we directly manipulate real DOM elements that are associated with the state, the state will be out of date, whereas it would be if it had been passed directly by React via the virtual DOM.

Access to DOM elements via the refs object

These precautions being taken, suppose that we still want to access the real DOM via a React program. Like the props object and the state object, React makes available the refs object, accessible in the class associated with the component by this.refs. This means that this this.refs object is only accessible in components created with a class, and is not available in components created with functions.

The this.refs object is an array that will contain all the ref attributes that are in the JSX code of our component. So just write a ref attribute (worth a string) into a JSX element, and the corresponding DOM element will be stored in this component's this.refs array.

The JSX element on which the ref attribute is set must correspond to a JSX element written in HTML, and not to a React component created via a class (otherwise no element of the actual DOM will correspond directly to it).

> The case where the ref attribute is positioned on a React component created by a class is discussed in the next section.

To illustrate this, let's write a React program that displays two lists of items in an <App> component. We have inserted ref attributes on some HTML elements of the lists. When the <App> component is ready (ie its componentDidMount() method is called), it means that the HTML code of the component has been displayed and the HTML elements are created. In the componentDidMount() method, the this.refs object contains references to the associated DOM elements.

Using ref attributes on HTML elements

```
class App extends React.Component {
 constructor(props) {
  super(props);
 }
 componentDidMount() {
  console.log(this.refs);
 }
 render() {
  return (
   <div>
    <ul ref="ref1">
     <li>Element1</li>
     <li>Element2</li>
     <li>Element3</li>
```

```
      <li>Element4</li>
      <li>Element5</li>
    </ul>
    <ul ref="ref2">
      <li ref="ref3">Element11</li>
      <li>Element12</li>
      <li>Element13</li>
      <li>Element14</li>
      <li>Element15</li>
    </ul>
  </div>
 )
 }
}
ReactDOM.render(
 <App />,
 document.getElementById("root")
);
```

The display of the `this.refs` object in the console is performed in the component's `componentDidMount()` method because the DOM elements of the component are ready.

We display the references associated with the three HTML elements on which the ref attributes are positioned.

Now that we have displayed the contents of this.refs object, what can we do with it? Each of the elements of this array is in fact a classic DOM element, on which all desired DOM manipulations can be performed. These DOM manipulations can be done directly in JavaScript, or with other libraries like jQuery for example.

Use jQuery to set the <li> element with the "ref3" reference in the JSX code to red color and font size of "20px". We must include the jQuery library in the HTML page.

Use jQuery to change the style of the element having ref="ref3"

```
<html>
<head>
<script crossorigin
  src="https://unpkg.com/react@16/umd/react.development.js"></script>
<script crossorigin
  src="https://unpkg.com/react-dom@16/umd/react-dom.development.js"></script>
<script src="https://unpkg.com/babel-standalone@6/babel.min.js"></script>
<script
 src="https://ajax.googleapis.com/ajax/libs/jquery/3.3.1/jquery.min.js"></script>
</head>
```

```
<body>
 <div id="root"></div>
</body>
<script type="text/babel">
class App extends React.Component {
 constructor(props) {
  super(props);
 }
 componentDidMount() {
  $(this.refs.ref3).css("font-size", "20px").css("color", "red");
 }
 render() {
  return (
    <div>
     <ul ref="ref1">
      <li>Element1</li>
      <li>Element2</li>
      <li>Element3</li>
      <li>Element4</li>
      <li>Element5</li>
     </ul>
     <ul ref="ref2">
      <li ref="ref3">Element11</li>
      <li>Element12</li>
      <li>Element13</li>
      <li>Element14</li>
      <li>Element15</li>
     </ul>
    </div>
  )
 }
}
ReactDOM.render(
 <App />,
 document.getElementById("root")
);
</script>
</html>
```

The jQuery library is included using the `<script>` tag, and jQuery statements are inserted into the `componentDidMount()` method so that DOM elements are accessible.

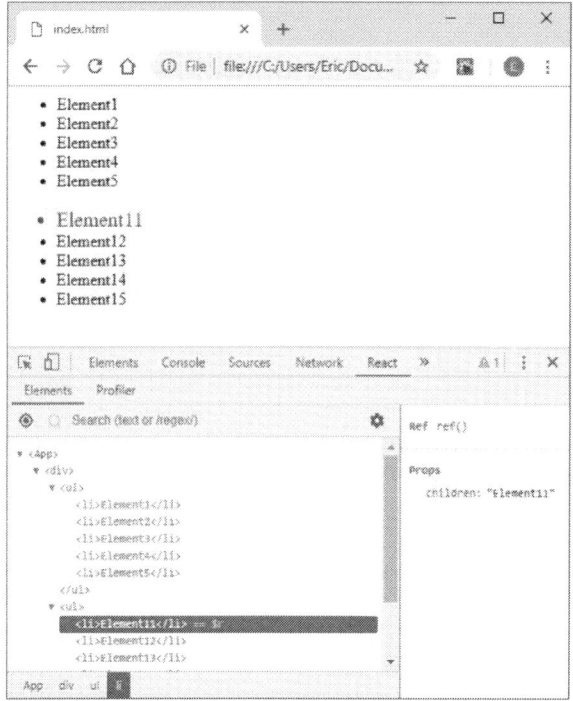

The element having ref="ref3" has its style modified, but one can see in the React tab that nothing indicates that this modification took place ... Hence the potential risks of errors between the virtual DOM managed by React and the real DOM modified via JavaScript.

For example, if you add the following jQuery statement in the componentDidMount() method:

Inserting a new item in the list
```
componentDidMount() {
  console.log(this.refs);
  $(this.refs.ref3).css("font-size", "20px").css("color", "red");
  $(this.refs.ref1).append("<li>Element6</li>");
}
```

Insert a <li> new list item into the first list displayed.

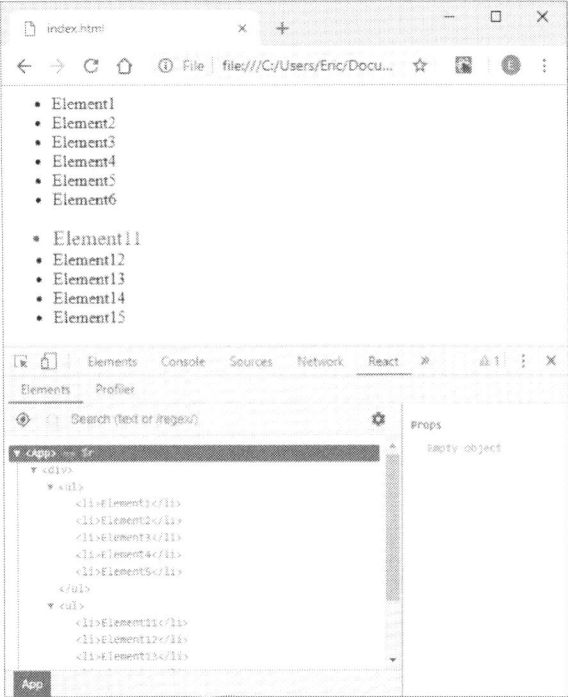

The "Element6" list item appears on the screen, but the React items displayed in the React tab do not reflect this new list at all!

Access to React components via the refs object

The this.refs object can also be used to access React components, children of this one. Just indicate a ref attribute (worth a string of characters) in the use of a component (which must be defined as a class, otherwise this.refs does not exist).

Let's write a list of elements using the <Element> component. We indicate the ref attribute on the first element of the list.

Using the ref attribute in a component

```
class Element extends React.Component {
 constructor(props) {
  super(props);
  this.state = { elem : props.elem };
 }
 render() {
  return <li>{this.state.elem}</li>
 }
```

```
}
class App extends React.Component {
 constructor(props) {
  super(props);
 }
 componentDidMount() {
  console.log(this.refs);
 }
 render() {
  return (
   <div>
    <ul ref="ref1">
     <Element elem="Element1" ref="ref2"></Element>
     <Element elem="Element2"></Element>
     <Element elem="Element3"></Element>
     <Element elem="Element4"></Element>
     <Element elem="Element5"></Element>
    </ul>
   </div>
  )
 }
}
ReactDOM.render(
 <App />,
 document.getElementById("root")
);
```

The `ref` attribute is used here in two places: on the `<ul>` element and on the first `<Element>` component. These two references are stored in `this.refs`, which is displayed in the console by the `componentDidMount()` method.

The "ref1" value is associated with the <ul> element, while the "ref2" value is associated with an object of class Element.

The interest here is to allow a parent component (here <App>) to access a child component (here <Element>), thanks to the reference indicated on the child component. Suppose we want to change the text of the element displayed in this component. Since the text of the <Element> component is in the state (in this.state.elem), we can use the setState() method on this <Element> component.

Use setState() on a child component

```
class Element extends React.Component {
 constructor(props) {
  super(props);
  this.state = { elem : props.elem };
 }
 render() {
  return <li>{this.state.elem}</li>
 }
}
class App extends React.Component {
 constructor(props) {
```

```
    super(props);
  }
  componentDidMount() {
    console.log(this.refs);
    this.refs.ref2.setState({elem : "New Element1"});
  }
  render() {
    return (
      <div>
        <ul ref="ref1">
          <Element elem="Element1" ref="ref2"></Element>
          <Element elem="Element2"></Element>
          <Element elem="Element3"></Element>
          <Element elem="Element4"></Element>
          <Element elem="Element5"></Element>
        </ul>
      </div>
    )
  }
}
ReactDOM.render(
  <App />,
  document.getElementById("root")
);
```

Thanks to the reference, we access the state of a child component.

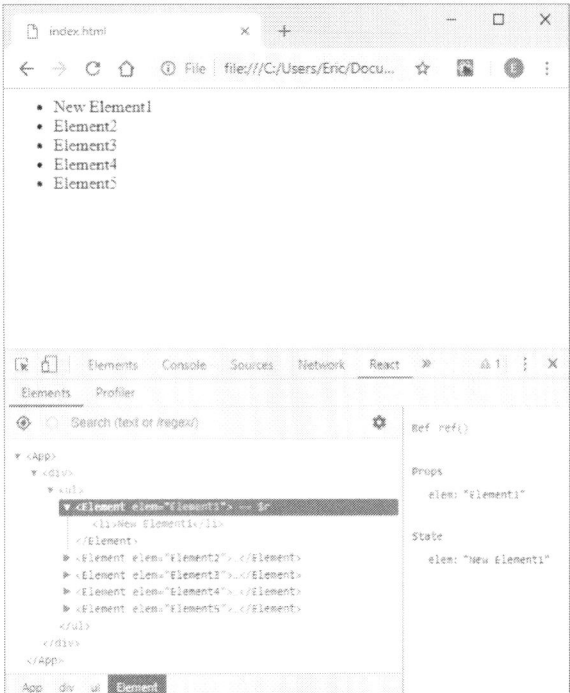

The text of the element has been modified ("Element1" becomes "New Element1"), as well as its state. The state and the display are therefore in agreement.

React and Ajax

Ajax is a concept to update a portion of the displayed HTML page by querying the server. This concept is widely used today in most websites, allowing a dynamic update of the page without having to reload it completely.

React does not integrate an API to perform Ajax queries, but allows without problems to use other APIs provided by other libraries, or even to use the internal API of the browser.

We study here these two possibilities:
- Using the Ajax API provided by jQuery (using the $.ajax() method),
- Using the browser's internal API (using the fetch() method).

In both cases, we use a PHP server that returns a list of elements in JSON format (any other server would work on the same principle).

The goal will be to retrieve this list of items on the server and then display it in the HTML page using React.

The PHP program that returns the list is the following (action.php file). It is deliberately very simple because the goal here is not to write complex server-side things, but rather to show how to retrieve them and then use them with React.

action.php file that returns data in JSON format

```
<?php
$result = array(
 array("text"=>"Element1"),
 array("text"=>"Element2"),
 array("text"=>"Element3"),
 array("text"=>"Element4"),
 array("text"=>"Element5")
);
echo json_encode($result);
?>
```

We return an array of objects in JSON format. The goal will be to display each element, in a list of the HTML page.

In the following two Ajax use cases, we use the `<Element>` component that is used to display a list item, and the `<App>` component that makes the Ajax call and displays the list retrieved from the server.

Use jQuery Ajax API

Let's use `$.ajax()` jQuery's method to make the Ajax call. The Ajax call is made in the `componentDidMount()` component's method as recommended in the React documentation (which makes sense because the DOM tree is then built and can be updated).

The jQuery library must of course be included to benefit from the `$.ajax()` method in our HTML page.

Inclusion of the jQuery library in the HTML page

```
<script
 src="https://ajax.googleapis.com/ajax/libs/jquery/3.3.1/jquery.min.js"></script>
```

Once the jQuery library is included, the component code including the Ajax call is as follows:

Ajax call with jQuery

```
class Element extends React.Component {
 constructor(props) {
  super(props);
  this.state = { elem : props.elem };
```

```
  }
  render() {
    return <li>{this.state.elem.text}</li>
  }
}
class App extends React.Component {
  constructor(props) {
    super(props);
    this.state = { elems : [] };
  }
  componentDidMount() {
    $.ajax({
      url : "action.php"    // server's URL
    })
    .done((response) => {    // server's response OK
      console.log(response);   // text response
      var elems = JSON.parse(response);  // conversion to JSON
      this.setState({elems : elems});    // update of the list
    })
    .fail((response) => {    // server's response Error
      console.log(response);
    })
  }
  render() {
    return (
      <ul>
        {
        this.state.elems.map(function(elem, index){
          return <Element key={index} elem={elem}></Element>
        })
        }
      </ul>
    )
  }
}
ReactDOM.render(
  <App />,
  document.getElementById("root")
);
```

The done() method chained with the Ajax call is executed if the Ajax call succeeds (a response from the server has been provided). The server returns a string that is transformed into a JSON object using JavaScript's JSON.parse() method. The array of retrieved objects is exactly in the {text: "value"} format used by the <Element> component (the <Element> component retrieves the text property and displays it in the render() method).

The fail() method is also chained with the Ajax call. It is used in case the Ajax call has failed. It displays the error message in the console.

The test of this program must be done using the http protocol, so you have to type the complete URL in the browser, here http://localhost/react, which displays the index.html file in the browser. The file protocol used so far to display our HTML page (drag & drop index.html file in the browser) does not work with Ajax.

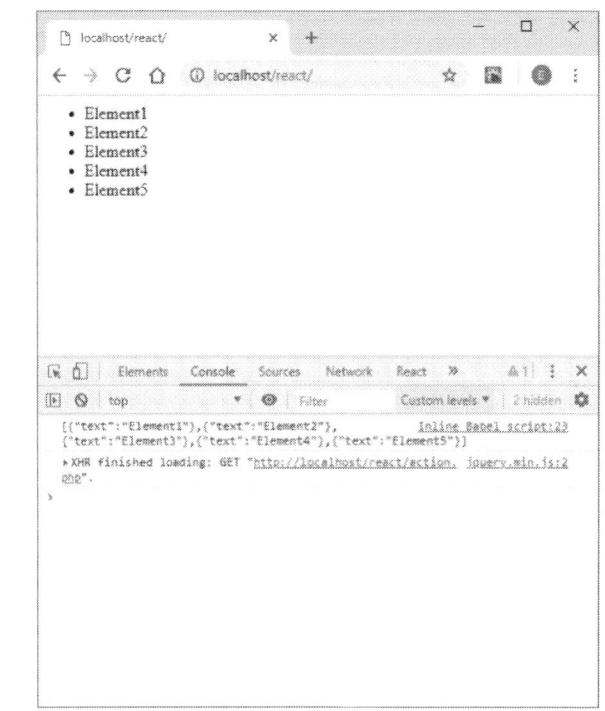

In the console the server response is displayed in text format.

| Notice the http://localhost/react URL used in the browser to display the page.

Use the browser's internal Ajax API

Let's use the fetch(url) method of the browser to make the Ajax call. The principle is almost the same as before, but the objects returned by the methods that follow the Ajax call are not the same in this case. And chaining methods to exploit the results have different names as well.

The principle of the Ajax call with fetch(url) is as follows: once the fetch() method is called, a response object is provided in a callback function chained by the then(callback) method of JavaScript. This response object is transformed into a JSON object using the response.json() method and is returned by the function to be exploited by another callback function that is also chained thanks to then(callback).

So we have the sequence of three JavaScript methods to use fetch(url):

Using fetch (url)

```
fetch(url).then(callback).then(callback)
```

The use in the React program is as follows: The used React components are the same as before (<Element> and <App>), and the Ajax call is made in the componentDidMount() method of the <App> component.

Of course, the inclusion of an external library such as jQuery is not necessary here.

Ajax call with fetch()

```
class Element extends React.Component {
 constructor(props) {
  super(props);
  this.state = { elem : props.elem };
 }
 render() {
  return <li>{this.state.elem.text}</li>
 }
}
class App extends React.Component {
 constructor(props) {
  super(props);
  this.state = { elems : [] };
 }
 componentDidMount() {
  fetch("action.php")      // server's URL
  .then(function(response) {
    console.log(response);   // Response class object
      return response.json();
  })
  .then(
    (result) => {        // JSON object
     console.log(result);
     this.setState({elems : result});
    },
    (error) => {         // error text
```

```
      console.log(error);
    }
  )
}
render() {
  return (
   <ul>
     {
      this.state.elems.map(function(elem, index){
        return <Element key={index} elem={elem}></Element>
      })
     }
   </ul>
  )
 }
}
ReactDOM.render(
 <App />,
 document.getElementById("root")
);
```

The second then() method uses two callback functions: the first is the one called when the Ajax call on the server is successful, the second is the one called in case of an error.

> Notice the use of the ES6 notation to indicate the processing functions: indeed, since we have to keep the value of this, we use the ES6 notation that allows it.

Let's display the HTML page using the http://localhost/react URL:

The result is the same as when using jQuery (or any other JavaScript library).

8 – USE CREATE-REACT-APP TO CREATE A REACT APPLICATION

For now, we have used a single HTML file (also containing JavaScript code) to write our React code. This approach is simple to explain React's operation through a few lines of programs concentrated in a single file, but is not a professional approach to write many components (let alone for a team of developers of several people).

The team that designed React has therefore developed a program to create a tree of files that will contain the code of our application. This program is a npm module and requires Node (which includes the npm command) installed on the machine that uses it.

Let's see how to install this application before using it.

Install the create-react-app app

The goal here is to install the create-react-app module to access the shell command of the same name.

First, make sure that you have Node installed on your machine by typing the following command:

Command to check the version of Node installed
```
node -v
```

We get for example (if Node is already installed, otherwise we get an error message):

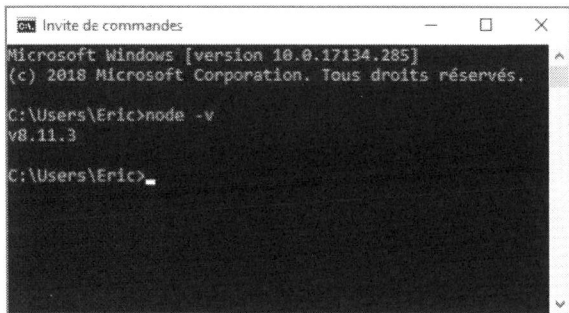

The version of Node is displayed, indicating that Node is installed.

Once Node is installed, you must install the create-react-app module to create applications for React. We type the following command:

Install the create-react-app module in global (-g option)

```
npm install -g create-react-app
```

The -g option used here allows to install this module globally on our machine, thus allowing access to the create-react-app command (provided by the installed module) from all the directories of our machine (and not just from the current directory from which this command is typed).

Once the command is typed, the modules (packages) composing the application are installed automatically:

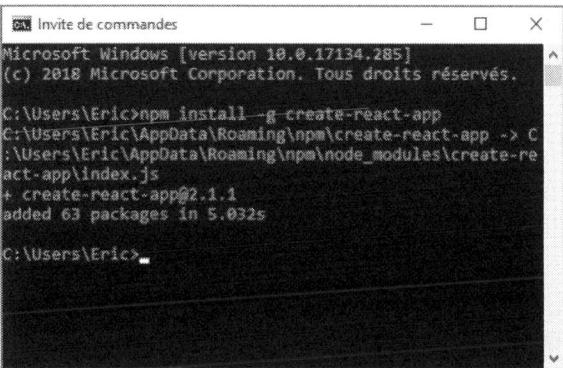

The modules that make up the create-react-app application are installed in the directories of our machine, making the create-react-app application accessible.

Type the following command to verify that the command is accessible:

Check that the create-react-app command is accessible

```
create-react-app -v
```

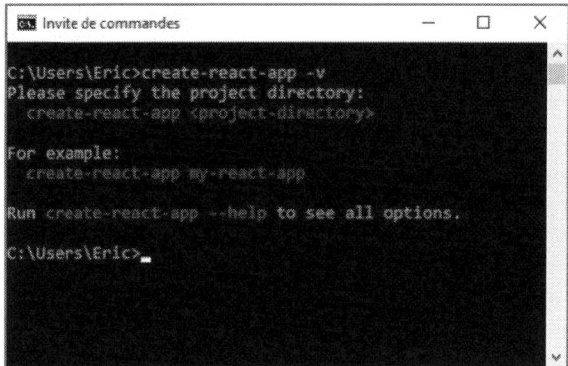

The instruction manual of the command is displayed.

The create-react-app command is ready to be used to create the tree of our React programs.

Create a React program with the create-react-app command

As indicated at the end of the download, just type the following command to create a new directory that will contain the React project tree.

Create the React project tree in a reactapp directory

create-react-app reactapp

This command creates the specified directory (here reactapp), in the current directory from which the command is typed.

Immediately after, the necessary modules are downloaded:

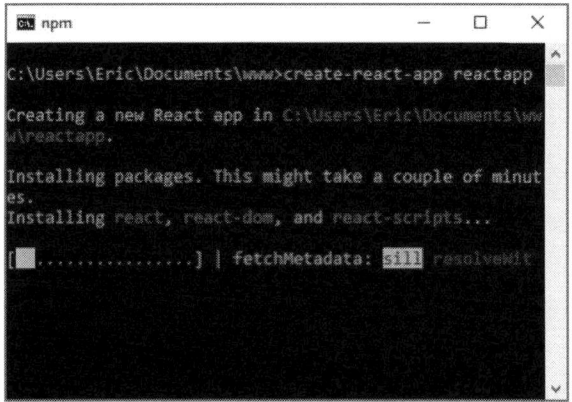

The React application is being created ...

After a few minutes, the following screen appears, showing how to use the created files.

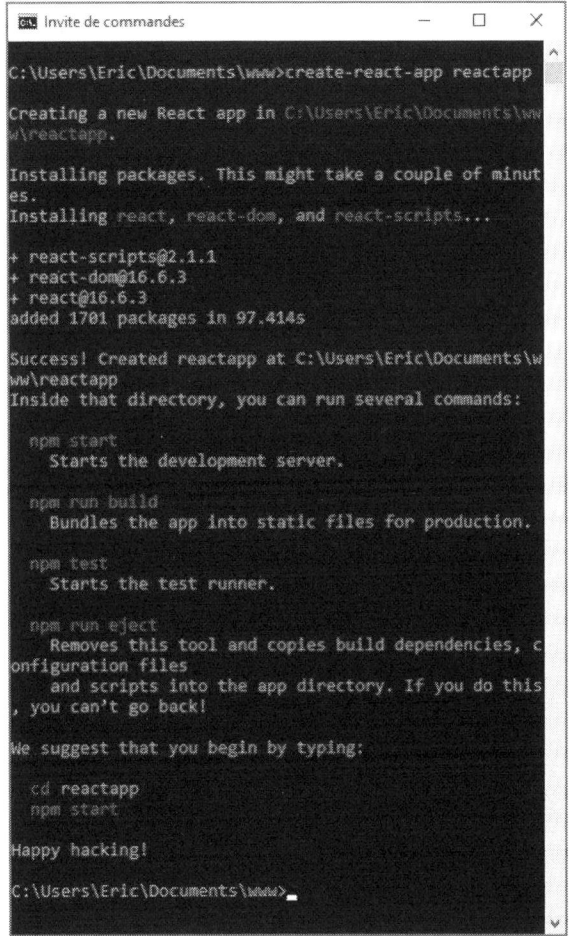

The screen displayed after the create-react-app command indicates the different npm commands possible.

Type the last two commands shown in the displayed suggestion:

Suggested Commands to Run the Basic React Program

| cd reactapp |
| npm start |

After a few moments, a browser opens, displaying the http:localhost:3000 URL.

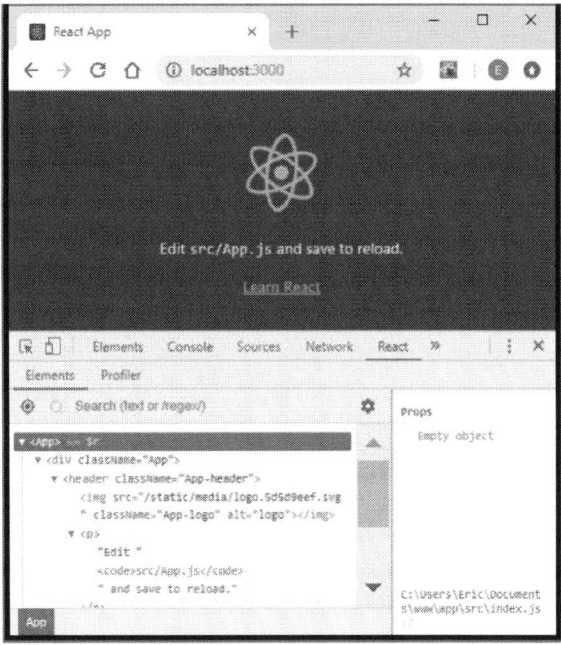

The displayed window is the default program created by the create-react-app command.

The module downloaded from npm, and associated with the create-react-app command, includes a web server that listens for port 3000, as shown in the URL of our page.

This server is started by the npm start command executed from a command window. If you close the command window, the server will no longer be active and the http://localhost:3000 URL will become inaccessible.

The reactapp folder contains all the programs needed to run the specified URL, which also includes the web server. This reactapp folder is organized as directories including:

• The node_modules folder (ie all the Node programs used to launch the server, but also the modules associated with React),

• The public folder including the main file of the default application displayed (index.html file),

• The src folder containing the .css (styles) and .js (React code) sources used for the application.

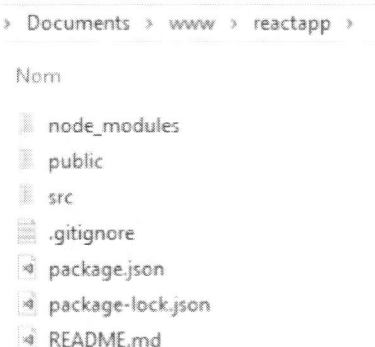

Previous figure displays the main directory of the application.

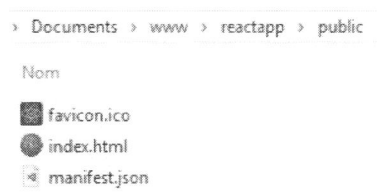

Previous figure displays the public directory of the application (index.html file).

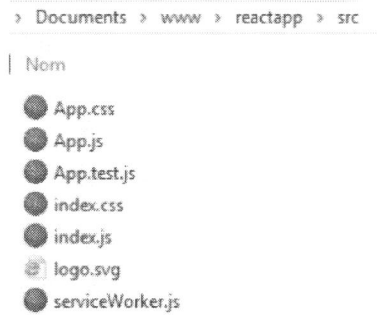

Previous figure displays the src directory of the application (.css and .js files)

Any application created from create-react-app must respect this tree:
- The public directory will contain the index.html file that is used when the application starts (usually never modified),
- The src directory (and any subdirectories) will contain the sources of the application (CSS code and JavaScript code).

Now let's take a look at the contents of the files created in each directory.

Analysis of the sources of the React application created by default

The main file of our application is index.html. This is the one that is responsible for running when starting the application (when accessing the http://localhost:3000 site URL).

public/index.html file

```html
<!DOCTYPE html>
<html lang="en">
 <head>
  <meta charset="utf-8">
  <link rel="shortcut icon" href="%PUBLIC_URL%/favicon.ico">
  <meta name="viewport" content="width=device-width, initial-scale=1,
     shrink-to-fit=no">
  <meta name="theme-color" content="#000000">
  <!--
    manifest.json provides metadata used when your web app is added to the
    homescreen on Android.
    See https://developers.google.com/web/fundamentals/web-app-manifest/
  -->
  <link rel="manifest" href="%PUBLIC_URL%/manifest.json">
  <!--
    Notice the use of %PUBLIC_URL% in the tags above.
    It will be replaced with the URL of the `public` folder during the build.
    Only files inside the `public` folder can be referenced from the HTML.

    Unlike "/favicon.ico" or "favicon.ico", "%PUBLIC_URL%/favicon.ico" will
    work correctly both with client-side routing and a non-root public URL.
    Learn how to configure a non-root public URL by running `npm run build`.
  -->
  <title>React App</title>
 </head>
 <body>
  <noscript>
    You need to enable JavaScript to run this app.
  </noscript>
  <div id="root"></div>
  <!--
    This HTML file is a template.
    If you open it directly in the browser, you will see an empty page.
```

```
       You can add webfonts, meta tags, or analytics to this file.
    The build step will place the bundled scripts into the <body> tag.

       To begin the development, run `npm start` or `yarn start`.
    To create a production bundle, use `npm run build` or `yarn build`.
  -->
 </body>
</html>
```

The most important line of the file is the one that defines <div id="root"></div> because React is known to use a <div> element of the HTML page where it renders the main React component . This React component is that of the application as a whole, which contains the other components. This component will be displayed in the <div> created here.

When loading the index.html file, the src/index.js file is also loaded (without having to indicate it in the HTML code), and finally contains the React code of our application. This tree (public and src directories), as well as the names of the used files (index.html and index.js) are to be kept if one modifies the source codes of the application by default, otherwise nothing will work.

src/index.js file

```
import React from 'react';
import ReactDOM from 'react-dom';
import './index.css';
import App from './App';
import * as serviceWorker from './serviceWorker';

ReactDOM.render(<App />, document.getElementById('root'));

// If you want your app to work offline and load faster, you can change
// unregister() to register() below. Note this comes with some pitfalls.
// Learn more about service workers: http://bit.ly/CRA-PWA
serviceWorker.unregister();
```

The main code for the React application is to execute the ReactDOM.render() statement, which renders the <App> component in the element whose id is "root" (defined in the index.html page previously). This is the same principle as what we did in previous chapters.

One difference from the code examples we previously wrote is that import statements are used here to import the corresponding modules (instead of the <script> tags used before).

- The first two import statements are linked to the code in the React library, which is now registered in the react and react-dom directories of the node_modules directory.

• The following two import statements (the third and fourth in the index.js file) allow you to include the corresponding css and js files. When the extension of the file is not indicated (here "./App"), it is by default .js (so "./App" means "./App.js").

• The last import statement is for the serviceWorker.js file, provided with the default application. There is no need here to run our React applications and we will not talk about it here.

The index.css file, as its name indicates, is used by the index.js file, and is used to define the global styles of the application. There is actually the definition of the style of the <body> tag and that of the <code> tag used in the <App> component.

src/index.css file

```
body {
  margin: 0;
  padding: 0;
  font-family: -apple-system, BlinkMacSystemFont, "Segoe UI", "Roboto", "Oxygen",
    "Ubuntu", "Cantarell", "Fira Sans", "Droid Sans", "Helvetica Neue",
    sans-serif;
  -webkit-font-smoothing: antialiased;
  -moz-osx-font-smoothing: grayscale;
}

code {
  font-family: source-code-pro, Menlo, Monaco, Consolas, "Courier New",
    monospace;
}
```

The interesting part of the application is in the <App> component definition, located in the src/App.js file. Note that the principle is to create a file (therefore a module) for each React component of our application. These components will all be located in the src directory (possibly in subdirectories of it), while the names of the files used are the names of the components. So the <App> component is described in the src/App.js file.

src/App.js file

```
import React, { Component } from 'react';
import logo from './logo.svg';
import './App.css';

class App extends Component {
```

```
  render() {
   return (
    <div className="App">
     <header className="App-header">
      <img src={logo} className="App-logo" alt="logo" />
      <p>
       Edit <code>src/App.js</code> and save to reload.
      </p>
      <a
       className="App-link"
       href="https://reactjs.org"
       target="_blank"
       rel="noopener noreferrer"
      >
       Learn React
      </a>
     </header>
    </div>
   );
  }
}
export default App;
```

Each component imports the files it needs, here the modules allowing to use the React and React.Component objects. Note the use of unstructured objects by writing {Component}, which means that you can use Component as the class name in the code instead of React.Component.

Rather than writing the lines:

By using the destructuring of objects

```
import React, { Component } from 'react';

class App extends Component {
 ...
}
```

With the destructuring of objects, we use the Component class instead of React.Component.

We can also write:

Without using the destructuring of objects

```
import React from 'react';
```

```
class App extends React.Component {
  ...
}
```

Without the destructuring of objects, we use the `React.Component` class.

The preceding code uses CSS classes (visible in the `className` attribute): App, App-header, App-logo and App-link. These classes are defined in the App.css file that is also imported into the App.js file. The rule is to use the same root filename for all the files of the same component, which will be distinguished by the extension used.

src/App.css file

```css
.App {
  text-align: center;
}

.App-logo {
  animation: App-logo-spin infinite 20s linear;
  height: 40vmin;
}

.App-header {
  background-color: #282c34;
  min-height: 100vh;
  display: flex;
  flex-direction: column;
  align-items: center;
  justify-content: center;
  font-size: calc(10px + 2vmin);
  color: white;
}

.App-link {
  color: #61dafb;
}

@keyframes App-logo-spin {
  from {
    transform: rotate(0deg);
  }
  to {
    transform: rotate(360deg);
  }
}
```

The last file analyzed here is the src/App.test.js file. It allows to test the <App> component. To run the test, you must enter the command npm test from the shell.

Command to test the React application

nmp test

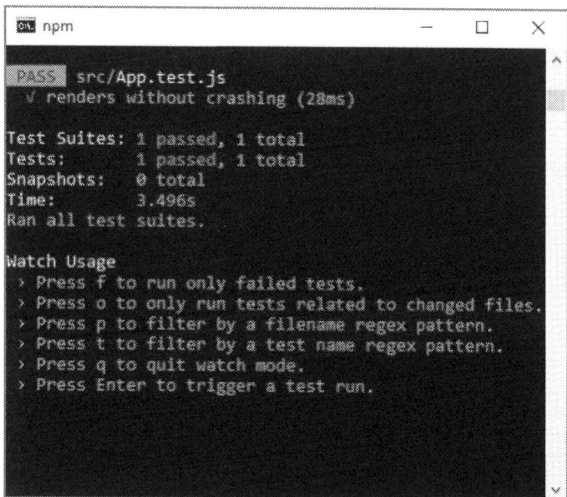

Create the sources of our React application

Once the application tree is created (by the create-react-app command), we must indicate the files of our real application (otherwise it is the default application that runs).

For example, consider the element list management application created in Chapter 6. Three components were used: <App>, <ElementsList>, and <Element>. The goal is to create a file for each component using the previous structure.

<App> component (src/App.js file)

```
import React from 'react';
import ElementsList from './ElementsList';

class App extends React.Component {
 constructor(props) {
  super(props);
  this.state = {
   elems : [],
   style : { fontSize : this.getFontSize() }
  };
 }
```

```
getUniqueKey() {
 var key = Math.random() + "";
 return key;
}
insertElem() {
 var elems = this.state.elems;
 var txt = "Element" + (elems.length + 1);
 var ukey = this.getUniqueKey();
 var elem = { txt : txt, ukey : ukey };
 elems.push(elem);
 this.setState({ elems : elems });
}
removeElem(objElem) {
 var elems = this.state.elems;
 elems = elems.filter(function(elem) {
  if (objElem.ukey != elem.ukey) return true;
 });
 this.setState({ elems : elems });
}
modifyElem(objElem, newValue) {
 var elems = this.state.elems;
 elems = elems.map(function(elem) {
  var { txt, ukey } = elem;
  if (objElem.ukey == ukey) elem.txt = newValue;
  return elem;
 });
 this.setState({ elems : elems });
}
getFontSize() {
 var fontSize;
 if (window.innerHeight < 150) fontSize = 12;
 else if (window.innerHeight < 200) fontSize = 13;
 else if (window.innerHeight < 250) fontSize = 15;
 else if (window.innerHeight < 300) fontSize = 16;
 else if (window.innerHeight < 350) fontSize = 18;
 else if (window.innerHeight < 400) fontSize = 20;
 else if (window.innerHeight < 450) fontSize = 22;
 else if (window.innerHeight < 500) fontSize = 24;
 else if (window.innerHeight < 550) fontSize = 30;
 else fontSize = 40;
 return fontSize + "px";
}
```

```
  handlerResize(event) {
   var fontSize = this.getFontSize();
   this.setState({ style : { fontSize : fontSize }});
  }
  componentDidMount() {
   window.addEventListener("resize", this.handlerResize.bind(this));
  }
  componentWillUnmount() {
   window.removeEventListener("resize", this.handlerResize);
  }
  render() {
   return (
    <div>
     <button onClick={this.insertElem.bind(this)}>Insert</button>
     <ElementsList elems={this.state.elems} app={this}
           style={this.state.style} />
    </div>
   )
  }
 }
 export default App;
```

Notice the import of the <ElementsList> component after importing React.

<ElementsList> component (src/ElementsList.js file)

```
import React from 'react';
import Element from './Element';

class ElementsList extends React.Component {
 constructor(props) {
  super(props);
 }
 render() {
  return (
   <ul>
   {
    this.props.elems.map((elem, index) => {
     var { ukey, txt } = elem;
     return <Element key={ukey} ukey={ukey} txt={txt}
           app={this.props.app} style={this.props.style} />
    })
   }
   </ul>
```

```
    )
  }
}
export default ElementsList;
```

Do not forget to export the component (defined here in a module).

<Element> component (src/Element.js file)

```
import React from 'react';
class Element extends React.Component {
  constructor(props) {
    super(props);
    this.ukey = props.ukey;
    this.state = {
       style : { ...this.props.style },
       removed : false,
      modifyOn : false,
      txt : props.txt
    };
  }
  mouseOver() {
    var style = { ...this.state.style, color : "red", fontStyle : "italic" };
    this.setState({style : style });
  }
  mouseOut() {
    var style = { ...this.state.style, color : "", fontStyle : "" };
    this.setState({style : style });
  }
  handlerRemoveElem() {
    this.props.app.removeElem(this);
  }
  modifyElem() {
    this.setState({ modifyOn : true });
  }
  handlerChange(event) {
    console.log(event.target.value);
    this.setState({ txt : event.target.value });
  }
  handlerKeyPress(event) {
    if (event.charCode == 13) {
      this.setState({ modifyOn : false });
      this.props.app.modifyElem(this, event.target.value);
    }
```

```
    }
    componentDidUpdate(prevProps, prevState) {
     if (prevProps.style != this.props.style) {
       this.setState({ style : this.props.style });
     }
    }
    render() {
     return (
      this.state.removed ? null :
        <li style={this.state.style}
            onMouseOver={this.mouseOver.bind(this)}
            onMouseOut={this.mouseOut.bind(this)}
         onDoubleClick={this.modifyElem.bind(this)} >
          { this.state.modifyOn ?
          <input type="text" value={this.state.txt}
             onChange={this.handlerChange.bind(this)}
             onKeyPress={this.handlerKeyPress.bind(this)}/> :
             <span>{this.state.txt}</span>
          }
          <button style={{margin:"10px", fontSize:"10px"}}
             onClick={this.handlerRemoveElem.bind(this)}
          >
            Remove
          </button>
        </li>
     )
    }
}
export default Element;
```

Do not forget to export the component (defined here in a module).

The src/index.js file still includes the `<App>` component.

src/index.js file

```
import React from 'react';
import ReactDOM from 'react-dom';
import App from './App';

ReactDOM.render(<App />, document.getElementById('root'));
```

We check that the operation of the application is identical.

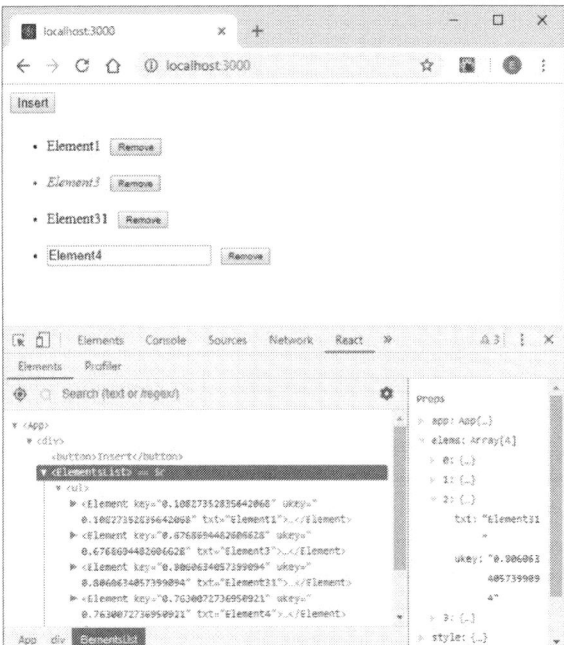

Note that the page is reloaded each time one of the server files is saved, which is handy for not manually reloading the page each time.

Create an application for a production server

The application tested on the server with the http://localhost:3000 URL is an application that uses development mode, and is not optimized for a production mode (hence the small loading time of the home page).

A real optimization would be to compact the files used, or to reduce the number by grouping them together. This optimization operation is available by typing the npm run build command, available through create-react-app.

Optimize the application for production mode
```
npm run build
```

Once the `npm run build` command is typed, the build directory is created containing the files that can be used in production mode.

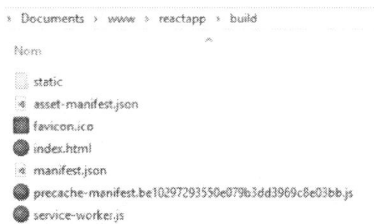

In addition, it is possible to immediately test these files by following the recommendations displayed on the screen of the command window:

Installing and commissioning a server in production mode

```
npm install -g serve
serve -s build
```

Once the `serve -s build` command is entered, it appears in the command window:

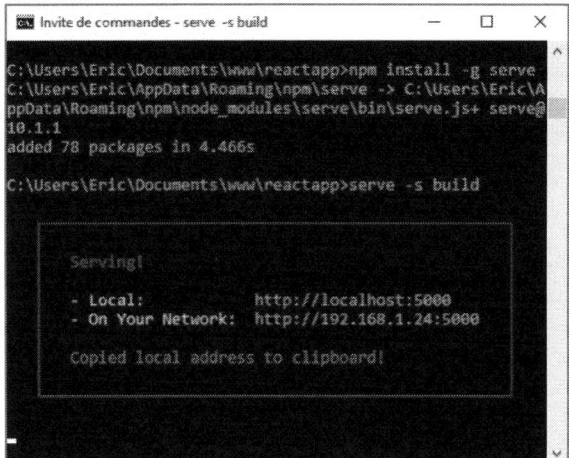

The server in production mode is accessible through the http://localhost:5000 URL.

Type in the browser the http://localhost:5000 URL indicated, it is displayed in a much faster way because of the file optimization performed.

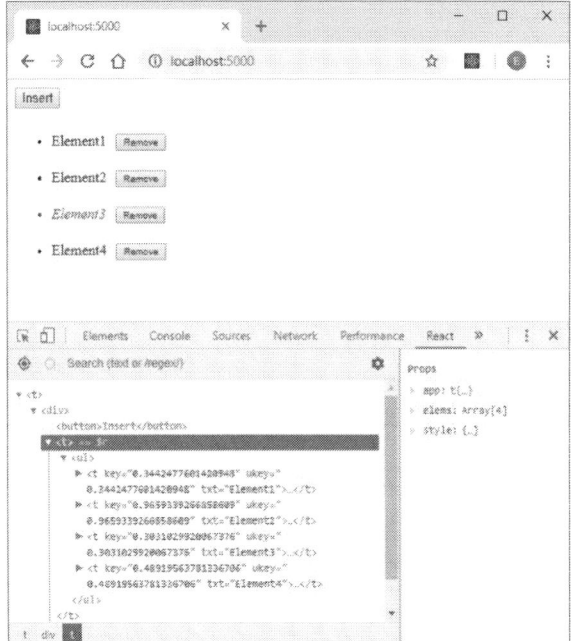

The application in production mode works the same way as in development mode, while being loaded faster in the browser.

Check the type of properties used in the components

The advantage of using `create-react-app` to create the React application is, for now:
- The ability to develop React components in separate modules, easily assembled using the import statement.
- The use of an internal server that restarts the application with each modification.
- The ease of deployment of the application through the `npm run build` command.

Another interest is that of using the React modules defined in the `node_modules` directory. We are currently using the `"react"` and `"react-dom"` modules imported into our modules, but the list visible in the `node_modules` directory makes us feel that we can use many others!

Among the available modules, use the `"prop-types"` module, which is very useful for writing React applications with as few errors as possible.

You will have noticed that when writing a component, it often happens that it uses other components. The use of these components is done through the properties passed in the `props` object.

It is essential to know the type of properties to be transmitted in a component: if it is waiting for a string of characters and something else is sent to it, some problems may appear!

React has planned to perform this verification (and many others) through the `"prop-types"` module. A description of the use of this module is available directly on the React website (see https://reactjs.org/docs/typechecking-with-proptypes.html) but we can already show how to use it here.

Let's take the simple example where we use the `<Element>` component used to display a list element. This component is used in the `<App>` component of our application. We write the simplest possible components because the purpose here is to show how we check the transmission of properties between them, not to write complex components.

When describing the `Element` class, we indicate in it the expected characteristics of the properties of the `props` object it receives. To do this, define the `PropTypes` property in the `Element` class. This property will be used by the `"prop-types"` module that we will have previously included.

Element class that verifies that the received elem property is an object (src/Element.js file)

```
import React from 'react';
import PropTypes from 'prop-types';
class Element extends React.Component {
  /* eslint no-useless-constructor: 0 */
  constructor(props) {
    super(props);
  }
  render() {
    return <li>{this.props.elem.text}</li>
  }
}
Element.propTypes = {
  elem : PropTypes.object
};
export default Element;
```

The elem property is an object with the text property. So we define the elem property in the Element.PropTypes object that is PropTypes.object.

The comment containing eslint allows you to stop displaying the warning that the written constructor is empty (outside the call of the parent constructor), because the server used by create-react-app displays this message to warn of a possible oversight.

App class that uses the Element class to display five list items (src/App.js file)

```
import React from 'react';
import Element from './Element';

class App extends React.Component {
  /* eslint no-useless-constructor: 0 */
  constructor(props) {
    super(props);
  }
  render() {
    var elems = [
      { text : "Element1" },
      { text : "Element2" },
      { text : "Element3" },
      { text : "Element4" },
      { text : "Element5" }
    ];
    return (
```

```
    <ul>
    {
      elems.map(function(elem, index){
        return <Element key={index} elem={elem}></Element>
      })
    }
    </ul>
  )
 }
}

export default App;
```

The elem property passed to the <Element> component is an object with a text property (as defined in the elems array).

Let's show the URL http://localhost:3000 in the browser:

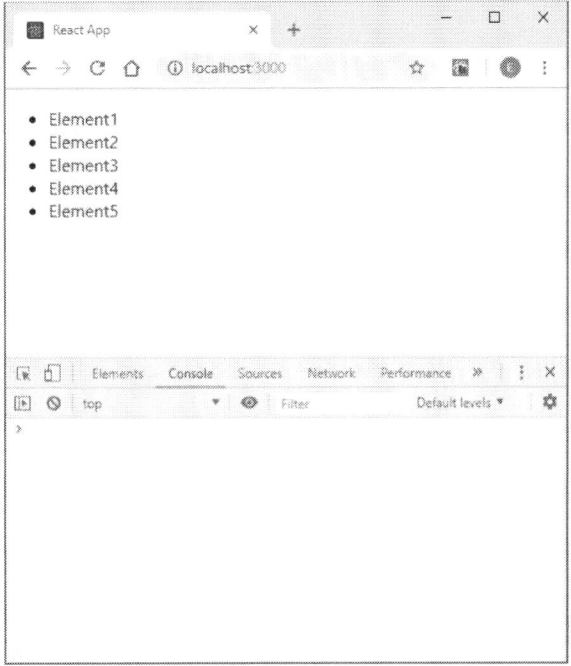

No error message is reported in the console.

Suppose now that the elem property expected in the <Element> component is a string of characters. We would have written in the Element component module:

Indicate that the elem property is a string
```
import React from 'react';
```

```
import PropTypes from 'prop-types';
class Element extends React.Component {
  /* eslint no-useless-constructor: 0 */
  constructor(props) {
    super(props);
  }
  render() {
    return <li>{this.props.elem.text}</li>
  }
}
Element.propTypes = {
  elem : PropTypes.string
};
export default Element;
```

One makes a mistake of type, in order to see what will be the reaction of React when displaying the page.

Let's go back to the http://localhost:3000 URL (it's actually showing itself again because the server refreshes the view each time the file is modified):

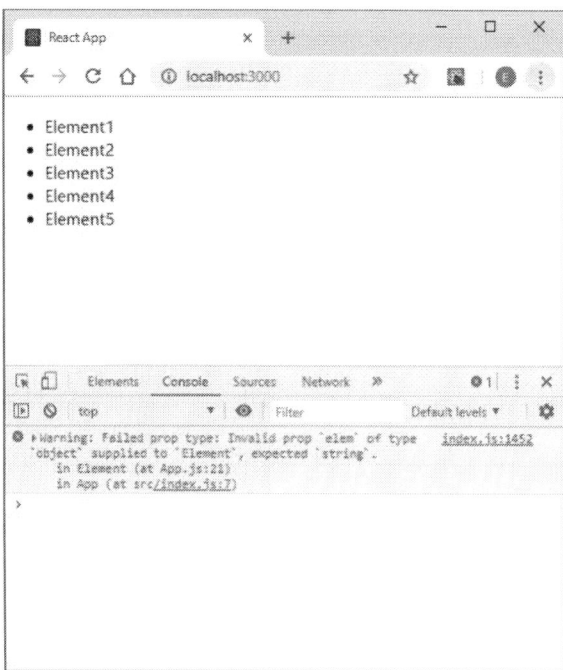

An error message is displayed in the console (detected thanks to the prop-types module).

9 – REDUX

Redux is a JavaScript library independent of React, but which is used a lot with React.
- With React, it allows to simplify the management of the state of the components of an application, by allowing a centralized management of all the states.
- Without React, it is also used in applications for which you want to use state management (such as the one used with React via the state object).

In order to understand the operation of Redux, it is used in this chapter independently of React, then we will see its use with React in the next chapter.

Purpose of Redux

Redux makes it easier to manage the state. We have seen in previous chapters that all React components (only those created by a class derived from `React.Component`), had a `state` property that reflects the state of the component. This state is used (among other things) to display the component. Any modification of the displayed component can only be done by modifying the state.

Sometimes, we have to update the state of another component, which is quite complex to do because we must have access to this other component. Moreover, we do not have access to a global state of the whole application but only to the states of the components that constitute it.

The idea of Redux is to centralize state management in a single object called the `store`, which centralizes all states of all components. This `store` object (unique for the entire application) is managed by the Redux methods.

Redux installation

Redux is an `npm` module that installs using the `npm install redux` command. Even if it is used here without React, we use the tree created by create-react-app in the reactapp directory (see previous chapter), in order to benefit from the installed structure (in particular module management).

Type the npm install redux command, located in the reactapp directory.

Install Redux as a module
```
cd reactapp
npm install redux
```

The "redux" module will now be accessible in our application.

In the following, we keep the original public/index.html file, and we only modify the src/index.js file (located in the reactapp directory).

Let's first check that the "redux" module is accessible to our application. For this we import the createStore() function of the module and we use it (for now without giving more explanation, they will come below).

Use the createStore() method of the "redux" module (src/index.js file)
```
import { createStore } from "redux";

var store = createStore(function(state, action) {
  return state;
});

console.log(store);
```

The createStore(reducer) function takes as parameter a callback function (called a reducer) with state and action parameters. The createStore(reducer) function returns an object called store.

The callback function used in createStore() parameters is therefore called a reducer. This function is studied below.

Let's run this program to see the contents of the store object in the console:

The store object returned by createStore() has the dispatch(), getState(), replaceReducer(), and subscribe() methods. These methods allow the operation of Redux.

How Redux works

The createStore() method returns a store object to hold and manage the state of the application. The state can only be read and updated through the methods provided on the store object, namely:

- The store.dispatch(action) method is used to modify the state, depending on the action specified. Indeed, only the actions allow to make a modification of the state. For example, an action could be "add this item to the list", or "remove the second item from the list".

The difference with React is that changing the state is not done directly by specifying its value (by this.setState()), but rather by executing an action that will cause the state to be modified (by store.dispatch(action)).

- The store.getState() method is used to retrieve the state (stored in the store) as an object. This store.getState() method looks like the operation of the this.state object used in React, except that this method returns the state of the entire application, not just the state associated with a component.

• The store.subscribe(listener) method is used to perform a processing, during each action. The processing is done in the listener() callback.

Overall, we see that we have actions that update the state, and we can "listen" any changes in state when the actions are executed.

The update of the state is carried out following the "dispatched" actions, but the procedure of update of the state is centralized in the callback indicated in parameter of the createStore(reducer) function. The reducer (method of the form reducer(state, action)) is therefore an important part of the application because it allows to indicate how the state is updated (depending on the old state and the action performed).

Actions in Redux

Actions are the elements of the application that modify the state. They correspond to anything that can produce a change of state of our application. For example, assuming our application maintains a list of items:

- Add a new item at the end of the list,
- Remove an item from the list,
- Reverse the order of the items in the list,
- Show only items that contain a search word.

These actions may or may not change the state. For example, if the list has only one element, inverting the list will not produce any changes to the display. But if you also want to keep the insertion order (ascending alphabetical order or not), the state will be modified internally (boolean indicating increasing or not) even if the display is not modified.

An action has parameters that describe it. So for the previous actions, we could have:

- Add a new item at the end of the list: description of the item,
- Remove an item from the list: index of the item to delete,
- Invert the order of the elements of the list: no parameter,
- Show only items that contain a search word: word to search.

An action in Redux is defined as a JavaScript object that is used to describe it. The only constraint is that each action must have a `type` attribute that will differentiate it from an action of another type. The `type` is an attribute of any type, but is often defined as an integer constant or string.

For example, considering the actions described previously:

Actions defined to manage a list of items (src/index.js file)

```
// constants defining the types of action
const ADD_ELEM = "ADD_ELEM";
const REMOVE_ELEM = "REMOVE_ELEM";
const REVERT_LIST = "REVERT_LIST";
const FIND_TAG = "FIND_TAG";

// add actions (at the end of the list)
var add_elem_1 = { type : ADD_ELEM, elem : "Element1" };
var add_elem_2 = { type : ADD_ELEM, elem : "Element2" };
var add_elem_3 = { type : ADD_ELEM, elem : "Element3" };
var add_elem_4 = { type : ADD_ELEM, elem : "Element4" };
var add_elem_5 = { type : ADD_ELEM, elem : "Element5" };

// remove actions
var remove_elem_1 = { type : REMOVE_ELEM, index : 3 };
var remove_elem_2 = { type : REMOVE_ELEM, index : 2 };

// inversion action
var revert_list_1 = { type : REVERT_LIST };

// search actions
var find_tag_1 = { type : FIND_TAG, tag : "Element3" };
var find_tag_2 = { type : FIND_TAG, tag : "Element4" };
```

The types of actions are defined here as constants, then each action is described with its parameters. Only the `type` attribute is present in each action, which allows to know what is the type of each action.

Moreover, since we can have several actions of the same type (for example `add_elem_1`, `add_elem_2`, etc.), it is simpler to create a function that constructs the action, indicating the properties of the action in the parameters of the function. So to replace the actions defined above, we would have the following creators:

Use action creators

```
// constants defining the types of action
const ADD_ELEM = "ADD_ELEM";
const REMOVE_ELEM = "REMOVE_ELEM";
const REVERT_LIST = "REVERT_LIST";
```

```javascript
const FIND_TAG = "FIND_TAG";

// action creators
function add_elem(elem) {
 return {
  type : ADD_ELEM,
  elem : elem
 }
}

function remove_elem(index) {
 return {
  type : REMOVE_ELEM,
  index : index
 }
}

function revert_list() {
 return {
  type : REVERT_LIST
 }
}

function find_tag(tag) {
 return {
  type : FIND_TAG,
  tag : tag
 }
}

// add actions (at the end of the list)
var add_elem_1 = add_elem("Element1");
var add_elem_2 = add_elem("Element2");
var add_elem_3 = add_elem("Element3");
var add_elem_4 = add_elem("Element4");
var add_elem_5 = add_elem("Element5");

// remove actions
var remove_elem_1 = remove_elem(3);
var remove_elem_2 = remove_elem(2);

// inversion action
var revert_list_1 = revert_list();

// search actions
```

```
var find_tag_1 = find_tag("Element3");
var find_tag_2 = find_tag("Element4");
```

Each action creator returns an action, according to the specified parameters.

Then the actions are created using the associated action creator.

Reducers in Redux

The reducer is the callback function used in the parameters of the `createStore(reducer)` function. It allows to indicate the changes of states of the application, according to the actions carried out.

Its role is thus the following: the `reducer(state, action)` function uses the current state of the application, and according to the action indicated in parameters, the function returns a new state. It must not do anything else, and especially it must not do:

- Update external values (databases, variables, etc.),
- Use variable data other than those indicated in parameters (state and action),
- Modify the current state (so we refrain from doing any action in the reducer, which would change the state).

In fact, a reducer is what we call a pure function: if we execute the function several times with the same arguments, its behavior must always be identical. And for that, the outside world must not influence its behavior.

Indicate the minimal form of a reducer. For the moment, it displays in the console the `state` and `action` parameters transmitted, and returns the same state as the one transmitted (no modification of the state for the moment).

General form of a reducer
```
import { createStore } from "redux";

createStore(function(state, action) {
  console.log("state =", state, "action =", action);
  return state;   // by default we return the current state
});
```

The role of a reducer being to return the new state, it is normal to return something, here the current state. If we do not return anything, it will be considered by Redux as if the new state was `undefined`.

It is of course possible to write the reducer as an external function, not directly integrated into the call to the createStore() function.

Reducer as an external function
```
import { createStore } from "redux";

function reducer(state, action) {
  console.log("state =", state, "action =", action);
  return state;  // by default we return the current state
}

createStore(reducer);
```

The reducer is defined here as an external function, and used as a parameter of the createStore(reducer) function.

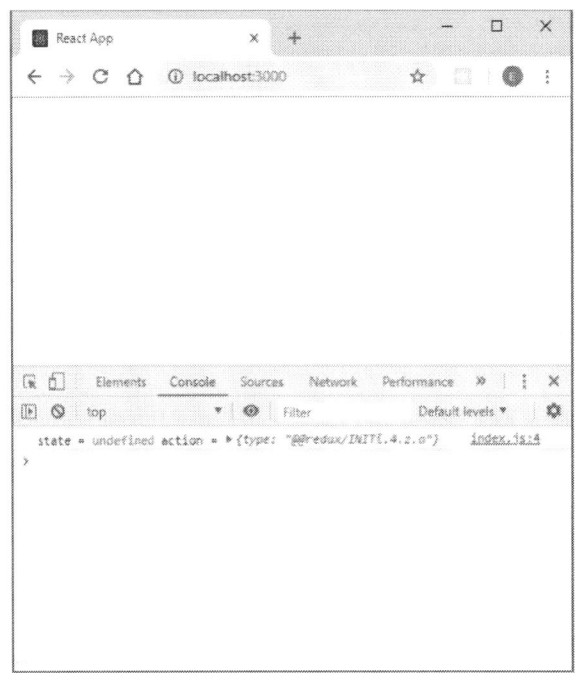

The reducer is called during initialization, using an action internal to Redux, while the state is undefined because it has not yet been defined.

Manage the state in the reducer

The role of a reducer is to return the new state, depending on the current state and the action to be performed (both passed as parameters).

The first step is to write the properties that must be defined in the state, according to the actions to be executed. Write the necessary properties to manage the ac-

tions on the list of elements. These actions were as follows:
- Add a new element at the end of the list: we need the elems array which will keep the list of inserted elements (initialized to []),
- Remove an item from the list: will use the previous elems array,
- Invert the order of the elements of the list: will use the elems array, and a revert boolean indicating if the array is inverted (true) or not (false, default value),
- Show only items that contain a search word: will use a new elems array (initialized to []) containing the elements containing the searched word, as well as the corresponding searched word (initialized to ""). To avoid name conflicts, we associate these two pieces of information in a find object of the form {elems, tag}.

This allows to define the initial state of the state:

Initializing the application state
```
const stateInit = {
  elems : [],    // elements of the list
  revert : false, // true if the list is reversed
  find : {
    tag : "",    // tag to search
    elems : []   // items containing the searched tag
  }
}
```

It remains to write the reducer that causes the changes in the state depending on the actions that occur.

Reducer managing list item states
```
import { createStore } from "redux";

// constants defining the types of action
const ADD_ELEM = "ADD_ELEM";
const REMOVE_ELEM = "REMOVE_ELEM";
const REVERT_LIST = "REVERT_LIST";
const FIND_TAG = "FIND_TAG";

const stateInit = {
  elems : [],    // elements of the list
  revert : false, // true if the list is reversed
  find : {
    tag : "",    // tag to search
```

```js
  elems : []    // items containing the searched tag
 }
}
function reducer(state = stateInit, action) {
 var newState;   // state returned by the reducer
 if (action.type == ADD_ELEM) {
  var elem = action.elem;   // item to add
  var elems = state.elems;  // current elements
  elems.push(elem);  // add the element
  newState = Object.assign({}, state, {elems : elems});
 }
 else if (action.type == REMOVE_ELEM) {
  var index = action.index; // index of the item to remove
  var elems = state.elems;  // current elements
  elems = elems.filter(function(elem, i) {
   if (i == index) return false; // remove the element
   else return true;         // keep the element
  });
  newState = Object.assign({}, state, {elems : elems});
 }
 else if (action.type == REVERT_LIST) {
  var elems = state.elems;  // current elements
  var revert = state.revert; // current order
  elems.reverse();   // invert the elements of the array
  newState = Object.assign({}, state, {elems : elems, revert : !revert});
 }
 else if (action.type == FIND_TAG) {
  var elems = state.elems;  // current elements
  var tag = action.tag;     // tag searched
  elems = elems.filter(function(elem, i) {
   if (elem.indexOf(tag) >= 0) return true;
   else return false;
  });
  newState = Object.assign({}, state, { find : { elems : elems, tag : tag }});
 }
 else {
  // unknown action
  newState = state;  // by default we return the current state
 }
 console.log(action, newState);
 return newState;
```

}

Note that for each action, the current state is never changed, but only the `newState` local variable which is then returned by the reducer.

The initial state of the state is initialized in the function definition, using the functionality of ES6. We see here the interest of treating the case of the unknown action in the reducer, which allows to take into account the internal initialization action of Redux.

Notice the use of `Object.assign(obj1, obj2, obj3, ...)`. This method is used to create a new object from the merging of properties of objects passed as parameters. However, this merge modifies the first object transmitted in parameters (here `obj1`), that is why this first transmitted object is an empty object `{}` so as not to modify an used object. The result of the merge is returned by the method.

In addition, another form of writing in ES6 could also have been used, using the destructuring of ES6 objects.

So instead of writing:

Merging the state object and the elems property
```
newState = Object.assign({}, state, {elems : elems});
```

We could also have written:

Merging the state object and the elems property in ES6
```
newState = { ...state, elems };  // ou newState = { ...state, elems : elems };
```

The properties of the state object are merged with the elems array into a new object.

Using actions with the reducer

The reducer is used to process state changes when actions occur. We will now integrate actions in our program, so that the reducer comes into play.

We use the action creators we previously defined, and we trigger the corresponding actions. The state display in the console allows you to see the corresponding state changes.

Use actions with the reducer (src/index.js file)
```
import { createStore } from "redux";

const ADD_ELEM = "ADD_ELEM";
const REMOVE_ELEM = "REMOVE_ELEM";
const REVERT_LIST = "REVERT_LIST";
```

```
const FIND_TAG = "FIND_TAG";

const stateInit = {
 elems : [],
 revert : false,
 find : {
  tag : "",
  elems : []
 }
}

function reducer(state = stateInit, action) {
 var newState;
 if (action.type == ADD_ELEM) {
  var elem = action.elem;
  var elems = state.elems;
  elems.push(elem);
  newState = Object.assign({}, state, {elems : elems});
 }
 else if (action.type == REMOVE_ELEM) {
  var index = action.index;
  var elems = state.elems;
  elems = elems.filter(function(elem, i) {
   if (i == index) return false;
   else return true;
  });
  newState = Object.assign({}, state, {elems : elems});
 }
 else if (action.type == REVERT_LIST) {
  var elems = state.elems;
  var revert = state.revert;
  elems.reverse();
  newState = Object.assign({}, state, {elems : elems, revert : !revert});
 }
 else if (action.type == FIND_TAG) {
  var elems = state.elems;
  var tag = action.tag;
  elems = elems.filter(function(elem, i) {
   if (elem.indexOf(tag) >= 0) return true;
   else return false;
  });
  newState = Object.assign({}, state, { find : { elems : elems, tag : tag }});
 }
```

```
  else {
    newState = state;
  }
  console.log(action, newState);
  return newState;
}

var store = createStore(reducer);

function add_elem(elem) {
  return {
    type : ADD_ELEM,
    elem : elem
  }
}

function remove_elem(index) {
  return {
    type : REMOVE_ELEM,
    index : index
  }
}

function revert_list() {
  return {
    type : REVERT_LIST
  }
}

function find_tag(tag) {
  return {
    type : FIND_TAG,
    tag : tag
  }
}

store.dispatch(add_elem("Element1"));
store.dispatch(add_elem("Element2"));
store.dispatch(add_elem("Element3"));
store.dispatch(add_elem("Element4"));
store.dispatch(add_elem("Element5"));

store.dispatch(revert_list());

store.dispatch(find_tag("Element5"));
```

```
store.dispatch(find_tag("Element2"));

store.dispatch(remove_elem(3));
store.dispatch(remove_elem(2));
```

The reducer is connected to the Redux store via the createStore(reducer) function. Once the action creators are defined, they are used via store.dispatch(action). We can see in the console the evolution of the state:

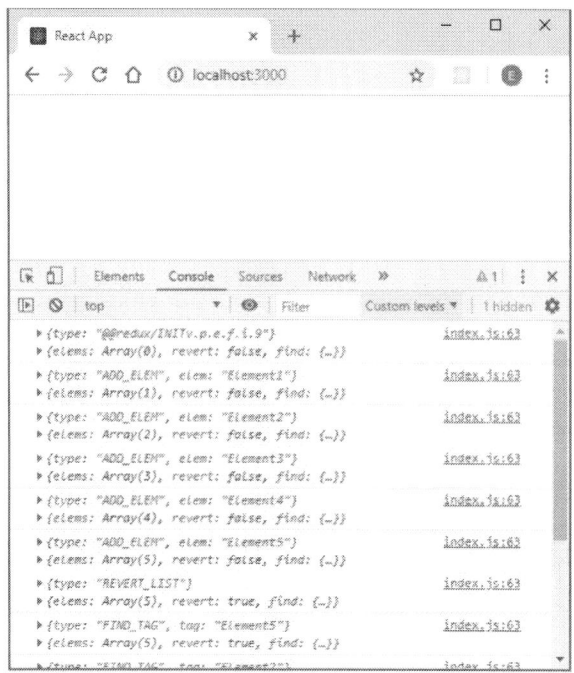

The state of Redux evolves as the actions are executed.

Taking into account the changes of the state in our program

The state is updated in the reducer as the actions follow one another. However, it remains to be able to take into account these changes in our program.

For this, we use the store.subscribe(callback) method. The callback function is called after each action (when the action is complete and the state is updated). Of course, this method must be executed before the first action is triggered (otherwise the action is triggered but no processing is written to take it into account).

<u>**Taking actions into account**</u>

```
store.subscribe(function() {
  console.log(store.getState()); // display the new state
});

// add actions
store.dispatch(add_elem("Element1"));
store.dispatch(add_elem("Element2"));
store.dispatch(add_elem("Element3"));
store.dispatch(add_elem("Element4"));
store.dispatch(add_elem("Element5"));

// inversion action
store.dispatch(revert_list());

// search actions
store.dispatch(find_tag("Element5"));
store.dispatch(find_tag("Element2"));

// remove actions
store.dispatch(remove_elem(3));
store.dispatch(remove_elem(2));
```

The `store.subscribe()` statement is set before the `store.dispatch()` statements.

Here we display the state, and the result is similar to the previous one.

Formatting the program in separate modules

All our program is contained in the src/index.js file. It would be nice to be able to separate the actions and reducer into separate files. We create the src/reducers.js and src/actions.js files which will be integrated in the main src/index.js file.

Moreover, the constants defining the actions are put in another src/actions_types.js file, so that they can be used in several other files.

Below is the content of each file. Let's start with the action constants file.

Constants defining the types of actions (file src/actions_types.js)

```
// constants defining the types of actions
export const ADD_ELEM = "ADD_ELEM";
export const REMOVE_ELEM = "REMOVE_ELEM";
export const REVERT_LIST = "REVERT_LIST";
export const FIND_TAG = "FIND_TAG";
```

Each constant is exported so that it can be used in another module.

The src/actions.js file allows to define the actions, and uses the file defining the previous constants. To import these constants from the actions_types.js file, we could write in the first line of the src/actions.js file:

importing action constants
```
import { ADD_ELEM, REMOVE_ELEM, REVERT_LIST, FIND_TAG } from "./actions_types.js";
```

Just list the constants of actions that are imported.

However, this syntax is a problem in case new actions are added because you have to update the imported list. It would be nice not to have to repeat this list each time you import constants into a new file.

The syntax of the import statement allows this, by defining a namespace for the imported data. So to import the constants from the actions_types.js file into the actions.js module, using the ACTIONS namespace (or any other name), we write:

Importing action constants using the ACTIONS namespace (src/actions.js file)
```
import * as ACTIONS from "./actions_types.js";
```

The ACTIONS namespace implies to use the imported data by prefixing them with "ACTIONS." For example ACTIONS.ADD_ELEM to use the constant ADD_ELEM.

The actions.js file can then be written:

File defining the actions (src/actions.js file)
```
import * as ACTIONS from "./actions_types.js";
// action creators
export function add_elem(elem) {
 return {
  type : ACTIONS.ADD_ELEM,
  elem : elem
 }
}
export function remove_elem(index) {
 return {
  type : ACTIONS.REMOVE_ELEM,
  index : index
 }
}
export function revert_list() {
 return {
  type : ACTIONS.REVERT_LIST
 }
}
export function find_tag(tag) {
 return {
```

```
  type : ACTIONS.FIND_TAG,
  tag : tag
 }
}
```

The action type is prefixed with the ACTIONS namespace, and each function defining an action is exported (so that it can be used in another module).

The reducer file is as follows:

Reducer file (src/reducers.js file)

```
import * as ACTIONS from "./actions_types.js";

const stateInit = {
 elems : [],
 revert : false,
 find : {
  tag : "",
  elems : []
 }
}

export default function reducer(state = stateInit, action) {
 var newState;
 if (action.type == ACTIONS.ADD_ELEM) {
  var elem = action.elem;
  var elems = state.elems;
  elems.push(elem);
  newState = Object.assign({}, state, {elems : elems});
 }
 else if (action.type == ACTIONS.REMOVE_ELEM) {
  var index = action.index;
  var elems = state.elems;
  elems = elems.filter(function(elem, i) {
   if (i == index) return false;
   else return true;
  });
  newState = Object.assign({}, state, {elems : elems});
 }
 else if (action.type == ACTIONS.REVERT_LIST) {
  var elems = state.elems;
  var revert = state.revert;
  elems.reverse();
  newState = Object.assign({}, state, {elems : elems, revert : !revert});
```

```
}
else if (action.type == ACTIONS.FIND_TAG) {
  var elems = state.elems;
  var tag = action.tag;
  elems = elems.filter(function(elem, i) {
    if (elem.indexOf(tag) >= 0) return true;
    else return false;
  });
  newState = Object.assign({}, state, { find : { elems : elems, tag : tag }});
}
else {
  // unknown action
  newState = state;
}
return newState;
}
```

You import the action constants using the ACTIONS namespace (or any other name), then this namespace is used in all uses of the action constants.

In addition, the reducer function is exported (export default) so that it can be used during the createStore(reducer) statement.

It remains to write the src/index.js file which uses the previous files. It is much shorter now that the other features are outsourced, and it focuses on the main processing.

src/index.js file

```
import { createStore } from "redux";
import reducer from "./reducers.js";
import * as ACTIONS from "./actions.js";

var store = createStore(reducer);

store.subscribe(function() {
  console.log(store.getState());
});

store.dispatch(ACTIONS.add_elem("Element1"));
store.dispatch(ACTIONS.add_elem("Element2"));
store.dispatch(ACTIONS.add_elem("Element3"));
store.dispatch(ACTIONS.add_elem("Element4"));
store.dispatch(ACTIONS.add_elem("Element5"));

store.dispatch(ACTIONS.revert_list());
```

store.dispatch(ACTIONS.find_tag("Element5"));
store.dispatch(ACTIONS.find_tag("Element2"));

store.dispatch(ACTIONS.remove_elem(3));
store.dispatch(ACTIONS.remove_elem(2));

Just import the reducer and the actions.

We verify that the execution of the program is identical to the previous one:

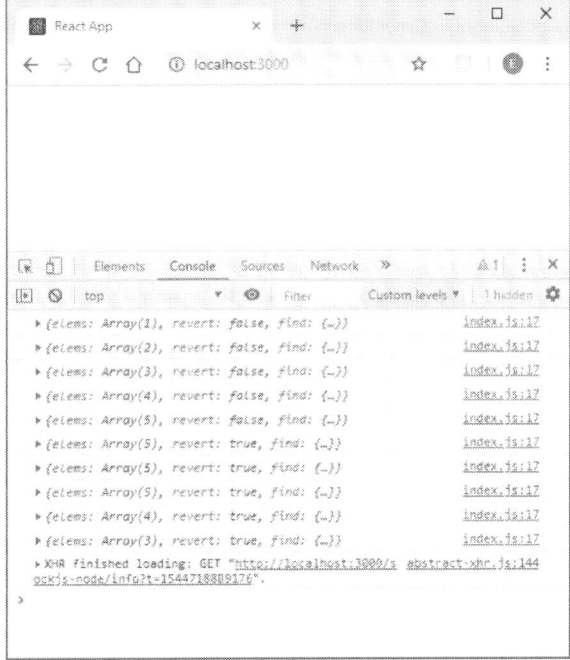

The state is displayed in the console after each action.

Conclusion

We have in this chapter studied the Redux module independently of React.

The Redux module allows:

- Manage the state of the entire application in a store object that contains it (in store.getState()),
- Then modify the state by means of actions (by store.dispatch(action)),
- And finally, to be notified of state changes when actions occur (by store.subscribe(listener)).

It remains to be seen how to couple the Redux module with React in our React applications, which is the subject of the following chapters.

10 – REACT & REDUX

The previous chapter showed how to use Redux in an application, regardless of React.

It remains to associate Redux with a React application. We will proceed in two steps to understand the operation:
- First by using Redux directly with React (in this chapter),
- Then using the new `"react-redux"` module which simplifies the code to write (in the next chapter).

Let's first look at using Redux directly with React. We use our element list management example, where you can insert, modify or delete elements.

Link React and Redux directly to manage a list of items

The principle of the association of React and Redux is simple. It consists of sharing the `store` object (which includes the state) with the various React components of the application (via the transmission in the attributes of the components, ie the `props` object). The components will be able to update the state thanks to the available actions (via the store) and will be able to know the state which is global to all the application. We no longer have to worry about passing the instance of a component to another component (so that it has access to the component's state) but only to transmit the `store` that gives access to everything.

We will create the Redux store in the most general React component of the application (often the `<App>` component) and send it to the other components via the `store` attribute created in the components that will use it. The components that will access the store will have access to the previous methods:
- `store.getState()` to retrieve the part of the state that the component needs,
- `store.dispatch(action)` to update the part of the state that depends on the ac-

tion performed by the component,
- store.subscribe(listener) so that the component is notified of state changes in another component.

Let's use these principles to manage the list of elements studied in chapter 6. We want to be able to insert an element in the list, delete it and finally modify it. And we also want to be able to reverse the order of the elements in the list.

Overview of the Redux App

The reducer written in the previous chapter handles these actions, except the action of modifying the list item. One adds this MODIFY_ELEM action in the file of the actions and in the reducer, keeping the tree of the application created in reactapp via create-react-app.

Also, we modify the parameters of the actions that use the index of the element in the list (to modify or delete it) because the index is modified in case of deletion of an element of the list (the index is modified for the following elements). Instead, a unique key assigned to each list item is used, as in the examples in Chapter 6.

If we do not make these adjustments, we will see a bug when a list item will be deleted if we try to modify the next element ...

src/actions_types.js file

```javascript
// constants defining the types of actions
export const ADD_ELEM = "ADD_ELEM";
export const REMOVE_ELEM = "REMOVE_ELEM";
export const MODIFY_ELEM = "MODIFY_ELEM";
export const REVERT_LIST = "REVERT_LIST";
export const FIND_TAG = "FIND_TAG";
```

The MODIFY_ELEM action has been added.

src/actions.js file

```javascript
import * as ACTIONS from "./actions_types.js";
// internal module function to return a unique key
function getUniqueKey() {
  var key = Math.random() + "";  // return a string
  return key;
}
// creators of actions
export function add_elem(txt) {
  var ukey = getUniqueKey(); // assign a unique key to the created element
  return {
```

```
    type : ACTIONS.ADD_ELEM,
    txt : txt,
    ukey : ukey
  }
}
export function remove_elem(ukey) {
  return {
    type : ACTIONS.REMOVE_ELEM,
    ukey : ukey
  }
}
export function modify_elem(ukey, txt) {
  return {
    type : ACTIONS.MODIFY_ELEM,
    ukey : ukey,
    txt : txt
  }
}
export function revert_list() {
  return {
    type : ACTIONS.REVERT_LIST
  }
}
export function find_tag(tag) {
  return {
    type : ACTIONS.FIND_TAG,
    tag : tag
  }
}
```

The unique key is assigned during the action of creation of the element of list (`ADD_ELEM` action).

The `MODIFY_ELEM` action takes in parameters the unique key of the element to be modified and the new value of this element.

The reducer is modified to take into account the management of the unique key and the addition of the `MODIFY_ELEM` action.

src/reducers.js file

```
import * as ACTIONS from "./actions_types.js";

const stateInit = {
  elems : [],   // { ukey, txt } array
```

```
  revert : false,
  find : {
   tag : "",
   elems : []
  }
 }

 export default function reducer(state = stateInit, action) {
  var newState;
  if (action.type == ACTIONS.ADD_ELEM) {
   var txt = action.txt;
   var ukey = action.ukey;
   var elems = state.elems;
   elems.push({txt, ukey});
   newState = Object.assign({}, state, {elems : elems});
  }
  else if (action.type == ACTIONS.REMOVE_ELEM) {
   var ukey = action.ukey;
   var elems = state.elems;
   elems = elems.filter(function(elem) {
    if (elem.ukey == ukey) return false;
    else return true;
   });
   newState = Object.assign({}, state, {elems : elems});
  }
  else if (action.type == ACTIONS.MODIFY_ELEM) {
   var txt = action.txt;
   var ukey = action.ukey;
   var elems = state.elems;
   elems = elems.map(function(elem, i) {
    if (elem.ukey == ukey) return {txt, ukey};
    else return elem;
   });
   newState = Object.assign({}, state, {elems : elems});
  }
  else if (action.type == ACTIONS.REVERT_LIST) {
   var elems = state.elems;
   var revert = state.revert;
   elems.reverse();
   newState = Object.assign({}, state, {elems : elems, revert : !revert});
  }
  else if (action.type == ACTIONS.FIND_TAG) {
```

```
  var elems = state.elems;
  var tag = action.tag;
  elems = elems.filter(function(elem, i) {
    if (elem.indexOf(tag) >= 0) return true;
    else return false;
  });
  newState = Object.assign({}, state, { find : { elems : elems, tag : tag }});
}
else {
  // action inconnue
  newState = state;
}
return newState;
}
```

The reducer is modified so that the elems array is now an array of {ukey, txt} objects allowing to associate to each element a unique key, which will be used to modify or delete the element from this key.

Once these additions and modifications are made, create the necessary components for our React application related to Redux. We will treat the following cases:
- Add an item to the list,
- Deleting an item in the list,
- Edit an item in the list,
- Inversion of the list to the display.

But before that, let's see how the application of the React side is organized globally.

Overview of the React side application

The files independent of the created code are the index.js and App.js files. They are described below.

src/index.js file

```
import React from "react";
import ReactDOM from "react-dom";

import App from "./App.js";

ReactDOM.render(
  <App />,
document.getElementById("root"));
```

We display the <App> component describing the application.

The App.js file describes the main component of the application. This component displays an Add button, allowing you to insert an item into the list, and also displays the list of items. This list contains by default five elements ("Element1", "Element2", ..., "Element5").

The <App> component is the one that creates the Redux store, and passes it to its child components.

src/App.js file (describing the main <App> component)

```
import React from 'react';
import ConnectedElementsList from './ConnectedElementsList';
import ButtonAdd from './ButtonAdd';

import { createStore } from "redux";
import reducer from "./reducers.js";

class App extends React.Component {
  /* eslint no-useless-constructor: 0 */
  constructor(props) {
    super(props);
  }
  render() {
    const store = createStore(reducer);
    // éléments de la liste initiale
    var elems = [
      "Element1",
      "Element2",
      "Element3",
      "Element4",
      "Element5"
    ];
    return (
      <div>
        <ButtonAdd text="Add" store={store}></ButtonAdd>
        <ConnectedElementsList elems={elems} store={store} />
      </div>
    )
  }
}
export default App;
```

The Add button is created as a <ButtonAdd> component, and the list of items is displayed with the <ConnectedElementsList> component (see below).

The `store` property is passed to all components that will need them (which will also pass them to their child components themselves).

Now explain the `<ConnectedElementsList>` component. It uses as attributes the initial `elems` list of the elements to display and the Redux `store`. In Chapter 6, we used only the `<ElementsList>` component that displayed the list of items. Let's not forget that now the list of elements is managed with the Redux store. It is therefore necessary that the list of the elements is refreshed if necessary during each action on the list (addition, suppression, modification, inversion). The `<ConnectedElementsList>` component will be used to take into account the actions of Redux and refresh the list, while the `<ElementsList>` component will be used only to display the list already updated.

src/ConnectedElementsList.js file (describing the `<ConnectedElementsList>` component)

```
import React from "react";
import ListeELements from "./ElementsList";
import * as ACTIONS from "./actions.js";
class ConnectedElementsList extends React.Component {
 constructor(props) {
  super(props);
  this.state = props.store.getState(); // recover in React the state of Redux
 }
 componentDidMount() {
  const { store } = this.props;
  // refresh the list for each Redux action:
  // refresh the React state
  this.unsubscribe = store.subscribe(() => {
   this.setState({ ...store.getState() }); // update the React state
  });
  // insert elements into the start list
  // ("Element1", ..., "Element5")
  this.props.elems.forEach(function(txt) {
   store.dispatch(ACTIONS.add_elem(txt));
  });
 }
 componentWillUnmount() {
  this.unsubscribe(); // call the method returned by store.subscribe()
 }
 render() {
  return <ListeELements elems={this.state.elems} store={this.props.store} />
  // or return <ListeELements {...this.state} store={this.props.store} />
 }
```

```
}
export default ConnectedElementsList;
```

This component really describes how to interface Redux with React.

We get in the constructor the state of Redux that is stored in React, because it is the modification of the state of React that refreshes the display.

Then we inquire by the `store.subscribe()` statement of the actions performed in Redux, in order to update the React state.

Finally we display the list of elements in the `<ElementsList>` component, thanks to the state of React updated.

The `<ElementsList>` component now becomes a simple display component (here described as a function).

src/ElementsList.js file (describing the `<ElementsList>` component)

```
import React from 'react';
import Element from './Element';

const ElementsList = function(props) {
  const { store, elems } = props;
  return (
   <ul>
   {
    elems.map(function(elem) {
      return (
       <li key={elem.ukey}>
         <Element text={elem.txt} ukey={elem.ukey} store={store} />
       </li>
      )
    })
   }
   </ul>
  )
}
export default ElementsList;
```

The `<Element>` component is also a simple display component described by a function.

src/Element.js file (describing the `<Element>` component)

```
import React from 'react';
const Element = function(props) {
  const { store, text, ukey } = props;
```

```
  return (
    <div>
      <span>{text}</span>
    </div>
  )
}
export default Element;
```

Finally, the Add button (to add an element in the list) is described by the <Button-Add> component, also as a function.

src/ButtonAdd.js file (describing the <ButtonAdd> component)

```
import React from 'react';
const ButtonAdd = function(props) {
  return <button>{props.text}</button>
}
export default ButtonAdd;
```

Let's check that these components work well with Redux. You should see a list of default items, and an inactive Add button for now.

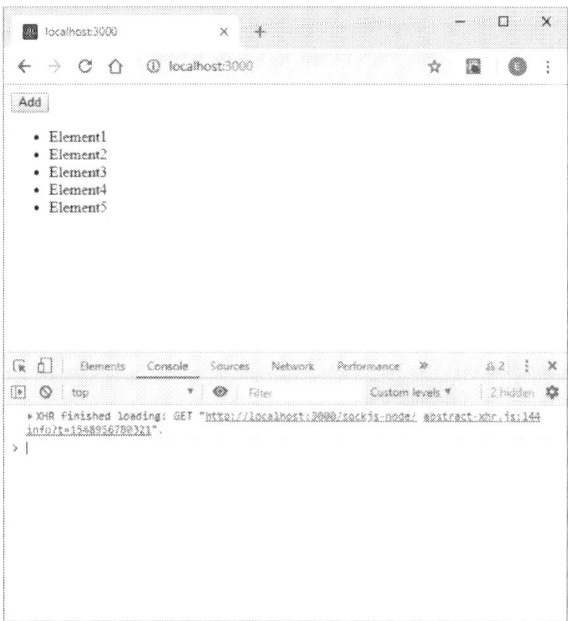

The default list of five items is displayed, along with the Add button for inserting. So for now what is written works (and the connection with Redux is done).

The click on the Add button does not work yet. Let's treat the click on this button.

Adding an item to the list

Adding an item to the list is done using the statement:

Adding an item to the list
```
store.dispatch(ACTIONS.add_elem(txt));
```

This instruction has already been used to insert initialization elements in the list. It is the fact of having done this.setState() in the callback function of the store.subscribe(callback) statement (in the <ConnectedElementsList> component) that allows the display to be refreshed at each insertion.

Therefore, each time you press the Add button, this add instruction must be called. The component to modify is <ButtonAdd> corresponding to the Add button.

<ButtonAdd> component that takes into account the click of the button (in src/ButtonAdd.js)
```
import React from 'react';
import * as ACTIONS from "./actions.js";
const ButtonAdd = function(props) {
  function handlerClick() {
    const { store } = props;
    var elems = store.getState().elems;
    store.dispatch(ACTIONS.add_elem("Element" + (elems.length + 1)));
  }
  return <button onClick={handlerClick}>{props.text}</button>
}
export default ButtonAdd;
```

The handlerClick() processing function is described internally in the function of the component. It is enough to call ADD_ELEM action with the text of the element to be inserted.

After clicking the button several times, new elements are inserted as a result:

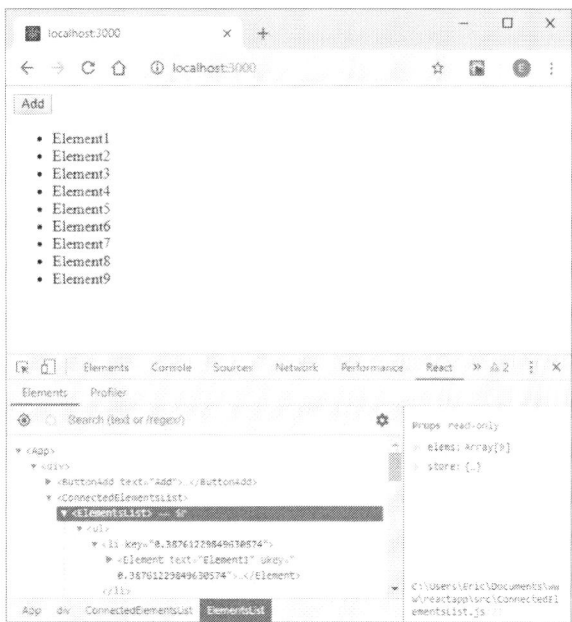

Deleting an item from the list

Deleting an item from the list is done using the statement:

Deleting an item from the list
```
store.dispatch(ACTIONS.remove_elem(ukey));
```

To do this, insert a Remove button in front of each list item, which will remove this item. Each Remove button is represented by a <ButtonRemove> component in which the item deletion processing will be performed.

The <Element> component is modified to integrate the Remove button in front of each list element.

<Element> component incorporating the Remove button
```
import React from 'react';
import ButtonRemove from './ButtonRemove';
const Element = function(props) {
 const { store, ukey, text } = props;
 return (
  <div>
   <span>{text}</span>
   <ButtonRemove style={{margin:"10px", fontSize:"10px"}} ukey={ukey}
        text="Remove" store={store}/>
```

295

```
    </div>
  )
}
export default Element;
```

The store object is passed to the <ButtonRemove> component so that this component can process the deletion of the list item.

Also the ukey property of the list item is passed to the component so that it knows which item to delete (from its unique key).

The <ButtonRemove> component is created to take into account the click on the Remove button. It is written as a simple function.

<ButtonRemove> component for deleting the list item (in src/ButtonRemove.js)
```
import React from 'react';
import * as ACTIONS from "./actions.js";
const ButtonRemove = function(props) {
  const { store, ukey, style, text } = props;
  function handlerClick() {
    store.dispatch(ACTIONS.remove_elem(ukey));
  }
  return <button style={style} onClick={handlerClick}>{text}</button>
}
export default ButtonRemove;
```

Clicking the button calls the handlerClick() method defined internally in the component. This method deletes the list item using the REMOVE_ELEM action.

You must of course import the actions file in order to use them in the component.

Note that we can also write the parameters of the function in the following form. This replaces the props object specified in parameters.

Another way of writing the function parameters of the <ButtonRemove> component
```
import React from 'react';
import * as ACTIONS from "./actions.js";
const ButtonRemove = function({ store, ukey, style, text }) {
  function handlerClick() {
    store.dispatch(ACTIONS.remove_elem(ukey));
  }
  return <button style={style} onClick={handlerClick}>{text}</button>
}
export default ButtonRemove;
```

The list of properties of the props object is directly indicated in an object as parameter of the function, as ES6 allows.

Let's test that it works. After removing some elements from the list, we obtain:

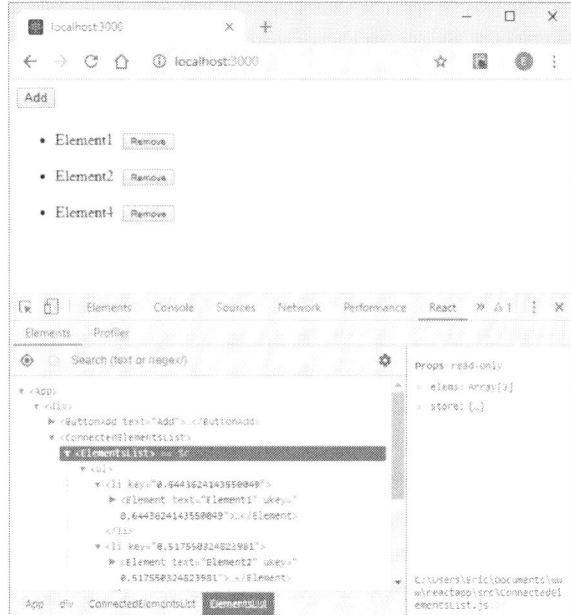

Items 3 and 5 have been removed.

Edit an item in the list

Editing an item in the list is done using the statement:

Edit an item in the list
```
store.dispatch(ACTIONS.modify_elem(ukey, txt));
```

To allow the modification of an element of the list, one allows the double click on each element of list, which will be then replaced by an input field allowing the modification. When leaving the field, the text associated with the element is modified.

Let's start by allowing the transformation of the text into an input field by double clicking. The display of the list will have to display either static elements which can not be modified, or elements which can be modified when double clicked inside. To do this, the state of each list element must indicate whether the element is being modified or not. So we see that we must introduce a new property in the state associated with each list item. This has already been done in the example discussed in Chapter 6 by introducing the modifyOn property into the state of each list item (in the Element class).

But here, the global state of the application is managed by Redux in the store. One could modify the state of each element inserted thanks to the elems property of the store (by introducing a modifyOn attribute), but it is better to directly manage the state of the element directly in the <Element> component (with this.state.modifyOn).

The state's modifyOn property is really local to the <Element> component, and there is no chance that another component will need to access it. If this were the case, then you would need to put this property in the Redux store to allow access to the other components.

In order to manage the internal state in the <Element> component, one must transform this component into an Element class (instead of the simple previous Element function). Indeed, this.state is only accessible in a class deriving from React.Component ...

Element class allowing double-click on the text of an element

```
import React from 'react';
import ButtonRemove from './ButtonRemove';
import * as ACTIONS from "./actions.js";
class Element extends React.Component {
 constructor(props) {
  super(props);
  this.state = {
   modifyOn : false
  }
 }
 handlerDoubleClick() {
  this.setState({modifyOn : true});
 }
 render() {
  const { store, ukey, text } = this.props;
  return (
   <div>
    { this.state.modifyOn ?
     <input autoFocus={true} value={text} /> :
        <span onDoubleClick={this.handlerDoubleClick.bind(this)}>{text}</span>
    }
       <ButtonRemove style={{margin:"10px", fontSize:"10px"}}
          ukey={ukey} text="Remove" store={store}/>
   </div>
  )
```

```
    }
}
export default Element;
```

We proceed as usual with React: we initialize this.state in the constructor of the class, then according to the value of this.state.modifyOn, we display (in the render() method) an <input> input field or a simple <span>, managing the double click on the <span> element.

Let's now check that the double-click on a list item replaces the item with an input field (the field is not modifiable at the moment because the onChange event on the field is not yet processed):

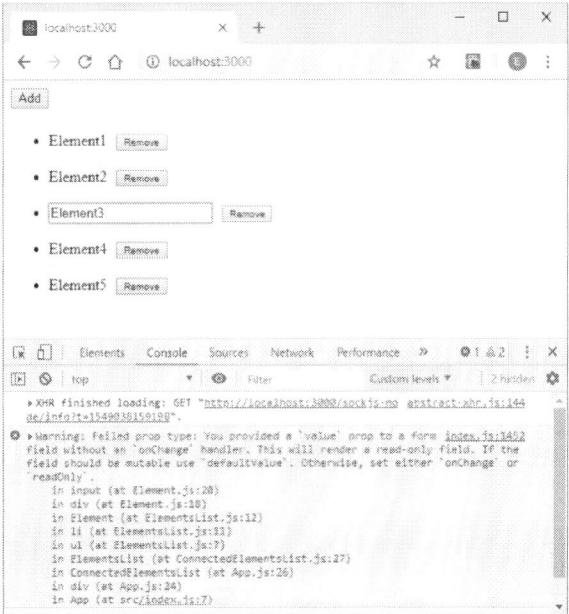

Double-clicking on a list item displays a non-editable input field, because as shown in the React error message displayed in the console, you need to implement the onChange event …

Let's implement the onChange event on the input field (as we learned in Chapter 6), and also the onBlur event on this field to process the modification of the Redux store (MODIFY_ELEM action).

Taking into account the modification of a list item

```
import React from 'react';
import ButtonRemove from './ButtonRemove';
import * as ACTIONS from "./actions.js";
```

```
class Element extends React.Component {
 constructor(props) {
  super(props);
  this.state = {
   modifyOn : false,
   value : props.text
  }
 }
 handlerDoubleClick() {
  this.setState({modifyOn : true});
 }
 handlerChange(event) {
  var value = event.target.value;
  this.setState({value : value});
 }
 handlerBlur() {
  this.setState({modifyOn : false});
  var value = this.state.value;
  const { store, ukey } = this.props;
  store.dispatch(ACTIONS.modify_elem(ukey, value));
 }
 render() {
  const { store, ukey, text } = this.props;
  return (
   <div>
      { this.state.modifyOn ?
        <input onChange={this.handlerChange.bind(this)}
             onBlur={this.handlerBlur.bind(this)}
         autoFocus={true}
         value={this.state.value} /> :
         <span onDoubleClick={this.handlerDoubleClick.bind(this)}>{text}</span>
    }
      <ButtonRemove style={{margin:"10px", fontSize:"10px"}}
         ukey={ukey} text="Remove" store={store}/>
   </div>
  )
 }
}
export default Element;
```

We see (in the handlerBlur() method) the use of the internal state of the component and that of Redux simultaneously.

Let's check that the elements are modifiable and that the output of the input field modifies them on the screen.

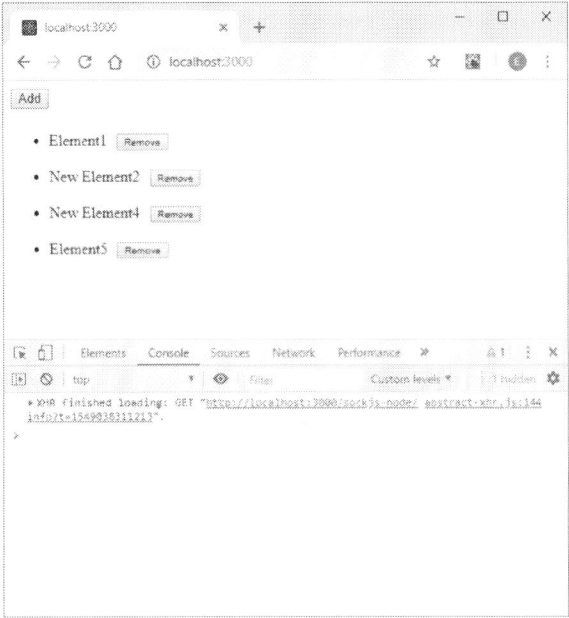

All the possible actions (insert, modify and delete) work!

Inversion of the list to the display

In order to train a bit more, let's add an Invert button that reverses the list. The RE-VERT_LIST action is used for this purpose.

Inversion of items in the list

```
store.dispatch(ACTIONS.revert_list());
```

The Invert button is inserted next to the Add button in the <App> component. To process the Invert button, it is associated with a <ButtonRevert> component.

<App> component with the Invert button

```
import React from 'react';
import ConnectedElementsList from './ConnectedElementsList';
import ButtonAdd from './ButtonAdd';
import ButtonRevert from './ButtonRevert';

import { createStore } from "redux";
import reducer from "./reducers.js";

class App extends React.Component {
  /* eslint no-useless-constructor: 0 */
```

```
constructor(props) {
 super(props);
}
render() {
 const store = createStore(reducer);
 var elems = [
  "Element1",
  "Element2",
  "Element3",
  "Element4",
  "Element5"
 ];
 return (
  <div>
   <ButtonAdd text="Add" store={store}></ButtonAdd>
     
   <ButtonRevert text="Invert" store={store}></ButtonRevert>
   <ConnectedElementsList elems={elems} store={store} />
  </div>
 )
}
}
export default App;
```

The principle of the Invert button is the same as that of the Add button. We import the file of the <ButtonRevert> component associated with the Invert button.

The processing of the click on the Invert button is done in the <ButtonRevert> component, which is a simple function.

<ButtonRevert> component to invert the list (in src/ButtonRevert.js)

```
import React from 'react';
import * as ACTIONS from "./actions.js";
const ButtonRevert = function({ store, text }) {
 function handlerClick() {
  store.dispatch(ACTIONS.revert_list());
 }
 return <button onClick={handlerClick}>{text}</button>
}
export default ButtonRevert;
```

When the button is clicked, the REVERT_LIST action defined in Redux is called.

Let's check that the list is reversed after clicking on the Invert button:

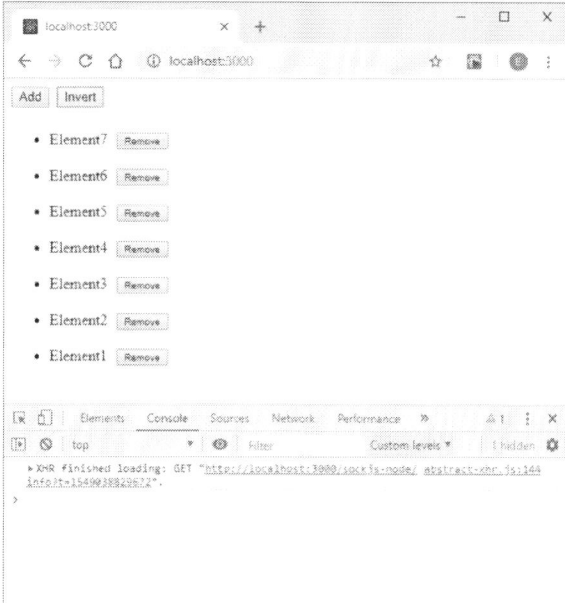

Each click on the Invert button reverses the list on the display. And other features (add, delete and change) are of course operational.

11 – USE THE REACT-REDUX MODULE

The use of Redux in React made it possible to simplify the use of the state by centralizing the state in the Redux store (see previous chapter).

However, to access the store (either to read the state, or to update it using the actions), it is necessary that each component has access to the store, which obliges to transmit it in the attributes of the components (via the store property as before).

In addition, we created an additional component that was responsible for listening for any state changes caused by the actions (`<ConnectedElementsList>` component). This component implemented the call to the store.subscribe(listener) method, in which the listener() callback function updated the state of the React component.

The "react-redux" module has been created to simplify this management:
- Deleting the `<ConnectedElementsList>` component that was only present to make it easier to use the store.subscribe() method.
- By giving access, to the components that request it, to the actions of Redux and to the properties of the state (for which the component wants access).

Install the "react-redux" module

The "react-redux" module is installed using the npm install react-redux command.

Install the "react-redux" module
```
cd reactapp
npm install react-redux
```

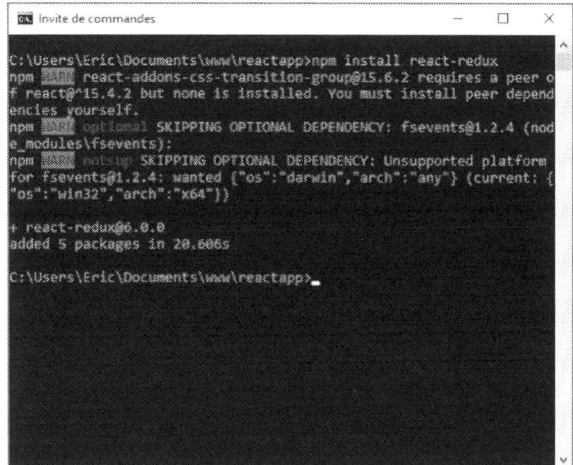

The "react-redux" module is installed in the reactapp directory.

Principle of the connect () method

The "react-redux" module mainly includes the connect() method, which will facilitate access to the store:
- To read the state,
- And to trigger actions that update it.

The state will no longer be read by store.getState() but by properties that will be added to the component (the connect() method adds them for us). For example, if in the Redux state the elems attribute has been specified, we can also access the elems property in a React component (even though this elems property was never created by us in the component).

The triggering of Redux actions follows the same principle. Properties (actually methods corresponding to actions) will be added to the component by the connect() method, which will allow to use these actions in the React component without going through the store (it's the connect() method that makes this invisible process). For example, if in the actions of Redux the add_elem(txt) action has been indicated which allows to insert a new element in the list, we will be able to access the add_elem(txt) method in a React component (and this although the add_elem property was never created by us in the component).

So we see that our main task, when using the "react-redux" module will consist of:
- To read the state: perform a mapping between the properties defined in the

state and those that you want to retrieve in the component (in the props object of the component). For each component, indicate the state properties used in the component and the name associated with them in the component (often the same). This mapping is done in a function called mapStateToProps(state) that returns an object mapping the names of the Redux state attributes to the names of the properties used in the component.

• To execute an action: perform a mapping between the actions defined in Redux and those that you want to use in the component (via the props object of the component). For each component, indicate the Redux actions used in the component and the name associated with them in the component (often the same). This mapping is done in a function called mapDispatchToProps(dispatch) that returns an object mapping the names of the Redux actions to the names of the properties (actually methods) used in the component.

Thanks to the established correspondences, we see that the store becomes transparent in the components, and that each component accesses the elements of the state and the actions that it wishes, without having to transmit information (such as the store) in the attributes of the components. This is the connect() method that will do it for us.

This implies, however, to write the reducer and the corresponding actions. The only facility provided by the "react-redux" module (via the underlying connect() method) is to easily make available in each component, the attributes of the state and the actions used in this component. But it's still a huge contribution!

Writing the connect () method

The connect() method, accessible through the import of the "react-redux" module, makes it possible to transform a component (thus written in the form of a function or class) in order to bring it new properties, which will allow access to attributes of the state and the desired actions. The store becomes invisible (hidden thanks to the connect() method) and no longer has to be transmitted by ourselves in the components.

However, the store must always be created by us via createStore(). And for its value to be passed into the components by the "react-redux" module, one must create a parent component of all the others (called <Provider>), to which the value of the store is transmitted in the store property.

The index.js file allowing to create the <App> component thus becomes (as part of the use of the "react-redux" module):

Use the \<Provider\> component with the store (src/index.js file)
```
import React from "react";
import ReactDOM from "react-dom";

import { Provider } from "react-redux";
import { createStore } from "redux";

import App from "./App.js";
import reducer from "./reducers.js";

const store = createStore(reducer);

ReactDOM.render(
 <Provider store={store}>
   <App />
 </Provider>
, document.getElementById("root"));
```

The `<Provider>` component is an internal component of the "react-redux" module, that's why it is imported from this "react-redux" module. It encompasses the main component of the application, here the `<App>` component.

In addition, the component's `store` property is initialized, and will be used internally by the module to allow the other components to access the Redux store (thanks to the `connect()` method studied below).

Once the `<Provider>` component is inserted, the `connect()` method can be used to allow access to the Redux store. Here is the general form of writing the `connect()` method, accessible by importing the method from the "react-redux" module:

General form of the connect() method
```
import { connect } from "react-redux";
MyComponent = connect(mapStateToProps, mapDispatchToProps)(MyComponent);
```

The `connect(mapStateToProps, mapDispatchToProps)` method actually returns a new function, which takes as parameter a component name (here called `MyComponent`). The component specified as a parameter is transformed according to the mapping rules specified in the `mapStateToProps(state)` and `mapDispatchToProps(dispatch)` functions. It is this transformed component that is returned by the `connect()(MyComponent)` method.

The `MyComponent` component specified as a parameter is either a function name or a class name (as we know how to create a React component).

Component transformation involves adding new properties to the component, allowing component access to the state and actions of Redux.

We must now study the functions mapStateToProps(state) and mapDispatchToProps(dispatch), which allow the addition of properties to the component to access the store of Redux.

For that, we will use the example of the timer which decreases with each second, until arriving at 0. We used this example in chapter 4 to illustrate the notion of state. We use it here to show the use of the "react-redux" module on a simple example.

For this example of the timer, we use the DECR_TIME action which decreases the time remaining by 1 second. The remaining time is put into the Redux state, as a time property of {min, sec}, min and sec indicating the number of minutes and seconds remaining before arriving at 00:00.

src/actions_types.js file describing the types of actions

```
// constants defining the types of actions
export const DECR_TIME = "DECR_TIME";
```

src/actions.js file describing Redux actions

```
import * as ACTIONS from "./actions_types.js";
// action creators
export function decr_time({min, sec}) {
 return {
  type : ACTIONS.DECR_TIME,
  time : {min, sec}
 }
}
```

src/reducers.js file describing the reducer

```
import * as ACTIONS from "./actions_types.js";

var stateInit = {
 time : { min : 2, sec : 0 }  // timer initialized at 02:00
}

function decrTime({min, sec}) {
 sec = sec - 1;
 if (sec < 0) {
  min = min - 1;
  if (min < 0) {
   min = 0;
   sec = 0;
  }
```

```
  else {
    sec = 59;
  }
 }
 return { min, sec };
}

export default function reducer(state = stateInit, action) {
 var newState;
 if (action.type == ACTIONS.DECR_TIME) {
   var time = decrTime(state.time);
   newState = { ...state, time };
 }
 else newState = state;
 return newState;
}
```

The reducer file processes the DECR_TIME action that will be used to decrease the remaining time by 1 second each time the action is called.

Previous files are typical for using Redux, with or without the "react-redux" module. On the other hand, the index.js file of starting of the application will be different according to whether one uses the "react-redux" module or not. In case the module is used, the index.js file is written:

src/index.js file using the "react-redux" module

```
import React from "react";
import ReactDOM from "react-dom";

import { Provider } from "react-redux";
import { createStore } from "redux";

import App from "./App.js";
import reducer from "./reducers.js";

const store = createStore(reducer);

ReactDOM.render(
 <Provider store={store}>
   <App />
 </Provider>
, document.getElementById("root"));
```

This file contains the import of the "react-redux" module and the use of the <Provider> component which encapsulates the <App> component (by passing the store attribute in the attributes of the <Provider> component).

It remains now to describe the file of the `<App>` component which displays the timer. We assume here that we use the "react-redux" module, so let's first see how the mapStateToProps() and mapDispatchToProps() functions are used.

Use the mapStateToProps (state) function

The mapStateToProps(state) function is passed as the first argument of the connect() method. It is used in the case where it is desired to allow the component to read access to the state (or part of the state) of Redux. In the case where the component does not wish to read the state of Redux, we replace this first parameter of the connect() method by null.

Calling the connect() method in case we do not use Redux's state reading in the component
```
MyComponent = connect(null, mapDispatchToProps)(MyComponent);
```

Specifying null in place of the mapStateToProps parameter in the connect() method means that you do not want read access to the Redux state.

The second parameter mapDispatchToProps will allow the component to access the actions of Redux (to modify the state of Redux, so in writing). This parameter will be studied in the next section.

In the case where the component needs read access to the Redux state, we must use the mapStateToProps parameter of the connect() method. This parameter corresponds to a function that returns an object that matches one or more attributes of the state to the properties that will be used in the component.

In the timer example, you want to display the value of the state (the time property) in the `<App>` component. So the mapStateToProps() function will be used here to match the time property of the Redux state with the time property (or some other name, but it's easier to keep the same name) of the `<App>` component.

This allows the `<App>` component to access the Redux store without having passed the store object to the `<App>` component.

The file describing the `<App>` component is then:

src/App.js file describing the `<App>` component
```
import React from 'react';
import { connect } from "react-redux";

function formatTime({min, sec}) {
  if (min < 10) min = "0" + min;
  if (sec < 10) sec = "0" + sec;
```

```
  return `${min}:${sec}`;
}

class App extends React.Component {
 /* eslint no-useless-constructor: 0 */
 constructor(props) {
  super(props);
 }

  render() {
  var time = formatTime(this.props.time);
  return (
    <div>{time}</div>
  )
 }
}

function mapStateToProps(state) {
 return {
   // the time property of the state becomes the time property of the component
   time : state.time
 }
}

export default connect(mapStateToProps)(App);
```

The `mapStateToProps()` function is specified as the first parameter of the `connect()` method, and the result of this call is applied to the `App` class, which is transformed and exported (for use in `index.js`).

This transformation process makes it possible to use the `time` property in the `<App>` component. This `time` property comes directly from the Redux state, so it will be updated every time the Redux state is updated by an action.

Let's run the program to see what happens:

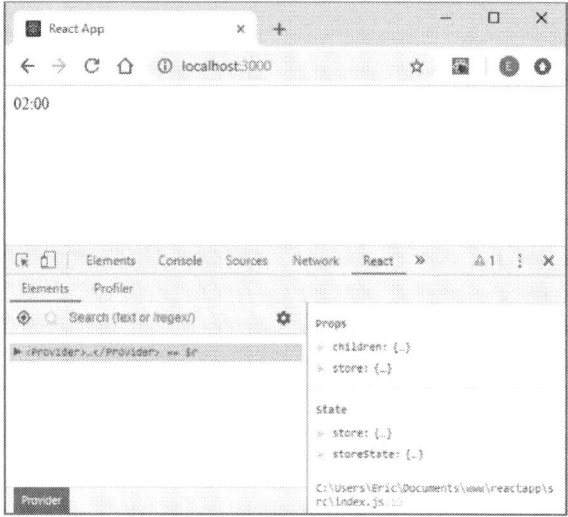

The timer is displayed at its initial value 02:00, but does not decrease. This is normal because you have to trigger the DECR_TIME action every second.

In order to update the timer every second, let's use the DECR_TIME action with the callback function of the setInterval() method triggered every second. This process is written to the index.js file, because it is the one that has the store variable defined (this store variable is needed to perform the DECR_TIME action via store.dispatch()).

src/index.js file that triggers the DECR_TIME action every second

```
import React from "react";
import ReactDOM from "react-dom";

import { Provider } from "react-redux";
import { createStore } from "redux";

import App from "./App.js";
import reducer from "./reducers.js";

import * as ACTIONS from "./actions.js";

const store = createStore(reducer);

ReactDOM.render(
 <Provider store={store}>
  <App />
 </Provider>
, document.getElementById("root"));

setInterval(function() {
```

```
  var time = store.getState().time;
  store.dispatch(ACTIONS.decr_time(time));
}, 1000);
```

Once the actions.js file has been imported, the ACTIONS.decr_time() method is accessible. It is used by telling it the time value of the state of Redux, which it decrements. This update of the state causes the new display of the <App> component because this component is linked to the change of the state of Redux via the connect()(App) method.

Let's check that the timer decrements on display:

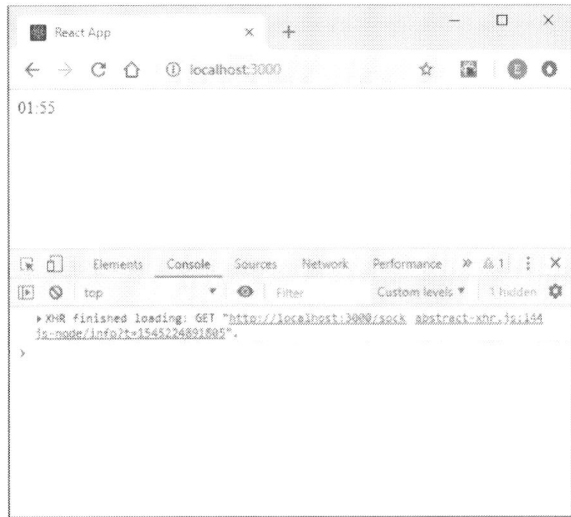

The timer decreases second to second until it reaches 00:00.

We showed how to use the mapStateToProps() function to allow a component to read the Redux state, using properties of the component. Each property of the Redux state that will be used in the component must be mapped to a component property name and can then be used through the component's props object.

However, this example also shows that we can not completely do without the store variable of Redux, especially to trigger the actions that update the state of Redux. It would also be more logical to write the setInterval() statement in the App class rather than in the index.js file. But for that, it would have been necessary to be able to access the store variable in the App class (to trigger the DECR_TIME action), but this store property is not transmitted in the <App> component ...

Following these last remarks, the mapDispatchToProps() function intervenes to allow the actions of Redux to be easily accessible in a component.

Use the mapDispatchToProps(dispatch) function

The mapDispatchToProps() function makes the Redux actions available in the component as properties (here, methods accessible through the props object). These actions allow to update the state of Redux (whereas the mapStateToProps() function seen previously makes it possible to make the state of Redux accessible in reading only).

The mapDispatchToProps() function is positioned as the second parameter of the connect() method. It returns an object indicating the new properties available in the component, related to the actions of Redux. For example, if the add_elem(txt) action exists in Redux actions, it is possible for a component to access this action by writing the following mapDispatchToProps(dispatch) function:

Component file that wants to use the ADD_ELEM action defined in actions.js

```
import React from 'react';
import * as ACTIONS from "./actions.js";
import { connect } from "react-redux";

// MyComponent defined as a function or class
//...
function mapStateToProps(state) {
 return {
   // ...
 }
}

function mapDispatchToProps(dispatch) {
 return {
   add_elem : function(txt) {
     var action = ACTIONS.add_elem(txt);
     dispatch(action);
   }
 }
}

// the action is available in MyComponent in the form:
// props.add_elem("New Element");       // if MyComponent is a function
// this.props.add_elem("New Element");  // if MyComponent is a class

export default connect(mapStateToProps, mapDispatchToProps)(MyComponent);
```

The `add_elem` property is now defined in the component, so it is accessible by the `props` object available in it.

Use the `mapDispatchToProps()` function to allow the `<App>` component defining the timer to access the `DECR_TIME` action. This allows setting the `setInterval()` function in the `App` class rather than using it in the `index.js` file (which was then required in order to access the Redux `store` object that was only visible in the `index.js` file where it was defined).

The `index.js` file is simplified because it no longer uses the `setInterval()` statement, which is reported in the `<App>` component.

src/index.js file

```
import React from "react";
import ReactDOM from "react-dom";

import { Provider } from "react-redux";
import { createStore } from "redux";

import App from "./App.js";
import reducer from "./reducers.js";

const store = createStore(reducer);

ReactDOM.render(
  <Provider store={store}>
    <App />
  </Provider>
, document.getElementById("root"));
```

The `<App>` component now incorporates the `setInterval()` statement, which is set in the component's `componentDidMount()` method.

`<App>` component managing the timer

```
import React from 'react';
import * as ACTIONS from "./actions.js";
import { connect } from "react-redux";

function formatTime({min, sec}) {
  if (min < 10) min = "0" + min;
  if (sec < 10) sec = "0" + sec;
  return `${min}:${sec}`;
}

class App extends React.Component {
  /* eslint no-useless-constructor: 0 */
```

```
constructor(props) {
  super(props);
}

  componentDidMount() {
  setInterval(() => {
    var time = this.props.time; // accessible through mapStateToProps()
    this.props.decr_time(time); // accessible through mapDispatchToProps()
  }, 1000);
}

  render() {
  var time = formatTime(this.props.time);
  return (
    <div>{time}</div>
  )
  }
}
function mapStateToProps(state) {
  return {
    time : state.time
  }
}
function mapDispatchToProps(dispatch) {
  return {
    decr_time : function({ min, sec }) {
      var action = ACTIONS.decr_time({ min, sec });
      dispatch(action);
    }
  }
}
export default connect(mapStateToProps, mapDispatchToProps)(App);
```

The connect() method is used to make the state readable (thanks to mapStateToProps) and writable (thanks to mapDispatchToProps).

The setInterval() method defines its callback function with the ES6 syntax (using =>) to preserve the this value in the callback function.

Let's check that the timer decreases second by second:

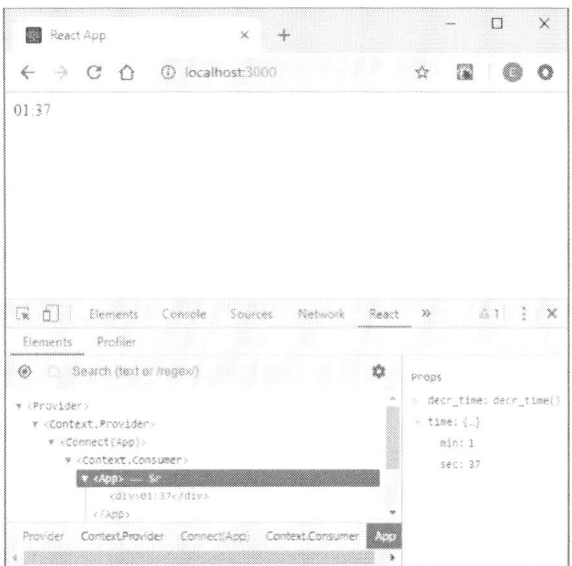

We see in the React tab that the <App> component has both the decr_time() and time properties, which shows that the connect() method actually added these two properties to our <App> component.

In this example, we see that the connect() method of the "react-redux" module makes it possible to manage the state of Redux without using the store, and especially without having to indicate the store attribute in the components (except for the <Provider> component for which it is mandatory).

Writing the list management example with the "react-redux" module

Let's use the "react-redux" module as part of a larger application (involving more React components). For example our list management application written in the previous chapter only with Redux, can also be written using the "react-redux" module.

This is for each component to write any mapStateToProps() and mapDispatchToProps() functions, depending on whether the Redux state is used in this component (read or write). And of course you no longer use the store attribute in the components, since you can access it now via the properties added by the connect() method.

For simplicity, we will consider that:

- Properties added in components have the same names as those in the Redux state (for properties added via mapStateToProps()),
- And that the methods added in the components have the same names as the actions defined in Redux (for methods added via mapDispatchToProps()).

These rules of simplification (and logic) are often those used everywhere ...

The names of the files and components are the same as those defined in the previous chapter, with the exception of the <ConnectedElementsList> component which no longer needs to exist because it is advantageously replaced by the functionalities provided by the "react-redux" module as we will see.

src/index.js file

```
import React from "react";
import ReactDOM from "react-dom";

import { Provider } from "react-redux";
import { createStore } from "redux";

import App from "./App.js";
import reducer from "./reducers.js";

const store = createStore(reducer);

ReactDOM.render(
 <Provider store={store}>
  <App />
 </Provider>
, document.getElementById("root"));
```

This file corresponds to the minimum index.js file of a program using React and Redux using the "react-redux" module.

src/actions_types.js file describing the types of actions defined in Redux

```
export const ADD_ELEM = "ADD_ELEM";
export const REMOVE_ELEM = "REMOVE_ELEM";
export const MODIFY_ELEM = "MODIFY_ELEM";
export const REVERT_LIST = "REVERT_LIST";
export const FIND_TAG = "FIND_TAG";
```

It's the same file as before ...

src/actions.js file describing Redux's actions

```
import * as ACTIONS from "./actions_types.js";
function getUniqueKey() {
 var key = Math.random() + "";
```

```
  return key;
}
export function add_elem(txt) {
 var ukey = getUniqueKey();
 return {
   type : ACTIONS.ADD_ELEM,
   txt : txt,
   ukey : ukey
 }
}
export function remove_elem(ukey) {
 return {
   type : ACTIONS.REMOVE_ELEM,
   ukey : ukey
 }
}
export function modify_elem(ukey, txt) {
 return {
   type : ACTIONS.MODIFY_ELEM,
   ukey : ukey,
   txt : txt
 }
}
export function revert_list() {
 return {
   type : ACTIONS.REVERT_LIST
 }
}
export function find_tag(tag) {
 return {
   type : ACTIONS.FIND_TAG,
   tag : tag
 }
}
```

It's the same file as before ...

src/reducers.js file describing the reducer

```
import * as ACTIONS from "./actions_types.js";

const stateInit = {
 elems : [],   // { ukey, txt } array
 revert : false,
```

```
  find : {
   tag : "",
   elems : []
  }
 }
 export default function reducer(state = stateInit, action) {
  var newState;
  if (action.type == ACTIONS.ADD_ELEM) {
   var txt = action.txt;
   var ukey = action.ukey;
   var elems = state.elems;
   elems.push({txt, ukey});
   elems = elems.map(function(elem) {
    return elem;
   });
   newState = Object.assign({}, state, {elems : elems});
  }
  else if (action.type == ACTIONS.REMOVE_ELEM) {
   var ukey = action.ukey;
   var elems = state.elems;
   elems = elems.filter(function(elem) {
    if (elem.ukey == ukey) return false;
    else return true;
   });
   newState = Object.assign({}, state, {elems : elems});
  }
  else if (action.type == ACTIONS.MODIFY_ELEM) {
   var txt = action.txt;
   var ukey = action.ukey;
   var elems = state.elems;
   elems = elems.map(function(elem, i) {
    if (elem.ukey == ukey) return {txt, ukey};
    else return elem;
   });
   newState = Object.assign({}, state, {elems : elems});
  }
  else if (action.type == ACTIONS.REVERT_LIST) {
   var elems = state.elems;
   var revert = state.revert;
   elems.reverse();
   elems = elems.map(function(elem) {
```

```
    return elem;
  });
  newState = Object.assign({}, state, {elems : elems, revert : !revert});
}
else if (action.type == ACTIONS.FIND_TAG) {
  var elems = state.elems;
  var tag = action.tag;
  elems = elems.filter(function(elem, i) {
    if (elem.indexOf(tag) >= 0) return true;
    else return false;
  });
  newState = Object.assign({}, state, { find : { elems : elems, tag : tag }});
}
else {
  // action inconnue
  newState = state;
}
return newState;
}
```

This is the same file as before, except for the parts highlighted in the code. Indeed, it has been found that the elems.reverse(); and elems.push({txt, ukey}); instructions did not cause a change in the state (!!!), hence the addition of the elems.map() statement which only returns the same array as the one received, but causes a change in the Redux State …

The previous files do not concern the React components, that's why the changes are minimal compared to the previous version. The actual changes will now occur when writing the components.

src/App.js file describing the <App> component

```
import React from 'react';
import ElementsList from './ElementsList';
import ButtonAdd from './ButtonAdd';
import ButtonRevert from './ButtonRevert';
import * as ACTIONS from "./actions.js";
import { connect } from "react-redux";

class App extends React.Component {
  /* eslint no-useless-constructor: 0 */
  constructor(props) {
    super(props);
  }
```

```
render() {
 var elems = [
  "Element1",
  "Element2",
  "Element3",
  "Element4",
  "Element5"
 ];
 elems.forEach((txt) => {
  this.props.add_elem(txt);
 });
 return (
  <div>
   <ButtonAdd text="Add"></ButtonAdd>
     
   <ButtonRevert text="Invert"></ButtonRevert>
   <ElementsList elems={elems} />
  </div>
 )
 }
}
function mapDispatchToProps(dispatch) {
 return {
  add_elem : function(txt) {
   var action = ACTIONS.add_elem(txt);
   dispatch(action);
  }
 }
}
export default connect(null, mapDispatchToProps)(App);
```

The insertion of the first elements of list is carried out by the ADD_ELEM action. This action is put in the properties of the <App> component so that it can use the method via this.props.add_elem().

src/ELementsList.js file describing the list of elements

```
import React from 'react';
import Element from './Element';
import { connect } from "react-redux";

const ElementsList = function(props) {
 const { elems } = props;
```

```
  return (
   <ul>
   {
    elems.map(function(elem) {
     return (
      <li key={elem.ukey}>
       <Element text={elem.txt} ukey={elem.ukey} />
      </li>
     )
    })
   }
   </ul>
  )
}
function mapStateToProps(state) {
 return {
  elems : state.elems
 }
}
export default connect(mapStateToProps)(ElementsList);
```

The list of elements (elems) is written in the state of Redux, so read access is allowed to this part of the state via the function mapStateToProps().

src/Element.js file describing a list item

```
import React from 'react';
import ButtonRemove from './ButtonRemove';
import * as ACTIONS from "./actions.js";
import { connect } from "react-redux";
class Element extends React.Component {
 constructor(props) {
  super(props);
  this.state = {
   modifyOn : false,
   value : props.text
  }
 }
 handlerDoubleClick() {
  this.setState({modifyOn : true});
 }
 handlerChange(event) {
  var value = event.target.value;
```

```
    this.setState({value : value});
  }
  handlerBlur() {
    this.setState({modifyOn : false});
    var value = this.state.value;
    const { ukey } = this.props;
    this.props.modify_elem(ukey, value);
  }
  render() {
    const { ukey, text } = this.props;
    return (
      <div>
          { this.state.modifyOn ?
            <input onChange={this.handlerChange.bind(this)}
                 onBlur={this.handlerBlur.bind(this)}
              autoFocus={true}
              value={this.state.value} /> :
              <span onDoubleClick={this.handlerDoubleClick.bind(this)}>{text}</span>
      }
          <ButtonRemove style={{margin:"10px", fontSize:"10px"}}
              ukey={ukey} text="Remove" />
      </div>
    )
  }
}
function mapDispatchToProps(dispatch) {
  return {
    modify_elem : function(ukey, value) {
      var action = ACTIONS.modify_elem(ukey, value);
      dispatch(action);
    }
  }
}
export default connect(null, mapDispatchToProps)(Element);
```

The MODIFY_ELEM action is used during the modification of a list element, it is put in property of the <Element> component.

src/ButtonAdd.js file to add an item to the list

```
import React from 'react';
import * as ACTIONS from "./actions.js";
import { connect } from "react-redux";
const ButtonAdd = function(props) {
  function handlerClick() {
```

```
  var elems = props.elems;
  props.add_elem("Element" + (elems.length + 1));
 }
 return <button onClick={handlerClick}>{props.text}</button>;
}
function mapStateToProps(state) {
 return {
  elems : state.elems
 }
}
function mapDispatchToProps(dispatch) {
 return {
  add_elem : function(txt) {
    var action = ACTIONS.add_elem(txt);
    dispatch(action);
  }
 }
}
export default connect(mapStateToProps, mapDispatchToProps)(ButtonAdd);
```

This component reads the elems property of the state (in order to know the number of elements already present in the list) and accesses the ADD_ELEM action. For this, we use the two mapStateToProps() and mapDispatchToProps() functions.

src/ButtonRemove.js file to remove an item from the list

```
import React from 'react';
import * as ACTIONS from "./actions.js";
import { connect } from "react-redux";
const ButtonRemove = function(props) {
 const { ukey, style, text } = props;
 function handlerClick() {
  props.remove_elem(ukey);
 }
 return <button style={style} onClick={handlerClick}>{text}</button>;
}
function mapDispatchToProps(dispatch) {
 return {
  remove_elem : function(ukey) {
    var action = ACTIONS.remove_elem(ukey);
    dispatch(action);
  }
 }
}
```

```
export default connect(null, mapDispatchToProps)(ButtonRemove);
```

This component accesses the REMOVE_ELEM action, hence the use of mapDispatchToProps().

src/ButtonRevert.js file to invert the displayed list

```
import React from 'react';
import * as ACTIONS from "./actions.js";
import { connect } from "react-redux";
const ButtonRevert = function(props) {
  function handlerClick() {
    props.revert_list();
  }
  return <button onClick={handlerClick}>{props.text}</button>
}
function mapDispatchToProps(dispatch) {
  return {
    revert_list : function() {
      var action = ACTIONS.revert_list();
      dispatch(action);
    }
  }
}
export default connect(null, mapDispatchToProps)(ButtonRevert);
```

This component accesses the REVERT_LIST action, hence the use of mapDispatchToProps().

Finally, we check that the program is working correctly, for example by deleting the last element and inverting the list:

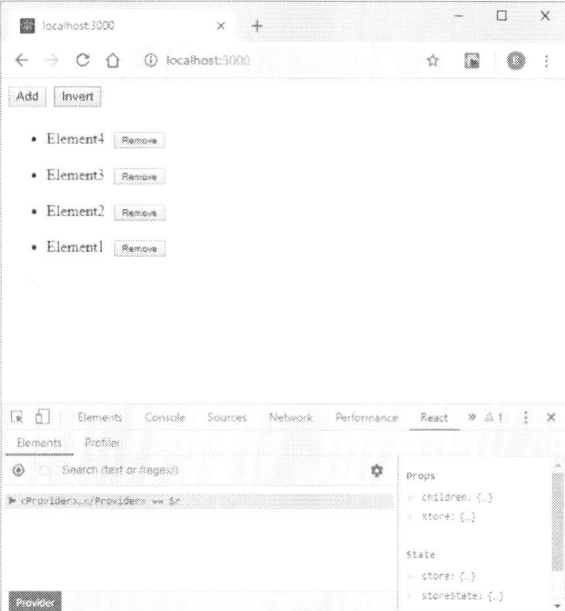

The last item in the list has been removed, and the list has been reversed.

Conclusion

We end here the use of Redux as part of a React project. Redux greatly simplifies access to the state in React components, especially if parts of the state must be shared in various components.

The "react-redux" module also provides a simplification layer by avoiding propagating the store attribute in the React components. The use of these two modules ("redux" and "react-redux") is done in the case of important projects that require to share a lot of data between the components, and became indispensable in projects using React.

12 – REACT ROUTER

React Router is a set of modules for using routes in a React application. A route represents a URL in the browser and corresponds to a display in the window, ie to the display of one or more React components.

The advantage of using the routes is that you can easily manage which components you want to display, according to the indicated URL. If the URL changes, the displayed components are not the same, and it seems to have changed HTML page, which is not the case.

In addition, a mechanism for the history of visited URLs is implemented in React Router, allowing you to go back in the history using the Back key of the browser. Without this mechanism, the rollback produces the output of the React application, because it is in a single index.html page, according to the SPA (Single Page Application) principle.

React Router exists in web version (used here) and version for native application (not used here). We will install the web version in the reactapp directory of the application created in previous chapters.

Install React Router (web version)

```
cd reactapp
npm install react-router-dom
```

Once the modules associated with React Router are installed, the React application that uses them (here the `<App>` component) must be inserted into the `<BrowserRouter>` component defined in React Router. The index.js file is modified as follows:

src/index.js file to use routes

```
import React from "react";
import ReactDOM from "react-dom";

import { BrowserRouter } from "react-router-dom";

import App from "./App.js";

ReactDOM.render(
 <BrowserRouter>
   <App />
 </BrowserRouter>
, document.getElementById("root"));
```

The `<BrowserRouter>` component is a component defined in React Router and included with the import statement above.

The `<App>` component of the application is directly inserted into the `<BrowserRouter>` component.

Note that the `<BrowserRouter>` component can have only one direct child, hence the interest of grouping the entire application in the `<App>` component.

Once the `<BrowserRouter>` component is positioned, the `<App>` component (and its internal components) can use the routes that will be defined.

Create the first routes with the <Route> component

The definition of a route is done using the `<Route>` component (defined internally in React Router).

As a first example of routes, let's define two routes in the `<App>` component:
- The route `"/"` displays `"Route /"`,
- The route `"/app"` displays `"Route /app"`.

It means that :
- If the URL in the browser is: http://localhost:3000, we display `"Route /"`,
- If the URL in the browser is: http://localhost:3000/app, we display `"Route /app"`.

The `<App>` component file is modified to take into account these two routes by means of two `<Route>` components.

src/App.js file defining / and /app routes

```
import React from "react";

import { Route } from "react-router-dom";

function App(props) {
 return (
  <div>
    <Route path="/" render={()=><div>Route /</div>} />
    <Route path="/app" render={()=><div>Route /app</div>} />
  </div>
 )
}

export default App;
```

The `<Route>` component uses both the `path` and `render` attributes here. The `path` attribute indicates the route that triggers the display associated with that route (described in the `render` attribute), while the `render` attribute indicates a callback function that returns the React elements to display (when this route is displayed). Other attributes of the `<Route>` component are available and discussed below.

The callback function specified in the `render` attribute is here written in ES6, but it is also possible to write it in a less concise form: `render={function () {return <div> Route / </div>}}`.

Let's run the program by typing the http://localhost:3000 URL:

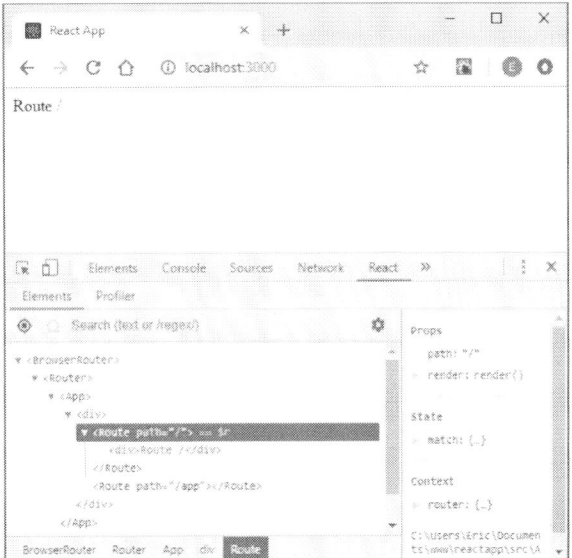

The render associated with the route "/" is displayed, and we see in the React tab the two <Route> components for which only the first contains the displayed <div> (the second <Route> component now has empty content).

It is the <BrowserRouter> component which according to the route indicated in the URL, displays the contents of the <Route> component corresponding to the route.

Now use the http://localhost:3000/app URL in the browser:

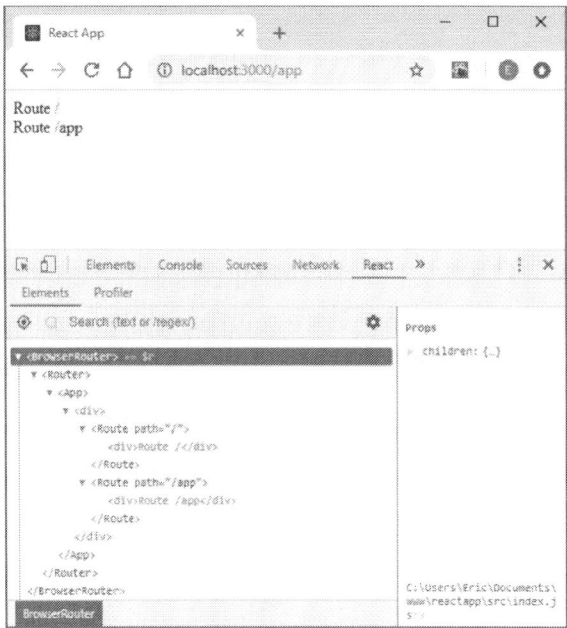

To our surprise, the displays of both routes occur, although the route indicated in the URL is "/app" ...

The reason for displaying both routes at once is simple: the path attribute specified in the <Route> component means that the URL must have that string, but that does not mean that it's exactly that value.

So in the case where we indicate "/app" in the URL, the first route with path="/" is appropriate because the indicated path is in the URL, and the second route with path="/app" is also suitable for the same reason. So all the suitable routes display their render, which is the case here.

So we see that when using <Route>, all routes whose path attribute matches with the URL will be displayed. To allow to display only one route among those which could correspond (in fact the first that corresponds), it is necessary to use in addition the <Switch> component.

Display the first route that matches with the <Switch> component

To avoid considering all routes that satisfy the path attributes (indicated in the <Route> components), <Route> components are surrounded by a <Switch> component. If multiple routes were to satisfy the specified path, only the first route in the list will be selected and displayed.

Let's surround the previous `<Route>` components with a `<Switch>` component:

Use the `<Switch>` component in routes
```
import React from "react";
import { Route, Switch } from "react-router-dom";
function App(props) {
 return (
  <Switch>
    <Route path="/" render={()=><div>Route /</div>} />
    <Route path="/app" render={()=><div>Route /app</div>} />
  </Switch>
 )
}
export default App;
```

The `<Switch>` component is imported in the same way as the `<Route>` component. It surrounds the two previous `<Route>` components.

Let's show again the http://localhost:3000/app URL:

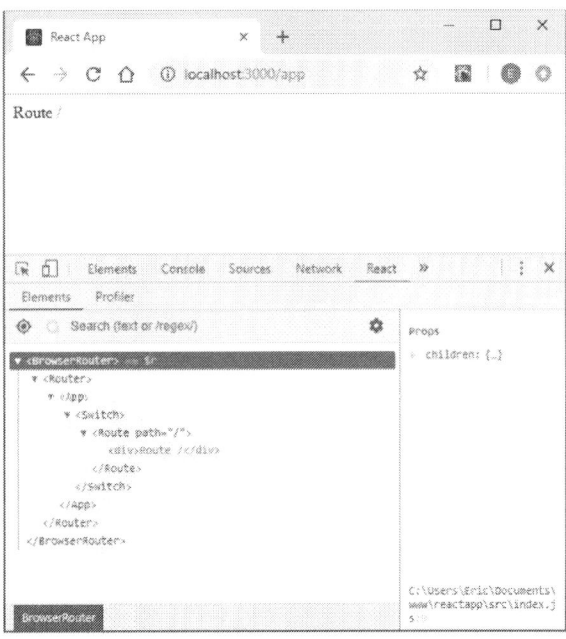

Only one route is now displayed (the first one whose path matches the URL)

333

In addition, the `<Switch>` component has removed the second `<Route>` component.

However, there is another problem. Indeed, it is not normal that when one indicates "/app" in the URL, it is the route having the path="/" which is selected (even if this behavior is normal in React Router). It would be more logical for the route with path="/app" to be selected first if the URL contains "/app". This is the role of the exact attribute in the `<Route>` component.

Use the exact attribute in the routes

The exact attribute (true or false) in a `<Route>` component allows you to indicate if you want the path to be exactly the same as the URL:
- If the exact attribute is true, the specified path and URL must be the same, otherwise the route is not chosen,
- If the exact attribute is false (the default), the behavior is the same as in the previous section.

In our example, you must specify the exact={true} attribute in the route whose path is "/", so that this route is not always selected first (because all URLs have at least a "/" in their value). With the exact={true} attribute, this route will only be chosen if the URL is "/" exactly.

Use the exact attribute in the `<Route>` component
```
import React from "react";

import { Route, Switch } from "react-router-dom";

function App(props) {
 return (
  <Switch>
   <Route exact={true} path="/" render={()=><div>Route /</div>} />
   <Route path="/app" render={()=><div>Route /app</div>} />
  </Switch>
 )
}

export default App;
```

The exact attribute is set to a boolean value of true or false. We consider in JSX that if the attribute is present, it is true if the value is not indicated (the presence of the attribute is sufficient). And if the attribute is not present, its value is false by default.

So we could have written too: `<Route exact path="/" render=... />`.

Let's use the http://localhost:3000/app URL again:

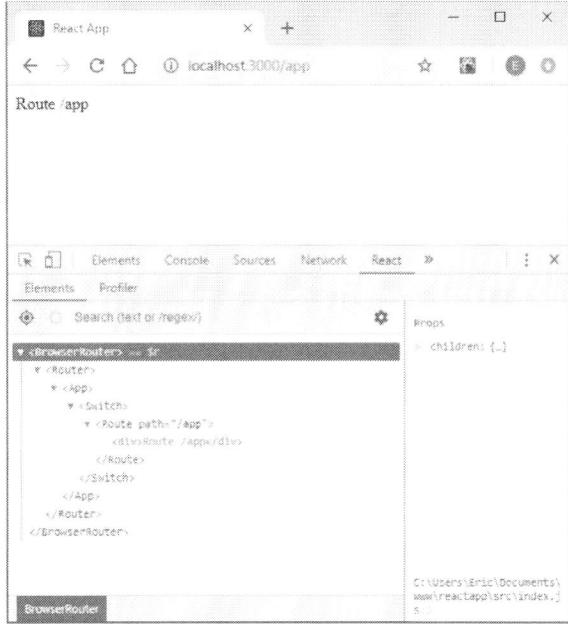

The route with the path="/app" is now selected if the URL is "/app".

Now use the http://localhost:3000 URL:

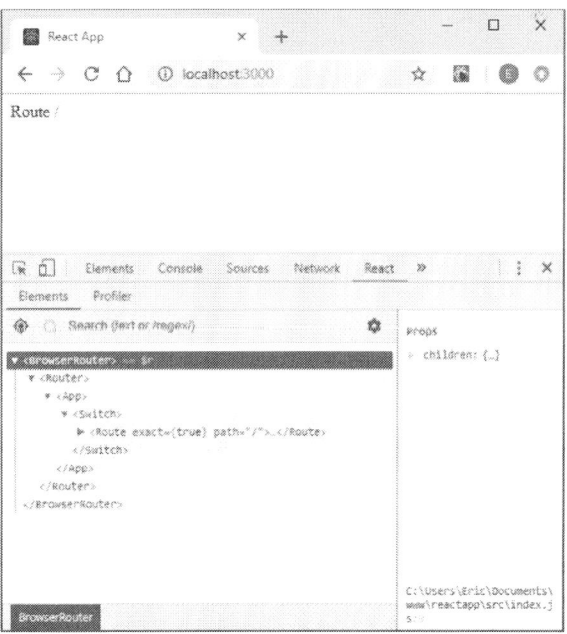

This is the route with path="/" which is chosen because the path of the route and the URL match exactly.

Use an unknown route

What happens if the URL indicates a value that is not associated with any path of any route? For example if we specify the http://localhost:3000/abc URL, the "/abc" value not being indicated in any path of the <Route> components?

So let's use the http://localhost:3000/abc URL:

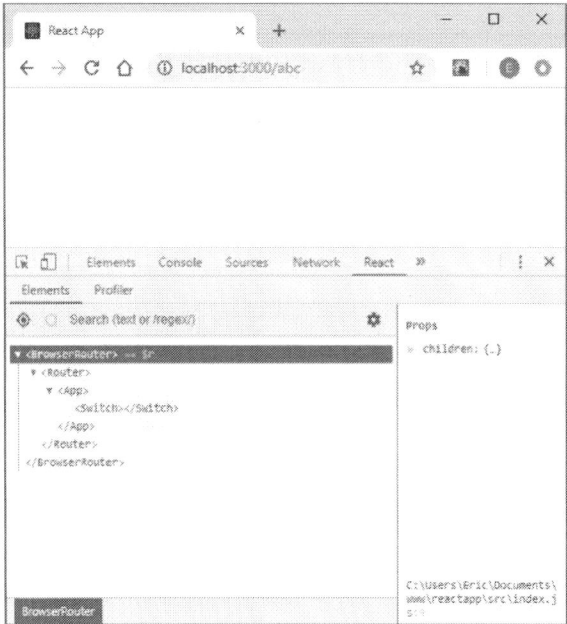

When the indicated URL is not recognized by any route, nothing is displayed, and <Route> components have been removed from the application by React Router.

Since the URL error is a common mistake, it would be good to display an error message to users.

To do this, just specify a route that does not have the specified path attribute (or path="") last in the route list. Indeed, if none of the previous routes is chosen, the last, not having the specified path, will necessarily be chosen by React Router because it can only agree.

Use a default route if no route is appropriate

import React from "react";

```
import { Route, Switch } from "react-router-dom";

function App(props) {
 return (
  <Switch>
   <Route exact={true} path="/" render={()=><div>Route /</div>} />
   <Route path="/app" render={()=><div>Route /app</div>} />
   <Route render={()=><div>Unknown Route</div>} />
  </Switch>
 )
}

export default App;
```

The pathless route is indicated last (because if it was indicated before, it would surely be suitable and would prevent the following routes from being taken into consideration).

Let's still use a URL with an unknown route, for example http://localhost:3000/abc:

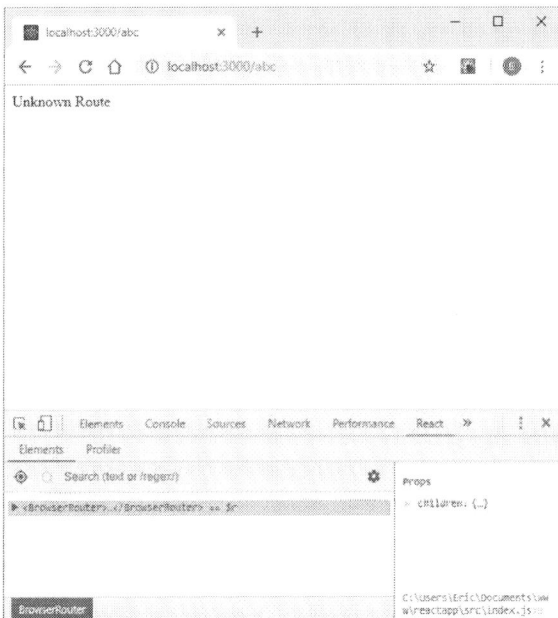

The last indicated route corresponds, so is displayed.

Display a component in a route

The `render` attribute used in the `<Route>` component can be used to display any

React elements, including those we have created ourselves (components created as functions or classes).

Let's use the "/" route to display a list of elements ("Element1", ..., "Element5"). We use for this the <ElementsList> component which is transmitted the array of elements to display in the elems attribute.

View a list of items in the route

```
import React from "react";
import ElementsList from "./ElementsList";

import { Route, Switch } from "react-router-dom";

function App(props) {
 var elems = [
  "Element1",
  "Element2",
  "Element3",
  "Element4",
  "Element5"
 ];

  return (
  <Switch>
   <Route exact={true} path="/"
       render={()=><ElementsList elems={elems} />} />
   <Route render={()=><div>Unknown Route</div>} />
  </Switch>
 )
}
export default App;
```

In the <ElementsList> component, the elems attribute containing the list of elements to be displayed is transmitted. The <ElementsList> component displays the elems array passed in its props object.

<ElementsList> component in src/ElementsList.js file

```
import React from 'react';
import Element from './Element';

const ElementsList = function(props) {
 var { elems } = props;
 return (
  <ul>
   {
```

```
    elems.map(function(elem, index) {
      return <Element elem={elem} key={index} />
    })
   }
  </ul>
 )
}
export default ElementsList;
```

While the `<Element>` component displays the value specified in the `elem` attribute that is passed to it:

`<Element>` component in src/Element.js file

```
import React from 'react';
var Element = function(props) {
 const { elem } = props;
 return <li>{elem}</li>
}
export default Element;
```

We display the http://localhost:3000 URL:

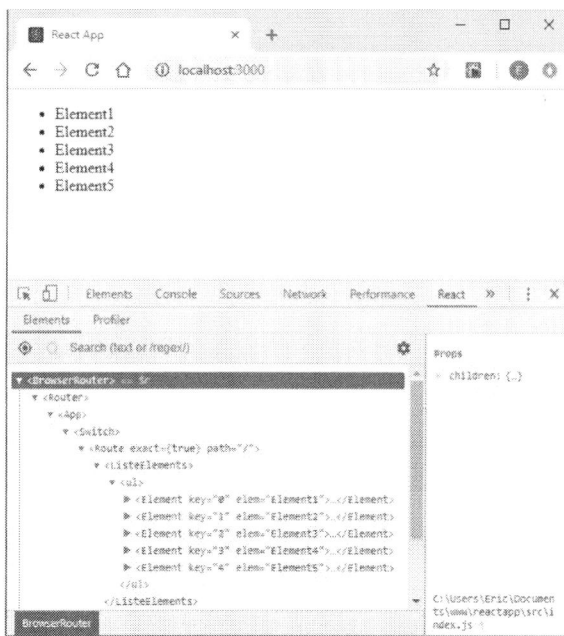

The list of elements transmitted is displayed in the route. This makes it possible to pass parameters when displaying a route (here the `elems` array of the elements to be displayed).

Use parameters in routes

We saw in the previous example how to pass parameters (actually attributes) to display a component in a route (the elems array). But the path attribute specified for the route can also be used to display the component.

Suppose we have the following two routes:
- The "/" route allows as before to display the list of elements in full,
- The "/edit/:index" route only displays the list item with this index (from 0). For example, the http://localhost:3000/edit/1 URL displays "Element2" (that is, the element with the index 1 in the list, the second in the list).

Note that to use variables in the definition of routes, prefix the name of the variable (here index) with ":", hence ":index". This is a rule of React Router.

The second route needs to be able to transfer the index of the element indicated in the URL to the component displayed by render. If we still use the <ElementsList> component to display this route, it will be necessary that this component also uses the index of the element if this index is transmitted (if the index is not transmitted the list is displayed in its entirety as in the first route).

The question is then how to transfer a value entered in the route (so in fact the URL) to the component used by the render attribute of this route? In fact the component retrieves in its props object (or this.props if the component is described by a class) elements that are added by React Router.

To check it, just create the "/edit/:index" route in our routes, and display for it the content of the props object received during the render.

Display the contents of the props object for the "/edit/:index" route

```
import React from "react";
import ElementsList from "./ElementsList";

import { Route, Switch } from "react-router-dom";

function App(props) {
  var elems = [
    "Element1",
    "Element2",
    "Element3",
    "Element4",
    "Element5"
```

```
];
  return (
  <Switch>
   <Route exact={true} path="/"
      render={()=><ElementsList elems={elems} />} />
   <Route path="/edit/:index"
      render={(props)=><div>{JSON.stringify(props)}</div>} />
   <Route render={()=><div>Unknown Route</div>} />
  </Switch>
  )
}
export default App;
```

The second route "/edit/:index" has been added to the route list.

Use the http://localhost:3000/edit/2 URL to display the result of this route:

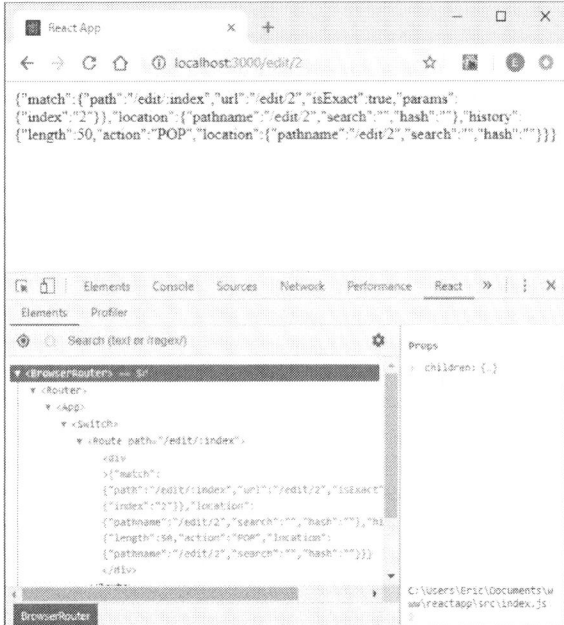

The content of the props object passed as a parameter in the render attribute is displayed. It is an object with match, location, and history properties.

The match property contains a params object containing the parameters specified in the URL, here {index: "2"}. So to access the value of the index, just write the expression props.match.params.index.

Write the <App> component file using the props object passed in the render attribute:

src/App.js file using the new route
```
import React from "react";
import ElementsList from "./ElementsList";

import { Route, Switch } from "react-router-dom";

function App(props) {
 var elems = [
  "Element1",
  "Element2",
  "Element3",
  "Element4",
  "Element5"
 ];

  return (
  <Switch>
   <Route exact={true} path="/"
       render={(props)=><ElementsList {...props} elems={elems} />} />
   <Route path="/edit/:index"
       render={(props)=><ElementsList {...props} elems={elems} />} />
   <Route render={()=><div>Unknown Route</div>} />
  </Switch>
  )
}
export default App;
```

The props object is passed in the attributes of the <ElementsList> component, so that this component can know the route that causes it to be displayed. And in order to concatenate this object with the already used elems attribute, we use the ES6 syntax with {... props} in both routes.

The <ElementsList> component used to display the list of elements or a single element (depending on the route used) is now written:

<ElementsList> component displaying a list or a single element (depending on the route used)
```
import React from 'react';
import Element from './Element';

const ElementsList = function(props) {
 var { elems } = props;
 return (
  props.match.path.match(/\/edit/) ?
```

```
    <ul><Element elem={elems[props.match.params.index]} /></ul> : (
    <ul>
    {
    elems.map(function(elem, index) {
      return <Element elem={elem} key={index} />
    })
    }
    </ul>
   )
  )
}
export default ElementsList;
```

If the URL contains "/edit" we display a single element (using the value of the index transmitted in the URL), otherwise we display the complete list as before.

Let's check the operation by first using the http://localhost:3000 URL, which displays the list as a whole:

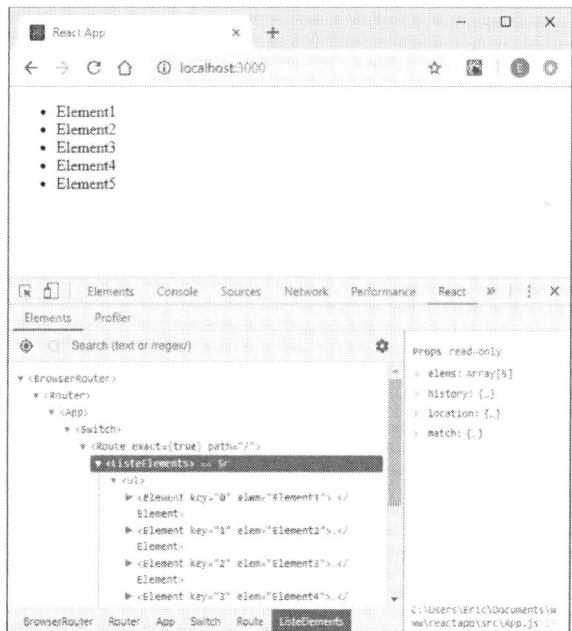

The list is displayed in its entirety.

Then use the http://localhost:3000/edit/2 URL to display a single item from the list:

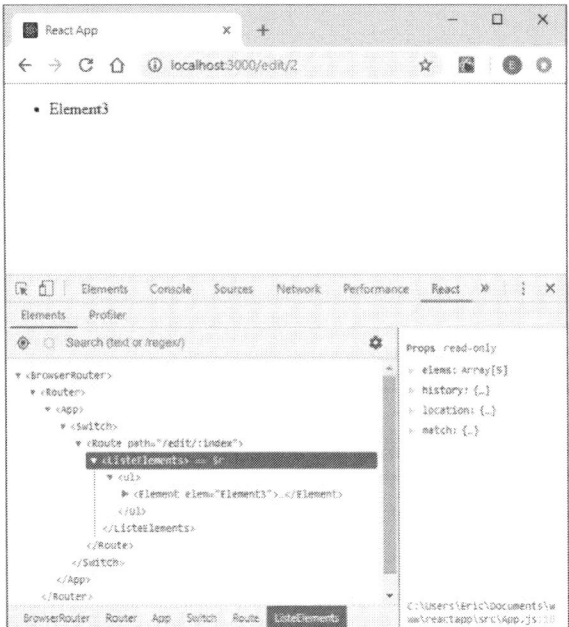

Only the specified index item is displayed by the route.

Use links to display routes with the \<Link\> component

The previous examples showed how to use multiple routes. The change of route was made by directly typing a new URL in the address bar of the browser.

However, it is rare to have to change the URL by typing it directly into the browser address bar. It is more common to click on a link in the page that directly effects this URL change for us.

For that we add in the page that is displayed the corresponding links:
- The first link is used to display the complete list of elements (corresponding to the "/" route),
- The second link is used to display the index element 2 for example (corresponding to the "/edit/:index" route).

Use navigation links in routes

```
import React from "react";
import ElementsList from "./ElementsList";

import { Route, Switch } from "react-router-dom";
```

```
function App(props) {
 var elems = [
  "Element1",
  "Element2",
  "Element3",
  "Element4",
  "Element5"
 ];

  return (
  <div>
   <a href="/">Full List</a>   
   <a href="/edit/2">Index 2</a>
   <Switch>
    <Route exact={true} path="/"
       render={(props)=><ElementsList {...props} elems={elems} />} />
    <Route path="/edit/:index"
       render={(props)=><ElementsList {...props} elems={elems} />} />
    <Route render={()=><div>Unknown Route</div>} />
   </Switch>
  </div>
 )
}
export default App;
```

The links here are simple `<a>` elements whose `href` attribute represents the route. Start the program by entering the `http://localhost:3000` URL:

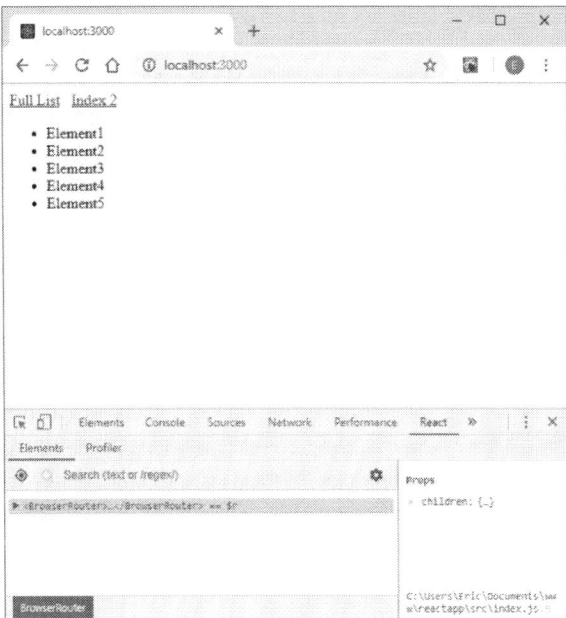

The complete list is displayed, as well as the two links.

Click on the second link to display a single list item:

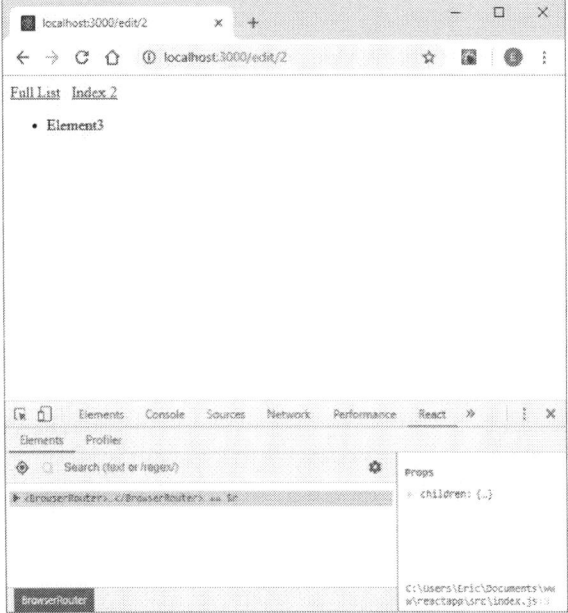

After clicking on the link, the index item 2 ("Element3") appears in the page.

The operation of the program seems normal. However, observing well, we realize that each click on one of the links, the complete page is redisplayed. In fact, clicking on one of the links reloads the entire page in the browser, regardless of the fact that it is already present.

In fact, this is not the behavior that you want to have when using React Router ... React Router provides a new component called `<Link>`, which replaces the `<a>` element in pages, and does not reload the page since it is already present.

The use of the `<Link>` component is similar to that of the `<a>` element. The href attribute is simply replaced by the to attribute.

Use the <Link> component for links in the page

```
import React from "react";
import ElementsList from "./ElementsList";

import { Route, Switch, Link } from "react-router-dom";

function App(props) {
 var elems = [
   "Element1",
   "Element2",
   "Element3",
   "Element4",
   "Element5"
 ];

  return (
  <div>
   <Link to="/">Full List</Link>  
   <Link to="/edit/2">Index 2</Link>
   <Switch>
    <Route exact={true} path="/"
        render={(props)=><ElementsList {...props} elems={elems} />} />
    <Route path="/edit/:index"
        render={(props)=><ElementsList {...props} elems={elems} />} />
    <Route render={()=><div>Unknown Route</div>} />
   </Switch>
  </div>
 )
}

export default App;
```

The `<Link>` component is imported like the other React Router components.

The `<a>` links have been replaced by the `<Link>` components.

The display is similar to the one using `<a>` links. But when clicking on a link, the page is not reloaded and the fluidity is maximum.

Note also, following the clicks on the links, that the `Back` button of the browser makes it possible to navigate between the various visited URLs, which was not possible outside React Router.

Use buttons to navigate in routes (instead of links)

It remains to show a final facet of React Router. In the previous section, it was shown how to display links to navigate in previously defined routes, using the `<Link>` component that keeps the same page in memory.

But what if we wanted to use buttons instead of previous links? A button does not have any `href` attribute (like the `<a>` element) or `to` atttribute (like the `<Link>` component). The question is: how to access a route dynamically (for example at the click of a button)?

It is necessary in this case to use a component of React Router which allows this kind of manipulations. This is the `<Router>` component, to be used instead of the `<BrowserRouter>` component. It allows more settings than the `<BrowserRouter>` component, and allows in particular to manipulate the browsing history.

So to display any route, just insert it in the array of visited pages named `history`:
- To display the `"/"` route, one carries out: `history.push ("/");`
- To display the `"/edit/2"` route, one carries out: `history.push ("/edit/2");`

It remains however to show now how one accesses the `history` array from the new `<Router>` component.

Setting up the <Router> component in the src/index.js file
```
import React from "react";
import ReactDOM from "react-dom";

import { Router } from "react-router-dom";

import App from "./App.js";

import createBrowserHistory from "history/createBrowserHistory";
const customHistory = createBrowserHistory();

ReactDOM.render(
 <Router history={customHistory}>
```

```
    <App history={customHistory} />
  </Router>
, document.getElementById("root"));
```

We import the `<Router>` component (instead of `<BrowserRouter>` as before), then we create a `customHistory` navigation history. This history will be used by the `<Router>` component because it is passed to it in the `history` attribute. If this attribute is not passed to the `<Router>` component, the Router produces an error.

Note that when using the `<BrowserRouter>` component directly, all these manipulations are hidden inside this component ...

This browsing history is also transmitted to the `<App>` component of our application, which will use it to display new pages visited following button clicks.

The `<App>` component is modified to display the two buttons instead of the two links, and manage the clicks on these buttons.

`<App>` component using buttons to display routes

```
import React from "react";
import ElementsList from "./ElementsList";

import { Route, Switch } from "react-router-dom";

function App(props) {
 var elems = [
  "Element1",
  "Element2",
  "Element3",
  "Element4",
  "Element5"
 ];

  function handlerClickFullList() {
   props.history.push("/");      // insert "/" route
  }

  function handlerClickIndex2() {
   props.history.push("/edit/2"); // insert "/edit/2" route
  }

  return (
   <div>
    <button onClick={handlerClickFullList}>Full List</button>   
    <button onClick={handlerClickIndex2}>Index 2</button>
```

```
    <Switch>
     <Route exact={true} path="/"
        render={(props)=><ElementsList {...props} elems={elems} />} />
     <Route path="/edit/:index"
        render={(props)=><ElementsList {...props} elems={elems} />} />
     <Route render={()=><div>Unknown Route</div>} />
    </Switch>
   </div>
  )
}
export default App;
```

The click on each button is handled by a function, which uses the `history` object passed in the attributes of the `<App>` component.

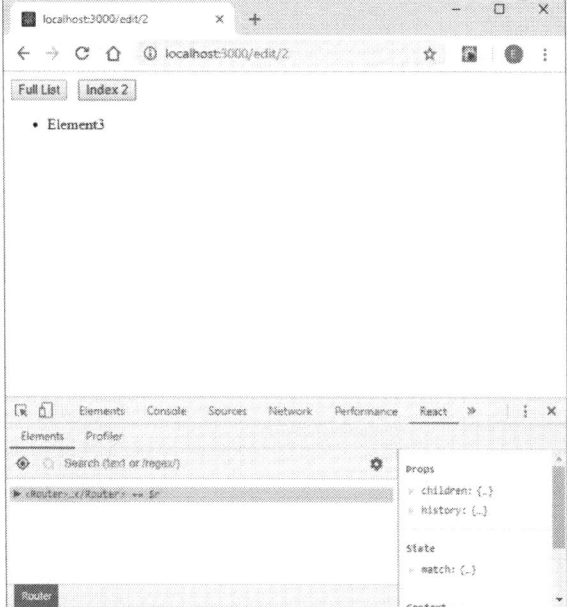

The change of route is now done by clicking on the buttons.

Made in the USA
Monee, IL
25 May 2021